P9-CLH-736

THE MEDITERRANEAN IN POLITICS

THE MEDITERRANEAN IN POLITICS

BY

ELIZABETH MONROE

NEW YORK

OXFORD UNIVERSITY PRESS

1938

Printed in the United States of America

TO

THE OLD AND NEW FRIENDS

WHOSE KNOWLEDGE AND ADVICE

ARE EMBODIED IN

THIS BOOK

PREFACE

THE people without whom this book would never have been written are all those to whom it is dedicated, but first among them is the Rockefeller Foundation, which financed and advised me throughout two long journeys round the Mediterranean. I have also to thank the Royal Institute of International Affairs in London for releasing me for fifteen months from my post in its Information Department, and the *Centre d'Étude de Politique Étrangère* in Paris for introducing me to Monsieur Robert Montagne, without whose encouragement and help I could not have seen and done what I did in the French territories which I visited.

The first journey was from Morocco to Syria, mostly by land and by bus, or by that cheap and universal means of travel in those parts—the hired seat in an Arab car. The second was by more hackneyed ways—to Italy, Albania, Greece, and Turkey—and after travelling through these different countries and régimes, I know that my remaining thanks are due to the fate that cast my lot in a democracy, and so enabled me to think what I like and say what I think.

E. M.

June, 1938

CONTENTS

TABLES

MAPS

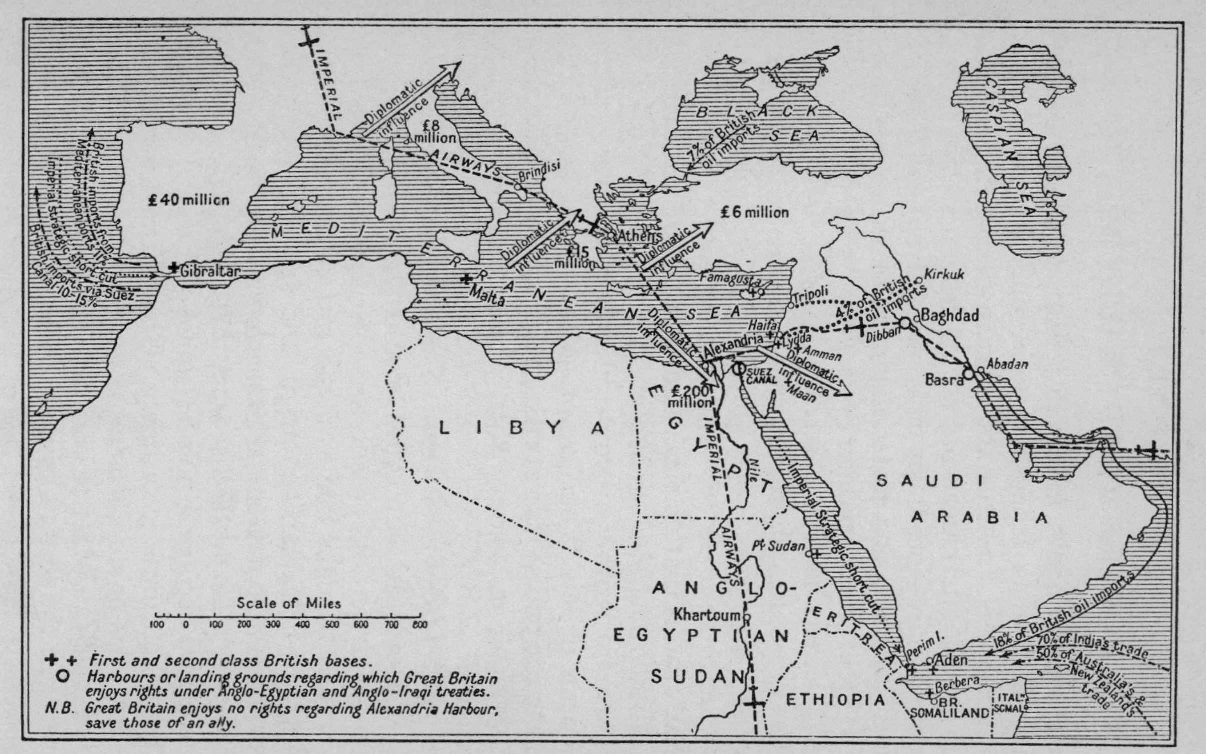

I. BRITISH INTERESTS

CHAPTER I

THE POWERS THAT REALLY MATTER

THERE are few books, except in Italian, on Mediterranean policy, and when I began to write one, I realized why. The subject is limitless and unmanageable because for years the Mediterranean has always been a means, and—except to Italy—never an end. Judged by standards of western business and materialism, its basin has not been a vital area. Heavy industry has almost passed it by. Its chief products are still the corn and wine and oil of the Bible. In politics, its significance has been that of a passage, or a megaphone, or a knuckle-duster. It has always been the route to somewhere, or the string which, when pulled, reveals that its other end is in India, Vladivostok, the Middle Danube, or Mosul. You cannot write on it without also writing on imperial policy, Moslem policy, European policy. You cannot write on it without considering the policy of five or six great powers, and as many satellites, all of whom, when a storm threatens, react differently.

In 1935, after fifteen years of uneventful history, just such a storm all but broke over Italy's *mare nostrum* policy—a dream which she had cherished for years but which was brought home to the rest of the world first during her Ethiopian campaign, and secondly when she gave official help to General Franco's forces in Spain. Her neighbours woke to the discovery that the Mediterranean, as such, had become a political issue and that they must readjust their ideas accordingly. Great Britain wondered whether to go or stay; France, at what point to jettison the eastern basin in order to concentrate on more important concerns in the west; Germany, how to get into the picture; Russia, how to get out of the Black Sea; Turkey, how best to glean advantages during these moments of uncertainty. Their calculations spread, as before, to Europe, Asia, Africa, and even Australasia, but they were obliged to make them in a new light—to take as a point of departure their attitude in the lands and seas between Suez and Gibraltar.

The Mediterranean scene is kaleidoscopic and confused in the years since 1935, but, looking back, an observer cannot fail to notice that some parts of the pattern are more constant than others. For instance, he sees that, of the states possessing Mediterranean territory, only four are strong enough to dictate Mediterranean policy—Great Britain, France, Italy, and that lesser but well-managed power Turkey, who has beaten Spain and is overhauling Poland in the race for European greatness. He sees that the action of every other Mediterranean state—Spain, Yugoslavia, Albania, Greece, Egypt—is subordinate either to the will of one of the big four, or to events in Europe. The smaller fry may band into ententes, but small-power ententes, which were strong things when they meant three or four votes cast in the same direction at Geneva, are weak things in face of rearmed might. Nowadays ententes hesitate and disband at the sound of siren calls from the great capitals. So this book concentrates on the interests of the four powers who alone can give a lead.

Our observer notices, too, that their leadership is not the enviable estate it used to be. Like modern masters with modern servants, they can no longer boss and bully. They must evolve a new and beguiling technique for dealing not only with the smaller states of Europe but with the restive Moslem peoples from Syria to Morocco.

From platforms in England and France and Italy, statesmen proclaim: 'We must defend our vital interests in the Mediterranean.' We give them a round of applause, but the phrase has become so usual that we accept it without thought. We repeat it, like a creed, without inquiring into the nature of the interests, or whether our money spent on their defence is well spent. My purpose is to describe these interests—to supply the reader with the chessmen so that, whenever a Mediterranean problem arises, he can pull out his book and set his chessboard, whether for an immediate match between the axis London-Paris and the axis Rome-Berlin, or for a more remote encounter between the powers with interests and possessions along the Suez route—Great Britain, France, Italy—and two competitors who may one day strike southwards—Germany and Russia.

Readers used not to puzzle their heads over diplomatic chess. They left it to statesmen who had at their elbow blue books and experts and documents marked: 'Cabinet: Secret.' But their habits have changed. They are no longer confiding and inert. When the British people rejected the Hoare-Laval plan in December 1935, they tasted a new power. They might be tempted to exercise it again, and, since history books bring them up to look upon the route to India as an article of faith, no subject would tempt them more than would a decision regarding the Mediterranean.

'Every man his own diplomatist.' The prospect is alarming; it would be less so if he had some facts at his disposal. Facts sadden, and wisen. But the pace and hubbub of modern western life leave him no time to read the two-volume studies, with appendices, in which the accurate material usually appears. What he asks for is a book cheap to buy, light to hold, and easy to read.

This is my excuse for producing so slight a book after fifteen months of work and travel given to me by the Rockefeller Foundation. Scholars may feel that I could have done them better service by publishing footnotes and tables, or by writing in greater detail on a less diffuse subject. My answer to them is that I have not neglected research. The light book, if it is to be accurate, demands long reflection upon the facts and figures which would fill the pages of a larger study. I have not set out these statistics and technicalities because I have thought it more important to try and write a book for ordinary people.

CHAPTER II

BRITISH INTERESTS

1. *War Strategy and Peace Policy*

WHEN the events of September 1935 changed the nature of Mediterranean politics, Great Britain was the nation to suffer the rudest awakening. Two generations of Englishmen had regarded the passage to India as an 'all-red route' and 'as safe as Gibraltar', yet a few weeks sufficed to prove that the conception was outworn, perhaps even a myth. British weakness stood revealed when the massing of the British Navy failed to prevent Italy from using the route for her Ethiopian campaign, and when the fleet, under threat of war with an air power, slipped out of Malta in search of a safer base.

The shock to opinion was the greater because insecurity was an unfamiliar sensation. Only once since the opening of the Suez Canal in 1869 had Great Britain had a fright about the route to India, but that incident had been forgotten in the long run of luck and success which had attended her Mediterranean diplomacy. In 1893, upon the announcement of the Franco-Russian alliance, she had gone through all the emotions which she was not to know again until 1935. France or Russia she was ready to deal with singly, but the thought of their combined navies had opened her eyes to her vulnerability. The consternation was so great that not a lip was sealed. Mr. Joseph Chamberlain announced to the House of Commons that in the event of war in the Mediterranean 'the British Navy would have to cut and run—if it could run'.

But on the whole the route had been remarkably secure. In the eighteen-seventies, the menace had been Russia, but while London sang: 'We don't want to fight, but, by jingo, if we do, the Russians shall not have Constantinople,'

Mr. Disraeli had headed off Russia by acquiring Cyprus. In the 'eighties, following the occupation of Egypt, the menace had become France, but Great Britain had secured herself against France by the Mediterranean Agreement of 1887, when she, Italy, Spain, and Austria had, with Bismarck's blessing, agreed to prevent further French expansion in North Africa. In the 'nineties she had had her fright, but she had recovered by rearming under the Spencer naval building programme. From then onwards, she had several times been blessed with fortune. Her route remained clear because when the clash with France occurred—at Fashoda in 1898—Russia was busy in the Far East and Paris with the Dreyfus case; because, by the time Germany's Morocco policy became serious, Great Britain and France were already firm friends; and because Italy, who might have been an awkward enemy once she had captured Libya and the Dodecanese islands from Turkey in 1912, hated Austria with so strong and public a hatred that she proved open to temptation to desert her anti-British allies. So the British controlled the main channel to the east even at the height of the World War, and in 1922 they reinsured it by acquiring Palestine among the spoils of victory.

Signor Mussolini's determined pursuit of his Ethiopian campaign therefore shattered the complacency of years. The British public, caught by surprise, was forced into some hasty thinking. If Malta were insecure in face of air armaments, were all small fortresses out of date, and if so, what about Gibraltar, Cyprus, Aden? Was the Mediterranean route essential? Would not the Government do better to concentrate its money and energy on the securer passage round by the Cape? Waking with a start, people expressed their ideas on these subjects in some confusion, mixing war strategy with peace policy, and talking in terms of the sea route to India as if there were no other reason for paying for a Mediterranean fleet.

Strategists and experts showed no way out of the wood, for they produced conflicting views as to what should be done. Some were for quitting the Mediterranean, on the plausible grounds that Great Britain, who was happy in the possession of an alternative route, would do well to limit her defence liabilities in time of war. Others pointed out that, quite apart from the fact that she possessed Mediterranean interests other than the sea route to India, to quit was to weaken her position because it reduced her power of attack.

The first or Cape School of thought based their reasoning on a truth which no one can deny: that, as far as merchant shipping is concerned, British control at the Mediterranean bottle-necks is of no avail in modern war since the menace of air and submarine attack have turned the whole 1,900 miles from Gibraltar to Port Said, not to mention the further 1,200 miles down the Red Sea, into a canal too narrow to allow of the defence device called evasive routeing.

For the sceptics who doubted this truth the experts produced a whole battery of arguments: they pointed out that even in the World War, when the enemy had boasted few or no Mediterranean bases, German submarines had been more successful in the Mediterranean than in any other sea; that five out of the thirteen million tons of allied and neutral shipping sunk by submarine had been caught somewhere between Gibraltar and Port Said; that one submarine alone had captured a bag of half a million tons; that commanders of German U-boats were, according to a German expert, 'much envied by their comrades in home waters owing to the extraordinary possibilities offered by operations in the Mediterranean', and that the success of these operations was such that a British decree of March 1916 had ordered all possible shipping to take the Cape route. They added that even if modern invention had provided the necessary defence devices, naval and air energy would always be better spent on its primary purpose of attack than on unnecessary convoying through the Mediterranean.

Starting from these foundations, the Cape School began to build their argument for abandonment. They pointed out that the British Mediterranean bases, most of which had been chosen with naval war in mind, were now dangerously commanded by foreign aerodromes, and had lost much of their old value. The safety of Gibraltar depended on a friendly Spain; Malta was dominated by the French base at Biserta and by the Italians in Sicily, South Italy, and the fortified islands of Pantelleria and Lampedusa; Cyprus and Alexandria were within range of the Italian fortresses in the Dodecanese—of which the chief is the secret island of Leros—and of their Libyan base at Tobruk.

They went on to argue that, since the British strongholds were not essential for the protection of merchant shipping, they might well be too costly to hold in war. In a crisis, the British Navy must be prepared to beat a strategic retreat. It must concentrate on sealing the Mediterranean at either end—if necessary, from Gibraltar and Aden—and confine its Mediterranean activities to small harassing operations carried out with aeroplanes and submarines.

They did not advocate abandonment of the Mediterranean fortresses. They simply held that Great Britain should cease to lavish money on bases there, and should spend instead upon the bunkering and port facilities which the Cape route lacked, on her bases at Sierra Leone and at Simonstown, near Capetown, and on bringing her merchant navy to a level which could meet the heavier demands made by the longer Cape route. Any other course, they said, was pandering to habit and prejudice. An expedient withdrawal might be check, if not checkmate, to enemy plans, whereas the holding of vulnerable islands against odds was gloriously futile.

The Mediterranean School disagreed. While admitting

that the route was impassable for merchant shipping in time of war, they pointed out that the despised bases had their uses. They might be open to attack, but they could also hit back. To abandon them was to abandon Britain's best chance of getting at her adversary. Blockade from Aden and Gibraltar was no substitute for attack, because a Mediterranean enemy—for instance, Italy or Turkey—could prosper within the blockaded area, since she could procure there all essentials except rubber and tin. She could get plentiful wheat and meat and dairy produce from the Balkans, coal from Russia or Germany, oil from Russia, Rumania, or Iraq, iron ore from French North Africa, Russia, or Spain, copper from Russia, Yugoslavia, or Cyprus, and cotton from Russia or Egypt. Obviously, some of these powers might join in the blockade, but Great Britain was far less likely to retain allies if she had retired to a distance. Italy, for example, would be in a position to browbeat her small neighbours into supplying her needs if there were no one left to dispute her local supremacy. Even as a war measure, therefore, the Mediterranean School held that the Cape theory was unsound.

As a peace measure, they condemned it as untenable. If a rival were to learn that Great Britain was slackening her Mediterranean hold in order to concentrate elsewhere, his acquisitive instincts would quicken at once. He would be the readier to risk attack if he had sighted an easy prize. In a world full of dictators preaching expansion, a war of succession would be inevitable. The Mediterranean School therefore concluded that there was no middle course between total abandonment and total maintenance, and that abandonment was impossible in view of Great Britain's interests other than the sea route to India.

The Government agreed with this conclusion. In the summer and autumn of 1936 they endorsed it out of the mouth of minister after minister. 'We are quitting nothing,' said the Secretary of State for the Colonies. 'Far from there being any question of our abdicating our position in the Mediterranean or scuttling from Malta, we intend to face these new and difficult problems—to make our future position secure,' said the First Lord of the Admiralty, after visiting Malta and Cyprus. The nation, almost unanimously and without complaint, subscribed to a rearmament programme of such magnitude that few states were rich enough to compete. Naval and air armaments were added to the Mediterranean stock; plans were laid for a base in Cyprus; a promise of harbours and landing-grounds was secured from Egypt, and the nervous voices of 1935, which had harped upon Great Britain's vulnerability, were drowned in a crescendo of expert talk —mysterious but confident—of developments at Malta and Gibraltar and their growing power of attack upon an adversary. The taxpayer trusted the experts and paid the bill almost without knowledge of the return which he was seeing for his money. The rest of this chapter is devoted to a description of the British interests which those new armaments defend, and is an attempt to show that he is paying for something more precious than the mere power to inflict counterblows in war.

2. *The Mediterranean as a Route*

Signor Mussolini, who is an honorary member of the Cape School, says that the Mediterranean 'is for Great Britain only a route, one of the many routes, I should say a convenient short cut'. And at first sight there is something to be said for his view.

We know that our merchant shipping will have to do without the Suez Canal route in any naval and air war in the Mediterranean. We are comforted to learn from experts that this privation will neither starve us nor wreck our industry; that diversion of traffic via the Cape will lengthen the voyage by as much as 80 per cent. from the

Persian Gulf, but by 10 per cent. only from Australia;[1] that while some dislocation of our flow of imports is inevitable, it will last no more than four to six weeks, and that we can live on our reserves of food and industrial materials over that period, suffering inconvenience, perhaps, but no serious shortage.

Yet the British Government contradicts Signor Mussolini and the Cape School. 'For us the Mediterranean is not a short cut but a main arterial road . . . a vital interest in the full sense of the word to the British Commonwealth of Nations.'

Here is a contradiction, but one which is easily explained: the two groups are arguing at cross-purposes. The first is reasoning only in terms of supply from beyond Suez. The second is reasoning in terms of British imperial security, and of Great Britain's position as a world trader and a political influence. It is thinking not only of the incoming traffic through the Canal, but of the two-way traffic both through and within the Mediterranean, the air routes to Asia and Africa which fork at Alexandria, and the oil route to the Mediterranean from the Iraq Petroleum Company's wells at Kirkuk. The first group is only seeing one part of the question. The other part is: whether Great Britain's presence in her Mediterranean bases in time of peace contributes to her national well-being and prosperity.

As to the supplies—though we know that we can exist without them, it is as well to know what they are.

Of the goods northward bound through the Suez Canal to all destinations, three-quarters normally consist of five

[1] Voyage increases via the Cape route to London are:

From the Persian Gulf . .	80 per cent.
From west coast of India . .	77 per cent.
From east " " . .	51 per cent.
From Mombasa . . .	45 per cent.
From Singapore . . .	44 per cent.
From Hong Kong . . .	37 per cent.
From Sydney	10 per cent.

main products. Over 20 per cent. of the volume consists of petroleum, and about 20 per cent. of vegetable oils coming to European factories to be made into a range of necessities running from soap through candles and margarine to varnish and paint. The other three commodities are cereals, textile fibres, and metals, each of which account for quantities ranging from 10 to 14 per cent. of the whole. Rubber, which is light, represents $3\frac{1}{2}$ per cent. only, and is followed at some distance by cane-sugar, tea, and frozen meat.

The exact percentage of British imports received via the Suez Canal is hard to estimate; it varies between 9 and 14 per cent. according to the period of days or weeks over which it is reckoned, and a calculation spread over a long period is a task the result of which would scarcely warrant the labour involved. Among the goods which Great Britain imports by this route, the largest in quantity is her petroleum from Iran; she takes about one-third of the total volume of oil passing Suez. But, though the Iranian petroleum is always mentioned in the first breath, it is less irreplaceable than are some of the other commodities. It represents 18 per cent. of the oil imported into the British Isles, but a far larger amount, and one which could be increased in a crisis, comes from the Caribbean. Even were the United States to apply the Neutrality Act, and to deny American exporters the right to sell Great Britain the 12 per cent. of her oil imports which they normally provide, she could satisfy her home needs, even in war time, from Venezuela, Trinidad, and from her principal supplier, the Dutch West Indies.[1] Less replaceable commodities arriving via Suez are the jute from Bengal—the unique source—which represents the livelihood of the

[1] Where the bulk of Venezuelan crude oil is refined. The chief suppliers of Great Britain's oil are (1937): Dutch West Indies and Venezuela, 35 per cent.; Iran, 18 per cent.; U.S.A., 12 per cent.; Trinidad and other Empire territories, 5 per cent.; Mexico, 5 per cent.; Rumania, 4 per cent.; Iraq, 4 per cent.; Peru, 3 per cent.; U.S.S.R., 3 per cent.

rope and sack makers of Dundee, the tin and rubber of which British Malaya and the Dutch East Indies are the world's great producers, and Indian manganese, rice, and tea. See table on p. 249.

So far as the Suez traffic is concerned, the Cape and Panama routes always provide a loop-hole. The imports which would be completely denied to Great Britain in time of war are those from countries within the Mediterranean. Surprisingly, these are almost equal in volume to the through traffic. They represent about 11 per cent. of the million tons of foodstuffs and raw materials reaching United Kingdom ports each week. Fortunately, however, the Mediterranean consignment consists chiefly of less vital commodities. The most important is the cotton from Egypt. More than three-quarters of the British cotton industry uses medium- and low-grade cottons from elsewhere, but the remaining mills work on the long, strong fibres which only the Nile can produce. Nevertheless, their machinery is easily adjustable to shorter or to rayon fibres, and a stoppage of the Egyptian supply would result rather in a loss of efficiency than in a dislocation of manufacture. Next in importance among Mediterranean purchases come two French North African products, phosphates and iron ore, but here again a blocked Mediterranean would not cause vital damage. In the event of war, Great Britain could secure adequate amounts of the former from the Atlantic ports of Morocco, and, though the latter is important, she could equally well obtain it from northern Spain or direct from the French mines in Lorraine. As regards petroleum, Great Britain now buys under 7 per cent. of her supply from the two big Black Sea producers, Russia and Rumania, and, although the pipeline from Iraq runs through territory under her rule, she is not its principal user, and does not count on it for more than 4 per cent. of her resources. Indeed, none of her Mediterranean dependencies is a great supplier of the mother country; Cyprus's copper is marketed chiefly in France and Germany, and the United Kingdom usually imports less oranges from Palestine than from Spain. Apart from the Spanish metals, most of which come from Atlantic ports, almost all the rest of her Mediterranean imports consist of pleasant but non-essential articles—fruits of the plants which help to make a Mediterranean view: grapes, wine, lemons, dates, olives, and olive-oil.

Of the supplies passing Gibraltar, therefore, there are none that Great Britain could not forego or receive by another route. Supply is not the reason why she is 'quitting nothing'. The point which the British Government has in mind when it talks of the main arterial road is, first, the part which the Suez Canal plays as a speed factor in imperial defence plans, and secondly, its contribution to imperial unity and to the prosperity of the British Isles.

When the taxpayer asks: 'Do I see a peace-time return for my money spent on ships and bases along the Mediterranean route?' the answer to his question is Yes; those ships and bases gain Great Britain more by creating British and Dominion confidence than they lose her by creating unpopularity abroad; they incline Dominion and Indian merchants to trade with Great Britain and to buy the goods which she must sell in order to live; they increase the earning chances of British shipping along a populous route, and they act as advertisement hoardings for British sellers everywhere from Spain to China. Here is a good reason why expansionist powers want to establish footholds of their own, and why they covet colonies and increase their fleets.

One practical peace-time value of the Canal is its convenience for imperial police purposes. The speed at which it enables protective forces to move from one part of the globe to another imparts a warm feeling of security to all those who like to go about their business undisturbed. One of the arguments that melted Tory opposition to the cutting of the Canal was the fact that its existence would have shortened the Indian Mutiny. It serves when extra forces are needed to cope with rebellion or epidemic or earthquake, to evacuate Cabul or to impart security to Hong Kong. This consideration applies equally to all nations, but Great Britain is at an advantage in possessing bases and forces all along the route. She knows that, in some colonial crisis, she can use the highway without fear of delay over polite formalities engineered by some ill-wisher at a foreign port. Very naturally, this advantage rankles among her rivals. It is in order to retaliate against a British stranglehold at Suez that Italy is fortifying the port of Assab, that she has made an alliance with the Yemen, and—above all—that she has acquired from France the strip of desert and the island of Dumeira which command the narrow channel at the exit from the Red Sea. As yet, few Englishmen seem to have considered the implications of an Italian closure of the back-door to Egypt and the Suez Canal.

Moreover, the British garrisons stationed along the main route to the east present another advantage. Troops from Malta or the Canal Zone can fill an eastern breach at shorter notice than can forces from home. They can save seven days to India, fifteen to Singapore.

Another imperial link lies in the confidence which Dominion and colonial merchants place in the chain of friendly fuelling stations and protective cruisers strung between Aden and Gibraltar. They see in them a protection against tiresome incident—against expensive delay of their goods in some foreign port, or against attack by pirate submarine. Malta or Aden is worth paying for if it creates satisfaction among a small but important class of Indians, and among sellers in Australia, New Zealand, or Kenya.

To India, unhampered use of the canal is more important than to any other great trading nation. It is the only route she uses for her trade with Europe, which represents 70 per cent. of her total trade. Australia normally relies upon the Canal for 25 per cent. of her imports and half her exports; she uses it for all the wool and meat, and most of the lead and zinc she sends to Europe, while about half her wheat comes by long sea—as any one who studies form in the Grain Race knows. New Zealand should, properly speaking, be out of the picture, because she is a thousand miles nearer England via Panama than via Suez. Nevertheless she uses the Suez Canal more than the American route because, in spite of lower canal dues at Panama, the Pacific lacks repaying ports of call.

This same confidence in a protected route applies to United Kingdom shippers and exporters.

Great Britain is like a merchant who buys and uses far more than he sells, and who makes up his deficit partly out of private income, but partly out of running a profitable business, letting out his vans on hire. Great Britain's subsidiary business is the shipping industry, on which she relies to make up about 30 per cent. of her trade deficit. For instance, in a year of large turnover like 1929, her adverse trade balance amounted to as much as £380 millions. Income from overseas investment met £250 millions of this; the shipping industry provided the remaining £130 millions.

Assured passage on the Suez route contributes to this figure. The route is second only to the North Atlantic in the volume of its traffic, and British shipping, carrying the goods and passengers of all nations, is by far its largest user. In amount, British traffic through the Canal has increased fairly steadily since the opening in 1869. In proportion, it has decreased owing to the growth of rivals, but it still accounts for 50 per cent. of the whole. Its preponderance is obvious even to a casual watcher of the ships that pass. First come the liners of the P. & O. group, flying their different house flags; then the British Tanker Company's vessels, riding high out of the water on their way south, and rolling north again clumsy and encumbered with their weight of oil; then ships of the Holt & Ellerman lines. The material advantage brought by their earnings is one British gain; the psychological advantage brought by their very passage is another. Reliable shipping services are a national advertisement, and the main sea route to the east touches more lands and serves more people than any other route in the world.

The advantages of assured passage apply equally to British export trade. In spite of Japanese competition, Mahatma Gandhi, hostility in Congress and other deterrents, India is, with the occasional exception of South Africa, the largest single market for British goods. Great Britain sells to her more than twice as much as to France, more than half as much again as to the United States. She takes about 9 per cent. of total British export trade, but the figure would fall quickly if the Suez route were to become uncertain.

Sales within the Mediterranean are less important than the sales beyond it, for all the countries of the Mediterranean basin combined do not buy as many British goods as does India alone. Yet, in spite of competition from cheap Japanese goods and from German selling devices, and in spite of the development of local industries, Great Britain for some time held her own in the Balkans and the Levant;[1] only in 1937 did she begin seriously to feel the effect of undercutting by the countries practising exchange-restrictions, who were able to trade at prices which bore no relation to world levels. The strong stand which she is making is partly due to her abiding asset—quality goods, whether West-of-England suiting or Welsh coal—but it is undoubtedly also due to the genial advertisement at which her Navy excels, and which you can watch if you come across a British battleship at Algiers, or two destroyers in a harbour on the Dalmatian coast.

British statesmen can argue convincingly, therefore,

[1] See table on p. 253.

that money spent on patrolling the sea route through the Mediterranean is well spent. They then add, as a makeweight, the need for protecting two other British interests—the imperial air route, and the oil route from Iraq to the sea. The analogy looks sound, and is accepted, but in fact their argument as applied to the air route and pipe-line is much weaker.

In both cases direct defence is impossible. In both cases indirect defence—that is, looking mighty in order to gain your end—is a psychological mistake.

Air lines are in a class apart in international relations, because the narrow margin of safety in the air means that technical considerations override all others. Nationalism cannot enter into an air liner's calculations. On its journey from London to Bagdad, an Imperial Airways machine calls only once—at Tiberias in Palestine—in a British dependency. The great air lines of the Mediterranean—Imperial Airways, Air France, the Dutch K.L.M., the Italian Ala Littoria and the Anglo-Egyptian Misr—are above discrimination as to the ownership of their ports of call. They all use Brindisi and Athens, and from there make, regardless of nationality, for Beirut, Haifa, or Cairo. Their only protection is the chivalry which the delicacy of their mechanism has created for them, and to argue that you must arm to protect your air routes is to introduce into the pleasant atmosphere of air relations that sinister note which has crept into modern politics.

The impossibility of direct defence, which is obvious in the case of the air route, is equally obvious to any one who has seen the pipe-line. When you visit it, you come away with two sharp impressions. The first is the simplicity of its works compared with the difficulty of the building feat which it represents; it is as easy to understand as a bathroom tap. The second is its vulnerability. The shining clumps of tanks on the beach at Haifa and in the low cup of hills behind Tripoli are undefended and look undefendable—a perfect target either from the sea or from the air, while a thousand miles of 12-inch pipe, buried only three feet deep and marked by a scar across the desert and a line of silver telegraph poles, must depend entirely, for its security, upon local goodwill. In the open desert it is relatively secure, for a leak is detected at once by the nearest pumping-station downstream, and can be located to within less than 100 miles, so that the company's air patrol can catch and identify a caravan escaping with the tackle necessary for puncturing the pipe. But in the hills and villages through which it passes near the coast, only a force standing almost shoulder to shoulder could ensure its safety at night. The damage which a malignant Arab can do with gimcrack gear presents no difficulty to an attacker equipped with modern apparatus; in war, the pipe can be put out of action so easily that no one can count upon it for supply.

In any case, proprietary British statements about defending the pipe are a mistake, because they provoke envy and animosity which are wrongly directed. The Iraq Petroleum Company is not a British but an international concern, controlled in equal shares by British, French, American, and Anglo-Dutch capital. To label the pipe British is to court useless damage to the Company every time that Great Britain is in bad odour—for instance, during any disturbance in Palestine. Moreover, contrary to the general belief in England, Great Britain scarcely relies on the pipe-line for her oil supply, for over three-quarters of the oil pumped both to Haifa and Tripoli is taken by France—an arrangement which has no political significance, and which is dictated by the situation and capacity of French refineries. The pipe is no one nation's property, and the international nature of its ownership is its most hopeful guarantee of security.

To sum up, whatever the state of British Mediterranean armaments, the air and oil routes depend not on the powers of the British Navy, Army, or Air Force to police or advertise, but on international good manners. Both involve establishments in foreign lands, and, with the Near East in its twentieth-century mood, policing and advertisement in the lands of others tends to do the policeman or advertiser more harm than good. But the sea route is in a different category. 'Whoever it belongs to, we shall profit,' said Mr. Gladstone of the Suez Canal. He was right, but the British purchase of the Khedive's Canal shares, and the presence of British forces in bases along the route, have increased that profit by an agreeable margin.

3. *Mediterranean Strength and British Diplomacy*

The British taxpayer, then, pays for a Mediterranean fleet more for reasons of imperial prosperity than to protect a channel of supply; but, looking back, he sees that both these motives hold good only since the opening of the Canal, whereas a Mediterranean fleet was a regular item of British expenditure long before 1869. There is an older and more primitive reason for showing the flag east of Gibraltar, and one which was noticed by a discerning Englishman as soon as British squadrons first rounded the south of Spain. 'Your fleets meeting here', wrote the ambassador at Madrid to Admirals Blake and Penn in 1651, 'is of no less admiration to other foreign kingdoms (into which reports fly to them daily) than to Spain, who much admire your quickness in such strength and fresh supplies. So I believe in a short time the Spaniards, through fear and love, will grow respectful to us.' His diagnosis, though nearly three hundred years old, still applies to-day. Great Britain's chief reason for maintaining Mediterranean strength is diplomatic; reports 'flying daily' increase her authority in Europe and in the Middle East, and secure her an influence which, were she to abandon the Mediterranean, she would no longer enjoy. This fact was eclipsed and forgotten during the post-War years of diplomacy by conference, but it resumed its old importance as soon as the conference method was flouted. In 1935, despite the moral support of fifty-one nations who had unanimously denounced Italy, Great Britain failed when she tried to exert authority because her Mediterranean strength was at a low ebb.

The announcement of the British rearmament programme acted like a blood transfusion into a weakened frame. Many people, both English and foreign, would have preferred a less war-like remedy, but to weep for the happier days of general pact and general conference is of little use; a 'Mediterranean Locarno' is for the time being an out-of-date conception. To-day, collective force is still stronger than individual force, but, since the value of treaties has depreciated to a record low level, the only basis upon which a collectivity of nations can be sure of acting quickly and together is that of immediate common interest. Therefore the only reliable international agreements are those formed to meet the needs of a moment.

Recent Mediterranean politics offer two successful examples of such agreements—the first, that of January 1936, by which Great Britain, France, Yugoslavia, Greece, and Turkey agreed to assist one another in the event of aggression by Italy; the second, the Nyon Agreement of September 1937, by which all the Mediterranean Powers (except Spain and, for a time, Italy) accepted a system of patrols in order to ward off the pirate submarines which, for a reason which baffles understanding, had taken to almost indiscriminate attack on merchant shipping all over the Mediterranean. Both these undertakings were intended to counter a temporary menace; both were designed to come to an end as soon as that menace was past.

Great Britain, when she took the lead in negotiating these two agreements, benefited not only herself but other people. She incensed the Italians, in the one case by the insinuation that they might perpetrate aggression elsewhere than in Ethiopia, in the other because she carried through the Nyon Agreement despite their refusal to attend the conference; but she pleased a cluster of smaller powers whose chief desire is to lead a quiet life in a calm Mediterranean.

Any Englishman who travels abroad must be aware that the British are not as a whole very popular people. Their casual manner is interpreted as national snobbery; they are thought to be smug and self-satisfied; however diffident their present feelings, they have to live down the repute of the generation that wrote 'Rule Britannia' and sang with conviction that Britain ruled the waves 'at heaven's command'. On the other hand, their desire to avoid violent changes in the map of the world annuls these foreign antipathies in any moment of stress, when to many weaker states they become a hope, a strength, and a very present help in trouble. This sentiment is more widespread in the Mediterranean than, for instance, in Central Europe, because in the former, where immediate British interests are at once affected, the smaller states know that they can rely on the British Government to act as quickly and as determinedly as they would wish. It accounts for Great Britain's greater popularity in the Mediterranean states than elsewhere. When you travel in Greece, for instance, you can bask in the warm affection of the Greek people. 'Can we ever forget a nation linked with the birth and development of modern Greece—the England of Navarino and the Treaty of London, of Canning and Gladstone, England whose friendly protection has never failed Greece in any moment of crisis'; so runs a typical leader in an Athens newspaper of January 1938, when, on the occasion of the marriage of the Greek Crown Prince to a German princess, the Government sought to popularize the wedding by instructing the press to emphasize the bride's descent from Queen Victoria. You will meet peasants who speak of Lordos Byron; you will find yourself living on a capital reserve of goodwill stored up in the nineteenth century and implemented whenever the British Navy joins in rescue work after an earthquake, or whenever a Greek speaks of the Duchess of Kent. Whatever the leanings of the Greek Government, the Greek people are true to their old loves, the English for strength and the French for culture.

Unfortunately pro-British feeling is not everywhere so profound. The opposite emotion prevails in Palestine, and the acute hatred of the English which now fires the Palestinian Arabs is being reflected with increasing violence in every Arabic-speaking country from Morocco to the Persian Gulf. 'We used to prefer the English to other Europeans, because they were simple, and dealt with us squarely and were not greedy of small gain, but now we do so no more, because they are betraying our brothers in Palestine.' This sentiment dogs you all along the south and eastern shores of the Mediterranean with a persistence which is the more disturbing because—until the British Government defines its Palestine policy—you can offer no convincing reply.

But between the zenith in Greece and the nadir in Palestine, Great Britain enjoys relations with a range of states in which British rearmament has quickened a sense of Mediterranean security. Among them, Yugoslavia is a borderline case, because her Mediterranean tactics are subordinate to her Central European policy, but the outstanding example is Turkey. Turkey was understandably anti-British in the days when Mr. Lloyd George sponsored Greek aspirations in Asia Minor and when her ministers haggled with Mr. Amery over the Mosul boundary dispute, but she has in the last two or three years changed her mind owing to her need of several decades of Mediterranean calm if she is to complete her programme for building a modern industrial state, and to her belief that this calm is more likely to be found in the wake of England than in the wake of Italy.

But in Turkey and Yugoslavia, in the Moslem countries and even in the faithful Greece, cordialities would dwindle and animosities grow if the British were to abandon the Mediterranean. Fear of their preying neighbours would cause each of these states to seek some other strong ally, and Great Britain would vanish from the front rank in Europe and the Middle East to reappear, alongside the Netherlands, as a nation on the fringe of the continent, with a rich empire in the tropics, but without influence beyond the Rhine or south of the Alps. Loss of Mediterranean friends would follow as inevitably as memory fades. 'Absence makes the heart grow fonder,' wrote a poet of a hundred years ago, but his pretty idea does not apply to politics. La Rochefoucauld's seventeenth-century scepticism was nearer to the brutal truth: 'Les absents ont toujours tort.'

4. *Business Interests*

Apart from the trade and shipping interests already described, Great Britain possesses another less mobile Mediterranean interest—her investment in the countries of the Levant.

The British are confirmed foreign investors. They led a fashion for investment abroad which started in the early years of the nineteenth century, and which gathered momentum at a steady pace until debts earned a bad name during the World War. That fashion was followed by other industrial countries with money to burn—first by France, Belgium, and the United States, then by Germany, and later and more gingerly by Italy—but Great Britain, its inaugurator, never lost the world lead.

'In 1914, the total value of British capital invested overseas amounted to over £4,000 million, half of which was in the Empire, a large part in the United States, and not more than 5 per cent.

in Europe. On the other hand France, with foreign investments valued in all at about £1,800 million, had more than 60 per cent. of her total investments in European countries. French investments were largely directed to Eastern European countries and to the Near East.'[1]

Of the two leading countries, therefore, France was the more heavily committed in the Levant, and though the British investor has been fast overtaking her since the War, he has not yet caught her up. But the difference between the pre-War and post-War situation is not so much in the amount as in the nature of the investments belonging to the capitalist powers. Before 1914 their moneys represented political influence—a hold which reduced a state like Turkey or Egypt almost to the level of a vassal. Post-War indebtedness has shed that subservient flavour; nationalist states of to-day resent and repudiate such debts, and it is they, not the creditors, who dictate the terms of payment. Investments which had a political complexion in 1914 have therefore lost it, while the new money invested takes the form of an ordinary commercial or industrial venture carrying with it no more political weight than do Mr. Henry Ford's factory at Dagenham or the Pirelli tyre works at Barcelona.

But though the *political* interest in measuring the stakes of the rival investors is largely gone, the *material* interest of making the calculation is as great as ever. Between £300 and £400 millions of British money is placed round the Eastern Mediterranean, and there is value in knowing where it lies, if only in order to assess the loss which must accompany any Mediterranean war.

British lenders are easily the largest foreign investors in Greece. They take first place not only in holdings of the public debt, but also in foreign lending to Greek industry and public utility companies. Apart from a

[1] Crouchley, *Investment of Foreign Capital in Egyptian Companies and Public Debt*, p. 2.

public debt of nearly £89 millions, more than half of which is said to be held by British nationals, the largest single interest is that of Whitehall Securities, Limited, which has invested nearly £5 millions in the lighting, tram, and bus services of Athens. Another £5 millions is sunk in loans to the chief Greek mortgage bank, while Hambro's Bank is interested in Greek concerns to the extent of over £1 million, placed in a chemical works and in loans to various branches of industry made through an Anglo-Greek credit institution called the Hellenic and General Trust. A British bank—the Ionian Bank, Limited—is one of the Greek 'big five'; other British companies have invested smaller sums in land reclamation, drainage and mining enterprises, and several British insurance companies have deposited in Greece the guarantee which the Greek Government demands before permitting them to open agencies there. In all, British capital sunk in private enterprises in the country must amount to nearly £15 millions.

Whereas Great Britain's Greek investment still retains vestiges of the old air of patronage, that in Turkey is of a new and ultra-modern stamp. The Turks have bitter memories of the foreign money-lender; they lived in his clutches for the sixty years before the War, fleeced mainly by Frenchmen, but also by Germans, Englishmen, and Belgians, in enterprises ranging from their railways to their light-houses and cigarettes. Those who resent the harsh verb 'to fleece' have only to travel over the Turkish railways built by foreigners on the basis of a kilometric guarantee, and to watch them twist their way in unnecessary curves over the flat plains of Thrace or Anatolia.

The new Turkey reacted against this foreign stranglehold; from the moment when she secured a revised peace treaty at Lausanne, she began to work for release from the old form of indebtedness. Between then and now, she has all but liquidated the former Ottoman Public Debt, partly by means of two reductions made in agreement with the bondholders, but partly also owing to a stroke of fortune—the fixing of the sum agreed at the time of the second reduction in terms of French francs, which boon is enabling her to pay off her debt at advantageous rates every time the franc falls to a fresh low level. Turkey's next move was to set about repurchasing the old concessions accorded to foreigners before the War. She offered prices far below the original value, but secured acceptance because the concessionaires preferred selling to risking further loss. In 1938, only a few minor concessions remain in foreign hands, and Turkey's chief liabilities abroad are the instalments due in payment of the various purchases, all of which are being punctually met, and which will be paid off within a few decades.

Lastly, sickened with every memory of the foreign capitalist, Kemalist Turkey was at first inclined to oust him from private enterprise also. The War had played into her hands; it had removed many French, British, and German concerns, and had reduced the business of the wealthy Greeks and Armenians of Istanbul and Smyrna—a process which was completed firstly by the sack of Smyrna in 1922, and secondly, by the exodus of Greek capital from Istanbul which accompanied the Turco-Greek exchange of populations. Such concerns as remained, and they were very few, are in theory as welcome as are Turkish private businesses, but are in fact dying a slow death as the Turkish state hastens national development by gathering the commercial and industrial life of the country into its own most competent hands.

Turkey permitted new foreign investment, but only in forms which bore no hint of foreign dominance. Her very understandable aim is to run Turkey to the profit of the Turk, and the form of foreign lending which she prefers is therefore the short- or medium-term credit system with which the British public is familiar through the advertisements of Mr. Drage—goods delivered in a plain van upon receipt of first payment, and cessation of all liability to the purveyor immediately the last instalment is paid. On this basis, she has borrowed all round Europe. Her largest and most important contract so far is that worth about £3 millions signed in 1936 with the British firm of Brassert for the erection of a Turkish national iron and steel industry—a transaction arranged not between government and government, but between a Turkish bank and Messrs. Brassert, though the risk taken by the latter was underwritten by the British Export Credits Department.

Such contracts are worth securing if they gain a reputation for reliable British service and so increase Anglo-Turkish goodwill. The stumbling-block to further such agreements is not Turkish unwillingness, nor yet British doubt as to Turkish integrity, but the difficulty of discovering a medium in which Turkey can pay, since she is short of foreign exchange, whereas the British Empire is already over-supplied with the goods which she can offer instead. British firms who offer tenders have therefore to compete with Germans, Swedes, or Dutchmen who are ready to take payment in currants or chrome. The Turk hesitates, for in his present frame of mind he prefers the British supplier; hence the visit of a group of Turkish bankers to London early in 1938. It seems worth Great Britain's while to stretch a point, and to enable the contractor to accept payment in Turkish goods, if necessary, by arranging for their re-export, for every transaction that contributes to Anglo-Turkish friendship contributes also to Mediterranean stability.

Travelling on round the Levant, we turn south from Turkey into Syria. Here Great Britain has few material interests, for even in the old days of catch-as-catch-can in the Ottoman Empire, the area was always a French preserve. The largest wholly British concern which operates there is the Nairn Transport Company, whose great silver buses at present carry all the *de luxe* and heavy traffic on the trans-desert motor road to the east; though this company represents but a small capital investment, it enjoys a certain political significance because of British interests in the part of Iraq which it serves. Of these, strategically the most important are the air bases retained by Great Britain under the treaty of 1930 which heralded the end of the Iraqi mandate, but financially the most valuable is the Iraq Petroleum Company, in whose capital the Anglo-Iranian and the Shell oil interests both participate, and whose installations include not only the wells at Kirkuk but the pipe-line to Haifa and Tripoli.

Perhaps because he was lured by more promising speculations in Egypt and Turkey, the British investor in the Mediterranean has been strangely diffident about investment under his own flag. Malta offered little scope for his enterprise, but nevertheless he was so preoccupied elsewhere that he never thought to cater for its many visitors by building a first-class hotel, while he seemed to forget or disdain Cyprus. The British Government has to thank American capitalists for some £2 millions invested in the copper mines there. No single British investment is so large, though some British money is sunk in smaller mines extracting copper, asbestos, and gold, in the telephone company, and in a number of banks which seem superfluous for the island's present activities.

On the other hand, in Palestine, which is in many ways a land of less promise than Cyprus, the British investment is much larger because funds have been drawn towards a country into which the Jews are pouring both capital and efficiency. Money attracts money. Investment by Jewish bodies and individuals is said to have totalled £80 millions during the first sixteen years of the mandate, and when to the magnetic power of that vast sum is added the draw of Jewish acumen and enterprise, the British investor proves ready and willing to stake his capital.

By no means all the capital placed in Palestine through purchases on the London market can be counted as British commercial investment; much of it is Jewish money invested for sentimental or religious reasons, and there is of course no means of distinguishing between the two. But sums which can with justification be classed as British are the £4½ millions of the Palestine Government loan; the large investments which British insurance companies have made in the country (the Prudential alone is said to have invested over £1 million); loans amounting to more than £3 millions which have been made by banks operating with British capital, and large though unspecified amounts invested in permanent installations by the Shell Company, the Iraq Petroleum Company, and—to a less extent—by Imperial Airways. Moreover, these concerns do not exhaust the list. There is British as well as Jewish money in the great Palestine Electric Corporation, which has put over £2 millions into the country, and in a mass of smaller concerns among which the most important is the Palestine Potash Company. When all these interests are added together, a total estimate of £15 millions of British as opposed to Jewish investment in Palestine is probably not unreasonable.

But the figures for Palestine, Cyprus, Syria, Iraq, Greece, and Turkey combined all pale to insignificance before the voluminous total of foreign investment in Egypt, which was estimated in 1937 at over £500 million pounds sterling—a sum contributed chiefly by France and Great Britain, though to no small extent by that lesser but vigorous overseas investor, Belgium.

The British share, which is believed to amount to some £200 millions, is difficult to describe because it is spread over a variety and confusion of enterprises, but if experts will forgive a few generalizations, it can be divided roughly into four or five categories which will serve to show the reader where it lies.

One item is the share of British holders in the Egyptian public debt. This interest is not as large as it was before the War, for between 1914 and the present day Egypt has undertaken a steady repurchase of holdings, and, out of a total debt ranging between £90 and £100 millions, has contrived to reduce the proportion held by residents abroad from 90 per cent. in 1914 to under 40 per cent. in 1936. The exact amount held by British bondholders cannot be given, for it cannot be judged from the only data available—namely, the cities in which coupons are presented for payment, but the sum undoubtedly runs into tens of millions.

Another large item is the British Government's holding in the Suez Canal Company—that famous prize originally worth the £4 millions which Mr. Disraeli borrowed in such haste from Mr. de Rothschild in order to snap up the Khedive's shares. But the bulk of the money has a less dramatic history, and lies in more humdrum though no less repaying ventures—banks, cotton, industry, land companies, mines, or the squat steamers from which the winter tourist sees the Nile.

These interests fall roughly into three classes. The first—which represents an unascertainable figure—comprises the interests of private residents in Egypt who, though British by birth, have lived and worked for so many generations in the luscious atmosphere of Alexandria that they have formed a justly famous breed of their own. For two or three generations Barker, Peel, or Carver have been names to conjure with on the Egyptian cotton bourse, just as is Whittall in Istanbul and Jardine or Swire in Shanghai. When you see their success and prosperity, you find it hard to believe that before the days of cotton a British Levant Company agent reported of Alexandria that 'if it rayned gold there wee should not think it worth the while to goe and fetch it'. Their businesses and house property, together with those of countless lesser families who run similar concerns, have thrived for decades under the wing of two institutions—the first, the Capitulations which freed them from the whim of Khedivial jurisdiction; the second, the Mixed Courts which provided them with a tribunal in which cases of 'mixed' nationality could be tried before neutral judges, and which further protected them by a veto on the application of Egyptian legislation to foreigners. These foreigners therefore had their hands free to develop the cotton trade, and this they did on a scale which raised cotton to the level of 75 per cent. of Egypt's exports, and therefore of her wealth. For the year 1935–6 the six biggest British exporting firms alone accounted for 30 per cent. of the total export of raw cotton from the country.

The second class covers interests more directly connected with the home-country and more specifically British because their operations in Egypt are liable to taxation in Great Britain—namely, the branches and agencies of British companies which show no separate balance sheet for their business transacted in Egypt. These concerns are innumerable, and include the investments made by British insurance companies in mortgage loans and blocks of property, the credits granted by British merchants to local commerce, and concerns such as Barclays (Dominion Colonial and Overseas) Bank or the huge and magnificent business which the Shell Company has built up all over the country.

The third class comprises the British capital invested in joint-stock companies registered in Egypt, and often operating with mixed British and Egyptian capital. Again the line stretches out to the crack of doom. Sums amounting to more than £30 millions are spread over forty or fifty enterprises from the National Bank of Egypt downwards. The only general statement that can be made about them is that the trend of the investment is changing. About half the money used to lie in mortgage and land companies, but these are now undergoing a steady reduction of capital, and the amounts directed into commerce and industry are on the increase.

Now that Egypt is fully independent and the Capitulations have been brought to an end, now that the Mixed Courts enjoy no more veto on legislation and are to disappear altogether in 1949, this last form of foreign investment—that of British linked with Egyptian capital—becomes the most interesting and the most promising of the three. For there is every indication that independent Egypt will extend nationalist principles to the business transacted on her soil, that she will subject the foreigner to unwelcome pressure and hope to retain his money while banishing his presence and his influence. She has a choice of devices at her command. She can tax him; she is already beginning to legislate against his western employees; she can, like Greece, allow him to make profits but refuse to let him export those profits beyond her frontiers. His defence against undue discrimination is to join with Egyptian capitalists in the financing and management of business enterprises—a practice which has already been adopted with success in Anglo-Egyptian combines such as Misr Airwork or the Egyptian Broadcasting Company, and of which a new and outstanding example is the cotton manufacturing and dyeing business which Bradford Dyers, Limited, opened in 1937 in conjunction with Egyptian business interests.

If the Egyptian Governments of the future can curb the nationalism of irresponsible supporters who cry: 'Out with the foreigner, capital and all'—if they can preserve at least the businesses in which Egyptian interests participate, they will bring benefit to every party concerned: to the British Empire, in that they will strengthen a link in its imperial chain; to the English capitalist, who will preserve something at least of his enormous stake in Egypt, and lastly, to Egypt itself. For though the Egyptian has capital and labour at his disposal, he lacks the third element of business success, which is enterprise, and needs an infusion of that precious quality from foreign associates if he is to keep his nation's economic machinery in its present running-order.

Meantime, does the presence of British troops and ships in the Mediterranean in any way contribute to the security of the British stake in the Levant? The answer is: Not as it used to do. Times have changed since one of Lord Palmerston's best speeches swayed the House of Commons into voting that a British Fleet had done right to bombard the Piraeus in order to support a claim advanced against the Greek Government by a Portuguese Jew, unsuitably named Don Pacifico, who was a British subject because he happened to be born in Gibraltar.

> 'The question the House has to decide is whether, as the Roman in days of old held himself free from indignity when he could say "*Civis Romanus sum*", so also a British subject, in whatever land he may be, shall feel confident that the watchful eye and the strong arm of England will protect him against injustice and wrong.'

The thunderous sentiments of 1850 sound strange in an age when a British ambassador can be wounded or an American gunboat sunk without evoking a retort more serious than a 'stiff note' or 'stern protest'.

Nevertheless, the Mediterranean fleet still plays some part in protecting British nationals and their interests in the Near East. So long as they retain homes and businesses there, they derive more out of the visit of an occasional battleship than a mere rosy glow of national pride, or a homely feeling when they hear the slurred accents of Plymouth bargaining and joking in an Egyptian bazaar. That battleship imparts to them something more than mere satisfaction or pleasure. It gives them standing; it adds to their 'face'; they would receive brusquer treatment if it were not there.

5. *Great Britain and Egypt*

Two hundred million pounds and a prosperous colony of British subjects are not Great Britain's only interest in Egypt. More important from an imperial point of view is her political and diplomatic link with the Egyptian Government—a link which plays no small part in her imperial defence plans.

That link has had a chequered history. In 1882, by which time the Suez Canal had proved its worth, Great Britain 'occupied' Egypt from motives which were at bottom strategic, and, largely from those motives, remained in occupation. In 1914, for the same reason, she changed the country's status to that of a protectorate. In 1922, when she declared its independence, the same reason again impelled her to reserve four points for later consideration—among them her imperial communications, Egypt's defence, and the Sudan. For fourteen years these questions were a stumbling-block to Anglo-Egyptian agreement; they wrecked four separate sets of conversations as to the terms on which Egyptian independence should become complete. The trouble was that the Egyptians, being good nationalists, resented the presence of British troops in their country, while the British, knowing the unstable, competitive atmosphere of Egyptian politics, feared that internal turmoil in Egypt might at some awkward moment upset their imperial defence schemes, and therefore sought to retain some hold not only on the defence of the Suez Canal but on that of the rest of Egypt. The deadlock was complete.

But in 1936 it dissolved into thin air. A few months sufficed to settle questions which had previously baffled the wiliest diplomats on both sides. The miracle came about through the agency of a third party—Italy.

The Italian attack on Ethiopia frightened the Egyptians almost more than it frightened any other nation. They saw in it a threat to the Sudan; they feared for their western frontier which marched with Libya; they even feared—though quite needlessly—for their Nile water-supply. They became painfully conscious of their weakness and their riches, and of their consequent desirability as a meal for a dissatisfied power. The danger united all the political parties for the first time in Egyptian history; their immediate reaction was to combine and seek a strong champion. Simultaneous nervousness overcame the British Committee of Imperial Defence. They pictured Italy, as the conqueror of Ethiopia, enjoying a pincer grip upon Egypt and therefore acquiring an influence over the Egyptian Government. They reasoned that, pursuing her expansionist plans, she might turn this influence to anti-British account, and then . . . what of the Suez Canal?

These mutual anxieties led to a mutual benefit agreement. By the Anglo-Egyptian treaty of August 1936 Egypt secured the removal of all British troops into the Canal Zone, a reaffirmation of the condominium with Great Britain over the Sudan, British support of her candidature for the League of Nations and, last but not least, a promise to secure abolition of the Capitulations—those ancient foreign privileges which, though they had done so much to create Egypt's wealth, were regarded by the twentieth-century Egyptian as a slight upon his dignity. Great Britain secured corresponding advantages—Egyptian recognition of her interest in the Suez Canal, the right to keep a force of 10,000 men and 400 pilots on its banks until the Egyptian army was strong enough to take over canal defence, a monopoly of foreign instruction and equipment of that army, and the right to use Egyptian landing-grounds and seaplane anchoranges. In the interests of both parties, a network of strategic roads, railways, and landing-grounds was to be built at Egyptian expense.

Both allies were on the whole pleased with their handiwork. The Egyptian, who is an ardent nationalist, of course remained anti-foreign, and therefore anti-British, but he preferred the British connexion to the Italian menace because Great Britain was a sated power whereas Italy was not, while the British naval and military authorities congratulated themselves on securing the safety of the Canal for an indefinite period. The foreign communities, however, were not so pleased; British, French, Italians, Greeks, Belgians, and the rest joined in upbraiding the British Government for its unconditional promise to promote the abolition of the Capitulations. They accused it of losing its head in a strategic emergency, of betraying a trust, and of jettisoning their interests in its flurry. Their case was not as strong as it sounds, for they had known for years that their Capitulatory privileges must go, but they were anxious to save something from the wreck. They argued that the Mixed Courts, at least, should remain, since they guaranteed a punctual and impartial justice which was just as valuable to Egyptians as to foreigners. But they argued in vain. Their other privileges had rankled for too long, and Egypt preferred to negotiate the abolition of every institution that was tainted with the old idea of foreign rights. At the Montreux Capitulations Conference of 1937 she secured terms which afforded the communities twelve years in which either to liquidate their businesses or else to make their own arrangements for carrying on their lives and work under Egyptian rule.

The year 1937 therefore saw the beginning of a new relation between Great Britain and Egypt. A dependency became an alliance; the Residency changed into an Embassy; students who had reviled Great Britain for years acclaimed her as a friend, and ministers who had viewed British control with suspicion and antagonism became willing to work with England on a basis of friendly cooperation.

Both sides stand to gain by a continuance of this

honeymoon. Egypt secures diplomatic and military support until she is strong enough to protect her frontiers and her riches; Great Britain secures a guarantee of safe passage to and from the east in an imperial emergency. The threat to harmony comes not from the staid, unemotional Englishman, but from his younger and more wayward partner.

Strong anti-foreign sentiments are the hall-mark of modern nationalism, whether in Europe, Asia, or Africa, and these sentiments are strongest in a country like Egypt which has known and disliked a foreign ruler. She forgot them in the panic of 1936 and the thankfulness which followed when she secured an ally, but fear and gratitude are both of them transitory emotions; they diminished as soon as the novelty wore off the Treaty. Among thinking Egyptians they revive whenever Italian policy smacks of expansion, but among the Egyptian crowd they are long since forgotten. One problem for Great Britain is, therefore: can she in any way contribute to her popularity in Egypt and so to her imperial security?

Her principal, indeed her only requirement as far as imperial defence is concerned is an internally stable Egypt—that is, an Egyptian Government with whom she can treat with some certainty, and an Egyptian people sufficiently under control to ensure that it will not knife its own leaders in the back. Whether this satisfactory state is achieved through a democratic government or through a dictatorship under a popular young king is not Great Britain's business; though most Englishmen, being liberally minded, would instinctively prefer a democracy, the point of interest to them is less the means than the end—namely, at least a moderate degree of stability in Egypt.

Some observers feel that to hope for this is to hope too much of the Egyptian. They point gloomily to a number of evil omens and say that if Great Britain needs a stable Egypt she will be obliged to step back, sooner or later, into Egyptian affairs, if only to prevent some other power from stepping into her vacated place. They instance as the characteristics which will prove Egypt's undoing the petty rivalries which pervade her politics, the personal ambitions which are placed before national needs, the violent transfers of allegiance from one leader to another in order to be on the right side of the next government, the family loyalties which demand that relations and friends shall receive an appointment to government office, and the consequent inefficiency and insecurity which pervade the civil service. But the fatal effect of these habits can be over-estimated. Judged by modern British standards they are nefarious and harmful, but they do not render a country unfit for independence. They prevail in several of the Ruritanias of South-eastern Europe and South America without calling for foreign intervention, while any one who has lived through a political crisis in Paris knows that one or two of them flourish in a great western state. They are not an insuperable bar to success as a nation.

On the other hand, Egypt's rulers have other and more formidable breakers ahead. The worst is the difficulty of controlling a crowd which has been born and bred on opposition and agitation. Fourteen out of Egypt's sixteen million inhabitants are an illiterate, cheerful peasantry, fully occupied with earning its bread—a slumbering volcano which is only just beginning to demand the rights which it has learnt to enjoy under British administration. But the remaining two million are different. They live in towns and follow politics, and for years have been accustomed to use mob tactics in order to express their dislike of foreign dominance. By nature excitable and irresponsible, they have difficulty in dropping this habit, and they clamour as lustily against their newly independent government as they did against British control.

Egypt is faced with the problem of curing these mob

habits—of instilling a sense of responsibility into the schoolboys and students who will in due course become voters. The educational task before her is not only one of quantity but of quality. She has just taken over sole control of that complicated mechanism, her government, but she is not yet in a position to educate enough skilled mechanics to run it. Her government schools teach facts, but not the art of reasoning from those facts. They therefore turn out a breed rich in clerks but short of administrators; they produce young men who are full of self-confidence, but who, when faced with a decision, often prove unwilling to take initiative or shoulder responsibility. Her best administrators are almost all to be found among the men who have worked shoulder to shoulder with British officials, or else have received a thorough education abroad.

Her more thoughtful public men recognize this difficulty, but are helpless in face of it because no one of them is in office for long enough to put through the necessary educational reforms, while a new minister is seldom loyal to the schemes of his predecessor. The wheel spins round in a pernicious circle as successive ministries discover that a modern state is not built in a day, and that their greatest difficulties often come from the unbridled behaviour of their own supporters.

This educational problem, which is enough to daunt the stoutest heart, does perhaps justify the pessimistic view that if Great Britain wants a tranquil Egypt she will have to take a hand in the tranquillizing process. The question is: what form should her assistance take? The pessimist prophesies that nothing short of a return to the old control will ensure stability, but here he is thinking in nineteenth-century terms. Present British and French experience in Moslem territories is proving that whereas Moslem allies are an asset, Moslem dependencies are a liability. Great Britain would saddle herself with a fresh burden of Islamic ill will if disorders in Egypt were to tempt her to turn busybody and to reassume the controls; all the advantages accruing to the Committee of Imperial Defence from the Anglo-Egyptian treaty would be threatened, and many of them undone. Great Britain's interest, therefore, is to prevent those disorders not by intervention, but by applying such influence as she may possess to calming passions and reconciling quarrels.

Popularity in Egypt is too much for a western nation to hope for, but since the Egyptian state is as yet too weak to surmount international crises unaided, her government must lean for diplomatic support upon one or other of the western powers. Chiefly because the Suez Canal runs through her territory, two powers in particular are ready to lend her that support; one is Great Britain, the other Italy. Egyptians, who have a liking and a flair for being on the winning side, will no doubt always incline towards the one of the two whose policy seems the more likely to promise success—towards the one who is strongest, and best able to defend her. Nevertheless, certain permanent considerations seem likely to weigh with her whenever she is confronted with the problem of choice.

Italians claim an advantage over Great Britain in that the Oriental mind is nearer to the Latin than to the Anglo-Saxon mentality; the assertion is true, but Great Britain seems to possess rival advantages which outweigh it. The first is one that those who know Egyptian society will appreciate, namely, the personal friendships which exist between individual Egyptians—statesmen, civil servants, lawyers, journalists—and individual British officials with whom they have worked or consorted. The respect and admiration cherished by the one for the other constitute an important bond between the two countries. The second is the fact that Great Britain is Egypt's best customer. The third and greatest advantage which Great Britain enjoys is her strong liking for the *status quo*; above all, she seeks no population outlets and makes no speeches about expansion.

6. *Security in Four Footholds*

In the days when Great Britain made her way along the Mediterranean, in a series of stately pounces, from Gibraltar to Malta, to Cyprus, to Egypt, to Palestine, she was in a position to hold each new fortress by her strength alone. To-day her position has changed. Subject populations have developed minds of their own, and she is obliged to depend for her security not only upon force of arms, but upon local contentment and goodwill.

Gibraltar is the colony in which these new conditions affect her least, for there the inhabitants outnumber the normal garrison by relatively little—only some three to one. Moreover, the size of the population is in any case unimportant, for the sentiments which it has acquired in the course of two centuries are markedly pro-British.

Its few leading families pride themselves on their loyalty to the Crown, and its working classes follow suit for material reasons if not from inner conviction; they have long been accustomed to pocketing British pay, and good wages have become a habit. Further, while they speak Spanish among themselves, they can most of them also talk English, and they therefore mix constantly with Englishmen; their women have intermarried over generations with British soldiers and sailors and policemen. Thus, though they are fond of criticizing British policy (which they do with a left bias) they instinctively buy poppies on Poppy Day, and stand up when they hear 'God Save the King'.

The value of their contentment is often under-estimated. It contrasts so favourably with the surly grumbling farther east that it is an asset not lightly to be discarded. Yet it is ignored by a minority who argue that Great Britain should seize the first opportunity of exchanging Gibraltar for Ceuta—its Spanish counterpart on the African side of the Straits.

The protagonists of Ceuta base their argument on the vulnerability of Gibraltar harbour. Nature, by placing this on the landward side of the Rock, made it a target for batteries mounted anywhere along twenty miles of the Spanish coast, and while it is easy for a gun to hit a harbour, it is another matter for the harbour to silence the gun. Strategically, Ceuta offers two advantages which Gibraltar lacks; it has a harbour protected on its landward side and it boasts an open space suitable for an aerodrome. These may or may not be great gains; all depends upon the power of defence which a small, isolated stronghold can put up against modern attack. But in one respect Great Britain would lose by the exchange.

Ceuta is a Spanish town of 60,000 inhabitants—as much a part of Spain as is Alicante or Cadiz. Its people are staunch Spanish nationalists. Quite apart from the important question of their rights, any strategic advantages gained by the change would be offset by an immeasurable drawback—that of acquiring a nest of irredentism of a kind unknown at Gibraltar.

Nowhere else in the Mediterranean does Great Britain enjoy the same comfortable measure of placidity. In each of her other three possessions anti-British influences stir the local population. Malta is the colony in which they do so with least success.

On the whole, the Maltese like being British. The majority prefer Great Britain to her rival—Italy—for two permanent reasons which do not apply in many colonies. In the first place, the vast sums of money which Great Britain spends in their island flow very directly into their pockets. She brings over £3 millions a year into Malta, of which more than half a million is paid in wages to local dockyard workers alone. The Maltese know that Italy, who has a surfeit of bases in the central Mediterranean, would employ them less freely. Secondly, under British rule they enjoy self-administration. They are an energetic and competent people, and—except for three British officials *de carrière*—the Maltese civil service is entirely Maltese-staffed. The holders of government posts from highest to lowest feel that they might not do so well under another flag.

Between inclination and force of example, they have adopted some very British ways. They keep public houses, not cafés, and drink beer, standing up, instead of apéritifs, sitting down. They wear English clothes, and if possible go to England for their holidays. Their papers give British sporting news. They christen their buses the 'Princess Elizabeth' and the 'Windsor Castle', and they know who won the Derby. Their jubilee demonstrations overtaxed the island's supply of electric light, and their applications for coronation illuminations had to be curbed. This exuberance is not all love of show. No one could doubt their emotion when King George V died; he was their king, and they mourned a personal loss.

Malta, bristling with armaments and surrounded with battleships and aeroplanes busy at target practice, is very naturally a thorn in the Italian flesh. It is only seventy miles from the coast of Sicily; it can be seen from Mount Etna on a clear day, and any power must dislike the presence of a foreign stronghold so near its shore. The inevitable reaction is to try and weaken that foreign strength, and this Italy began to do long before the Anglo-Italian quarrel of 1935.

Italians like to think that they can appeal to the Maltese on grounds of race and kinship, but in this belief they are wrong. Their theory is disproved by that reliable indicator—language. Maltese, which has been sufficiently virile to survive centuries of conquest, even though it lacks such preservatives as a folk-lore or a literature, has adopted some Italian words, but is in fact a Semitic and not a Latin tongue. Even an amateur can see this at once; for instance, the Lord's Prayer in Maltese begins:

Missierna li inti fis-smewwiet,
Jitqaddes ismek,
Tigi saltnatek
Ikun li trid Int, kif fis-sema hekda fl-art.

The languages to which this is most nearly related are Syriac and Arabic, and a Maltese can make himself understood in Tunis but not in Rome.

But Italy, though she fails to claim kin, can appeal to the Maltese through two other channels—their Church and their culture. Either method can be effective, for on the one hand, the Maltese are very devout, and on the other, Italian has been their language of manners and learning since the eighteenth century, spoken by the nobility, the priests, and in the courts of law. Its use has never died out because, unlike most imperial powers, the British are diffident about imposing their own language upon their colonies. Thus, when they took over Malta—which they did by invitation in 1814—they allowed Italian to stand, ranking it on the same level as English in schools and in the administration. Italy was therefore well placed for sapping British strength should she so wish, and at one time she did so with vigour. During the years in which she first began to spread Fascist propaganda overseas, she intervened in Maltese politics with a success which twice forced Great Britain to suspend the constitution which in 1921 gave Malta responsible government.

In fairness to Fascism it must be confessed that the first Anglo-Italian brush, which arose not with the Italian Government but with the Vatican, was in great part due to lack of tact on the Maltese side. A Maltese premier, Lord Strickland, quarrelled with the local clergy and crossed swords with the Pope—a rash act which caused the Church to influence voters against him at the elections of 1930. Faced with a form of foreign intervention, Great Britain suspended parliamentary government for two years, during which time she tried to minimize Italian propaganda by curtailing the teaching of Italian.

But the thin edge of a wedge had been inserted. Fascism was growing more active, and, when elections were reinstituted in 1932, the Maltese, moved by Church bias against Lord Strickland, returned some of his pro-Italian opponents to power. The new cabinet set about reviving pro-Italian sentiments. It evaded the British restrictions on the teaching of Italian by giving 'voluntary' instruction after school hours, and it encouraged Fascist agents to offer the Maltese free holidays in Italy, free medical aid, and the hospitality of a princely Italian club, the *Istituto de Coltura*. The British grew apprehensive, and in 1933 once more suspended the constitution, which was finally repealed in 1936.

The curve of Italianism reached its zenith in 1933; from then onwards it began to decline, partly owing to outside factors, but largely because the British authorities, abandoning their former *laissez-faire*, began to adopt a cultural policy which gave the Maltese their due. For instance, they set about demolishing the social barrier which divided the British residents from the Maltese aristocracy. Prejudices on both sides were broken down on the day when thirty Maltese were elected to that hyper-British institution, the Union Club, and as many Englishmen to the *Casino Maltese*.

But the most far-reaching change they made was the substitution of Maltese for Italian in the law-courts—a tardy measure of justice which enabled the inhabitants to stand their trial in a language which they could understand. Just as a natural force thrusts to the surface the moment artificial restraint is removed, so the vernacular began to gain ground. The advocates of Italian found themselves swimming upstream when a new Maltese orthography was adopted by the Government, in the schools and in the press, and when the Church, recognizing the advantages of the new medium, translated the Bible and catechism into Maltese.

The Italo-Abyssinian dispute helped the British authorities in their task. It put an end to the former tug-of-war between the Colonial Office (struggling with Italian propagandists) and the Foreign Office (anxious to maintain friendship with Italy). It enabled the governor to expel Italian undesirables, to close Italian schools, and to shut down the *Istituto de Coltura*.

The reception given to these measures indicates the weakness of pro-Italian feeling. A few vociferous leaders complained bitterly of British high-handedness, but most of their followers accepted the decisions from London. They were undergoing an anti-Italian reaction because they had been deeply shocked by two happenings in the early spring of 1936. The first was the hearing of some rather ignoble evidence in a spy case in which the Italian consul was implicated; the second, the arrest of two Maltese in Libya for making statements which an Italian informer had overheard them utter in Tunis. This second revelation convinced most Maltese that they were freer under British than under Italian rule. Even their annoyance at the British failure to restore their self-government has not since given them reason to change this view.

Moreover, many of them had never gone through the Italian phase. Though foreigners may be sceptical, it is a fact that large numbers of Maltese have come to feel as much a part of the British Empire as does an Englishman, and enjoy the feeling, and would not wish to be otherwise. They cherish these sentiments more easily than does a colony like Rhodes or Cyprus because they are a people apart—a European race, but without racial affinities in Europe. And where their feelings towards Great Britain are luke-warm, their personal interests usually turn the scale. A Maltese likes the British passport which enables him to migrate from his over-populated island to other parts of the British Empire, and he is far too practical to turn down the advantages offered by a rich and rearming nation. Thus, he goes smilingly through air-raid drill, bustles about in a gas-mask, and tells you with relish that his son is among the new Maltese recruits to the Royal Engineers, and is learning to work the searchlights.

Even the few ardent pro-Italians recognize the advantages of a British currency. They admit that they want to have their cake and eat it. 'What we would really like', said one, 'is the Italian language but the pound sterling,' and, if confronted with a choice between these blessings, those who would forego the latter could be counted upon the fingers of one hand.

Whereas in Malta an active foreign influence has to labour to make headway, in Cyprus the position is the opposite. A passive but far more potent influence stirs the population to its depths, and the British find imperial loyalty harder to capture. For, excepting a Turkish minority which forms 20 per cent. of the whole, and which is staunchly pro-British, the Cypriot population is Greek to the core—Greek by sentiment, Greek by language, and Greek by church. Cypriot families are proud to trace Greek ancestry. Nationalist societies vaunt their 'great Greek fatherland and immortal Greek civilization'. They share Greek joys and sorrows, take an interest in Greek athleticism, and buy the Greek press.

They cherish no such feelings for Great Britain. She weakened her hold upon them when, in 1915, she offered their island to Greece as a bribe for entering the war in order to save Serbia. Moreover, she has not so far tempted them with any material advantages such as she has brought to Malta. On the contrary, they consider her to be not only niggardly, but a robber. There is some truth in the allegation. The trouble is that she acquired Cyprus for a purpose for which it proved useless. She therefore lost interest in it, and allowed it to degenerate into a Cinderella, and the Fairy Godmother, though announced two or three times, has not yet put in an appearance.

Cyprus was leased from the Turks in 1878. Though never used for countering the Russian menace in Asia as it was meant to do, it could not be abandoned because it lay too near the Suez Canal. Great Britain therefore retained it on leasehold, but, being a tenant and not an owner, she spent as little as possible on the fabric. She rubbed along like a caretaker. Even after she annexed the island when Turkey entered the War, she continued to be as economical as was compatible with keeping the Cypriots contented. She made amends for her parsimony by offering them moral joys. She smiled while they flew Greek flags and kept Greek Independence Day and talked about *enosis*—union with Greece. Inevitably, they drifted under the influence of the Greek priest and the Greek money-lender; they drifted steadily from 1878 until 1931.

In 1927 a new and energetic governor started using his influence in Whitehall in order to give Cyprus its due. Sir Ronald Storrs made roads; he secured a loan in order to provide the island with a harbour; he advertised it with new stamps; he proclaimed its beauty and the possibilities of its tourist traffic. He delighted the cultured classes by his ability to quote Homer, and he promised the island prosperity. No one had paid it so much attention since Disraeli had called it 'the rosy realm of Venus' and 'the key to Western Asia'.

Perhaps the Cypriots would have gone on living on promises if they had not had one bitter and legitimate grievance against Great Britain. The story of the Cyprus Tribute is long, and shows the British Government in the unbecoming role of Shylock, but, long though it is, it affects Cypriot opinion, and therefore must be told.

The Turks had made an annual profit on Cyprus, and Great Britain, under the original lease agreement, undertook to pay them the equivalent of that profit as rent. The sum was fixed at the average amount received in the last five years of Turkish rule, namely, at £99,799. 11*s*. 3*d*. But this arrangement failed to allow for Turkish methods. While the Turkish tax-collector had extracted the maximum out of the Cypriots, the Turkish administrator had spent the minimum on their welfare. British ideas of administration were more lavish, and the Cypriots soon found themselves paying both the Tribute money and the extra cost of British rule. The burden on the island's revenues left nothing over for development; in fact, the British taxpayer usually had to put his hand in his pocket to make good a deficit.

Meanwhile, to the annoyance of Turkey, Great Britain did not pay over the Tribute in cash. She kept it in London, and used most of it to pay the interest on an old Ottoman Loan which she had guaranteed in 1855. The small unexpended surplus she put into Consols against the rainy day when Turkey might default on some other obligation.

In the eyes of the Cypriots Great Britain was an extortioner, and was robbing their pockets to pay the interest on a debt with which Cyprus had nothing to do. The bald British reply was that, taking into account the help from Great Britain which yearly met the Cyprus deficit, the Cypriots were no worse off than in Turkish days, that they were in any case much better ruled than formerly, and that how the Tribute money was used was nothing to do with Cyprus.

Great Britain might have been expected to make a

change when she annexed the island in 1914; but she did not. She simply changed the Tribute's name to 'Share of Cyprus of the Turkish Debt Charge', and continued to collect and use the money as before. She did not relieve the pressure until, in 1927, she undertook to pay the island an annual grant-in-aid equivalent to the exact amount of the Tribute, receiving in return an annual £10,000 from Cyprus as a contribution towards imperial defence. She then stated that she regarded the question as closed. Not so the Cypriots. They claimed that she owed them two sums: first, the unexpended surpluses which she had been investing in Consols since 1878, and secondly, the Tribute money for the thirteen years during which Cyprus had been a British colony. They rightly argued that there was no reason for starting the new arrangement in 1927; if legitimate then, it had been legitimate since 1914.

The climax came in 1931. The British, after years of humouring Greek sentiment, had little control over the crowd, and the Cypriot extremists were able to advance plenty of inflammatory arguments. Sir Ronald Storrs's promises were many of them unfulfilled; the British Navy was said to be mutinying at Invergordon; Great Britain was a dying nation; she had left the gold standard and Greece had not. But the most rousing anti-British argument arose out of an incident in the Tribute controversy. In answer to a question in the House of Commons, the British Chancellor of the Exchequer had announced that the unexpended surpluses invested in Consols had been 'disposed of for the sinking fund of the Turkish loan of 1855'. This reply enraged the Cypriots; the interest on the loan in question had been guaranteed, but not the principal, and they felt that Great Britain had unwarrantably used their money to pay off some undeserving nineteenth-century speculators.

In October 1931 they marched to Government House to protest. There some one set fire to a car parked outside the door, and some one else threw a blazing fragment through a window, and they burnt down the house.

The insurrection which followed waked the British to a more active policy. They exiled turbulent bishops, they forbade Greek flags, and they imposed a stern D.O.R.A., the repeal of which was not announced until 1937.

To-day the Cypriots are still discontented, but their discontent is different in nature from that which prevailed in 1931. A metamorphosis happened during the Italo-Abyssinian dispute, which stirred them into some logical thinking. They reasoned that Greece, though attractive, was impotent, and that unless they wanted to belong to Italy, they had better support Great Britain. 'When's the war,' the peasants asked the officials, 'because we are on your side.' They have several reasons for considering Italian rule undesirable. They are taught to do so by their priests, who tell them that, once upon a time, Italians subjected the Orthodox to the Latin Church. Their Church has a long memory, and has not forgotten the Bulla Cypria of 1260, or the dethronement of the Archbishop of Cyprus by the Venetians in the sixteenth century. These displeasing memories are confirmed by more recent events; the Cypriots were pro-Turk in the Italo-Turkish war of 1911, and resented the Italian capture of the Dodecanese. Moreover, they hear that Italy is over-populated; they know from sponge-fishers and itinerant merchants that she has settled Italian peasants in Rhodes, and they do not want such settlements in Cyprus. Even the ardent nationalists who still cry out for Greek sovereignty now include in their demands provision for a British base on Cypriot soil.

But Great Britain did not derive the advantage that she might have done from this change of heart. She failed to seize upon and encourage it among the educated, cultivated classes. She continued to administer them as if they were black sheep, or, worse, the backward tribes among whom too many of her officials have had all their training. You hear echoes of Greek resentment on this score not only in Cyprus, but as far away as Athens and Alexandria.

Individual officials succeeded in changing their tactics, but they could not make bricks without straw, and Westminster furnished no straw. Till the British Government imparts some impetus to the island's development by helping it to build a proper commercial harbour or a good hotel, Cyprus's great possibilities as a tourist centre will remain unexploited, shipping and air services will continue to pass it by, and there will still be no funds available to build a proper hospital or to stamp out malaria. Only a sated power could possess so neglected a colony—a place of beauty but of disenchantment owing to hard beds, crumbling monuments, and a disillusioned, zestless administration which can only patch the fabric because it has not the wherewithal to renew it.

Presumably that wherewithal will be provided if the British Admiralty and Air Force adopt the colony. If the Cypriots cannot be united to Greece, they ask nothing better than that their central plain should become an air base and Famagusta a naval harbour. They would like to be a second Malta and to enjoy the prosperity which that distinction implies. But, until bases are built and sailors and airmen are spending their pay in the island, the Cypriot Greeks are merely putting up with British rule for fear of falling into worse hands. At the coronation review at Nicosia in 1937, a Union Jack on the bastion above the saluting troops was flying from a blue-and-white Greek flagpole. As an illustration of the present Cypriot state of mind, the symbol could not be bettered.

In Palestine, the task of preserving British security is on quite another plane. Whereas in Malta or Cyprus the problem is practical, and is soluble in terms of pounds, shillings, and pence, in Palestine it is psychological, because, in the case of both Jews and Arabs, national passions have come to transcend material interests.

The English are at their worst when confronted with a situation of this sort. Their own phlegmatic patriotism is governed by self-interest and common sense, and when they meet emotional nationalism, they cannot imagine its essence. They are baffled when they try to deal with it. Thus, they can take a general strike or an abdication in their stride, but they bungle the trial of three Welsh nationalists on a charge of arson and rouse the primitive instincts of half Wales. They understand the South Africans, but not the Irish. Unfortunately for British imperial well-being, the Palestine problem falls within the Irish class. Still more unfortunately, it looms larger and more formidable than ever the Irish question did, for on its solution hangs the goodwill of two great powerful faiths—Islam and Jewry.

Great Britain originally decided to extend her imperial commitments into the Arab territories of the Ottoman Empire because she was alarmed at the threat which the Turkish advance in 1915 had caused to the Suez Canal. She and France therefore agreed in a secret treaty of 1916—the Sykes-Picot Agreement—that they would divide the lands between the Mediterranean and the Persian Gulf into two 'spheres of influence' in the event of victory. During her pursuit of other War interests, Great Britain also made two further promises affecting this same territory. In 1915, in a correspondence between Sir Henry McMahon—then Commander-in-Chief in Cairo—and the Sherif of Mecca, she promised the Arabs independence over a wide area if they would revolt in the desert against the Turks. Two years later, partly out of a long-standing regard for the Jews, but partly also to gain the support of the Jews of the United States for the allied cause, she made the famous Balfour Declaration of November 1917, by which she promised a 'National Home in Palestine' to the Jewish people.

Promises given under stress sometimes prove awkward when the stress is past, but Great Britain, in thus committing herself to the Jews and Arabs, had no fears for the future. The undertakings added to her immediate chances of victory, but, as far as she could see, they also added to her ultimate security. She counted on establishing two friendly populations whose gratitude would further her strategic interests.

Palestine in 1938 constitutes so complete a reversal of these hopes that it reduces the original British calculations to a mockery. Two bitterly antagonistic populations dislike Great Britain only slightly less than they dislike one another. You sense hatred exuding from the passers-by as you tread the streets. You feel as if a pall had lifted the moment you cross the frontier into the Lebanon or Transjordan and meet a smiling policeman. Nowhere can you escape the oppressive atmosphere. Tragic to relate, Jerusalem is no longer built as a city that is at unity in itself.

Great Britain's failure to secure a contented Palestine is in part her own fault, for an analysis of her policy since the War reveals two disastrous weaknesses. For those equipped with a knowledge of the events of eighteen years, it is easy enough to look back and be wise, to denounce mistakes and to criticize decisions which were taken in the dark, because the situation was without precedent. But Great Britain's cardinal error seems to have been her failure to recognize the danger inherent in the vague wording of her promises to the Jews and Arabs. Her imprecision led to fears and uncertainties, and roused the passions which she has now to try and quell.

Her promise to the Arabs covered an area which she defined so vaguely that Arab leaders have a good case for maintaining that it included Palestine, despite her affirmations that she never intended it to do so. Further, she assured them that they could rely on her to safeguard their rights, but she never explained what she understood those rights to be. To the Jews, she never said what she meant, either in size or nature, by a 'National Home'. She told them in 1922 that it did not mean 'a wholly Jewish Palestine', but, apart from that general statement, she let them preach and plan for a return on an unlimited scale. The Palestinian Arabs, therefore, began to fear the day when they would be overwhelmed by Jewish numbers, and she allowed this fear to grow until it turned to violence and bloodshed.

Her second weakness lay in her refusal to read the signs of the times. When she undertook the mandate, she calculated that she could simultaneously fulfil a triple promise—giving to the Jews a national home, to the Arabs protection of their rights, and to the joint community self-government. Obviously, fulfilment of this programme hung upon one essential condition—namely, that the Arabs could be brought to submit to a Jewish incursion. But when events began to prove that this was not to be, she closed her eyes to their significance. She failed to interpret the fact that every time the Jewish graph was on the down-grade, the Arabs were quiet, and that every time it took an upward curve they struck or rebelled. She persisted in hoping that the populations would settle down, and in time enable her to muddle through. Thus, even though tempers were rising on both sides, she pursued a lenient, conciliatory policy designed to create as little ill-feeling as possible. Herself full of capacity for compromise, she failed to see that she was dealing with two peoples belonging to the most uncompromising race in the world.[1] She patched and placated until both sides began to interpret her policy as weakness—until the Arabs were encouraged to violence, and the Jews, distrusting her powers of protection, exerted

[1] Both are Semitic peoples. Cf. T. E. Lawrence: 'Semites had no half tones in their register of vision. They were a people of primary colours, or rather of black and white, who saw the world always in contour. . . . They knew only truth and untruth, belief and unbelief, without our hesitating retinue of finer shades.' *Seven Pillars of Wisdom*, p. 38.

themselves to strengthen their position by the admission of more Jews. This was the pitch which matters had reached when armed rebellion against her rule broke out in 1936.

Great Britain is to blame for her policy far more than for her original assumption that the Arabs would accept an influx of Jews. At the time when she took over the mandate, there were grounds for belief that they might do so. The leaders of the two groups—the Emir Feisal on the one hand and Dr. Chaim Weizmann on the other—expressed 'a perfect understanding'.[1] Both peoples were the seed of Abraham; they were living side by side elsewhere—in Algeria, for instance, and in Mesopotamia—and they had done so in Palestine itself before the War, where colonies of Jews had been successfully planted at the expense of Baron de Rothschild and other philanthropists. Great Britain realized that the type of Jew migrating to the new National Home would be different, because he would be richer and more westernized, but she hoped and believed that his money and enterprise would act as a lubricant and enable him to slip easily into place.

And indeed, for some years after mandatory rule began, she still had some reason for holding this view. On the one hand, she could not foresee the volume which Jewish numbers were later to acquire; as lately as 1927 more Jews left Palestine than entered it. On the other, some Arabs liked the brisk atmosphere which the new-comers were importing into the country. The Jews were hated from the outset by a handful of *effendi* families, who saw in Jewish riches and power a threat to their own feudal position, but the Arab business man and Arab worker were attracted by the prospect of higher wages and better trade. Arabs from the neighbouring deserts began to migrate into Palestine, while impoverished states next-door (notably the Lebanon and Transjordan) actively

[1] Letter of December 10, 1918, from the Emir Feisal to Sir Herbert Samuel, quoted in the House of Lords, July 20, 1937.

expressed a desire to receive Jews. The British took heart, and felt that harmony might in the end prove possible.

Events have since demonstrated that they lacked imagination as to future requirements. They left out of account a phenomenon the full force of which was foreseen by no one, not even by the Jews themselves. That phenomenon was the immense motive power of Zionism which was unleashed during the building of the National Home.

This force took some years to acquire momentum, but to-day it has to be seen to be understood; it is much the most impressive thing in Palestine—magnificent, but overwhelming. It depends not only on money, but on inspiration, labour, and sacrifice. It reaches its highest manifestations in the renaissance of the Hebrew language—which has been revived and raised to the level of a national vernacular in less than twenty years—and in the Jewish agricultural colonies, where faith of the kind that moves mountains has turned sand dunes into vegetable gardens and orange groves. The spirit which it has engendered is, in its force and its conviction, as powerful as that reigning in Elizabethan England or Nazi Germany. It is an unleashing of the pent-up emotions of two thousand years—of desire to escape persecution coupled with longing to return to the Promised Land.

Its very potency was the factor which upset Great Britain's calculations. It swept, like a tide, over all the types of Jew upon whom her original assumption had been founded—the religious Jews who had always lived unobtrusive lives in the holy cities of Palestine, the pre-War agriculturists who spoke Arabic and employed Arabs, and the far-seeing, scholarly Jews who thought that the surest way of fulfilling the Messianic Promise was to join with the local population in forming a covenant of peace. It brushed aside every consideration that did not contribute to the immediate increase of the National Home. In its might and its haste it increased the natural tendency of the Jews to be exclusive. 'It is the duty of every Jew', they said, 'to make room for another Jew. If, as a by-product of this process, the Arabs benefit, so much the better; if they do not, it cannot be helped.' Some Zionists, indeed, went much farther: 'If the Arabs do not like us, let them go elsewhere; they have plenty of other states to which to go, whereas we Jews are homeless.' Only the great Jews, the Jews of insight and political wisdom, realized that no Arabs would be willing 'to leave the land in which they and their fathers have been settled for a thousand years, where they have their mosques and where they have their graveyards'.[1]

The arrival of moneyed Jews undoubtedly brought some material benefits to the Arabs—not to the peasants of the inland hills (for, except at Jerusalem and in the holy cities of Galilee, Jewish settlers have scarcely penetrated the hill country), but to the landowners and villagers in the plains. Those who disbelieve this assertion have only to compare the level of Arab life along the coastal strip of Palestine with the similar districts farther north in the Lebanon and the Latakia province of Syria.

Where the Jews made their fatal mistake was in their failure to exploit this advantage, and to turn it into a general Arab desire for their presence. They are psychologically at fault when they argue that the high prices which they paid for land should have been enough to make them welcome. There comes a point when the value of the gift is outweighed by the manner of the giving. In their exclusiveness, they surpassed that point, and they are reaping the consequences of their unwisdom. Seeing them and hearing their arguments in Palestine, even an admirer of their great qualities is forced to the conclusion that they are politically an obtuse people—that the very characteristics which give them such force as preservers of a race, a religion, or a business are a hindrance

[1] Speech by Viscount Samuel in the House of Lords, July 20, 1937.

in social intercourse or in the give-and-take of democratic politics.

Viewed from the narrow standpoint of immediate gain, their policy can claim to have been a success. It secured, in the shortest time, admission of the largest number of Jews into Palestine that the mandatory power would allow. But, viewed on the long-term basis of the future of the Jewish race, it was hasty and ill considered. It allowed spiritual exaltation at the fulfilment of an ancient longing to get the better of prudence and common sense. It saddled the race, which has few friends, with a new and bitter enemy; it closed Arab frontiers which would have been open to Jews for their money; it weakened the security of the Jews settled in Palestine, and it jeopardized the lives of all Jews living elsewhere in the Moslem world. As far away as Algeria and Morocco, ugly murmurings against the local Jews accompany every fresh item of news from Palestine.

Jewish and British policy are the more to blame because at one time the acquiescence of the Palestinian Arabs would not have been impossible to win. The great majority were not a very noble type; they were poor, improvident, hungry for immediate gain, the first to liquidate their heavy debts by selling their land to Jewish bidders, but, unless rightly managed, the first also to complain against the Jews when it was sold. They were not a proud, pure stock like the Arabs of Arabia, but a mongrel breed evolved in the course of countless invasions, another of which they might have been brought to accept had the Jews and the British played their cards aright. As it was, clumsiness on the part of both Briton and Jew enabled the disgruntled Arab *effendi* to secure a hearing among the other classes, and made it worth his while to apply himself to stirring up the Arab peasant and worker. These, who had suffered under *effendi* tyranny for generations, would not have listened so readily to his exhortations had they in the meantime found a better employer. But they had not, so when the *effendi* began to preach revolt against the Jews and the British, he was able to do so with success.

These trite strictures may sound unreal to the Jew in a Palestinian colony who is living in hourly danger from Arab snipers, or to the Englishman who is struggling to administer the mandate without any very clear idea of the policy which Westminster would like him to pursue. 'How can we work with the Arabs,' says the first, 'an ungrateful people who murder a Jewish doctor when he goes to an urgent case in one of their villages.' 'We have done our best to mix the races,' says the second, 'but we have had to give it up, and deal with them separately.' True, the moment for racial co-operation has passed, but it once existed, and Jewish and British policy are both to blame for its passing. The Arab—the least developed of the three types concerned—was mismanaged by both the others, and, because he lacked the intellectual equipment for meeting them on their own ground, he fell back upon primitive methods—murder and pillage. Deplorable as these methods are, they have proved his best means of checking the relentless tide of Jewish immigration, to which the British have set no limit, and which, unless he protests, will submerge him by force of its numbers, its wealth, and its efficiency. Hence the Arab rising against the Jews in 1929, and the armed revolts not only against the Jews but against Great Britain which took place in 1933, 1936, and 1937–8.

Even this cursory analysis of events should be enough to show that the trouble is indigenous to Palestine—that, though it may be aggravated by foreign factors, it is essentially a local growth. Since 1933 it has been intensely aggravated from abroad, firstly by the rise of Arab nationalism in neighbouring states, and secondly, by the persecution of the Jews in Europe, which increased the Jewish need for sanctuary and caused a sympathetic British

Government to double the rate of immigration into Palestine. But neither of these circumstances, nor yet Italian propaganda, was the cause of the disturbances; outside factors merely precipitated a crisis which had been growing more inevitable with every year of British oscillation and Jewish intransigeance.

Is there a solution to a dilemma in which Great Britain has promised the same bread to two peoples and neither will accept half the loaf? In 1937 a Royal Commission set out to find one, and, in a report which for its frankness was a credit to the British nation, dissected the faults of all three parties and concluded that 'the only solution offering at least a chance of permanent peace' was Solomon's judgement—namely, the division of Palestine into two states, with Jerusalem, which is a holy city not only of Christendom but of the Jewish and Islamic faiths also, as neutral ground under British mandate.

The British Government gave its approval to the Royal Commission's scheme, which, unfortunately for those who have to grapple with the ultimate solution, included a map which threatens to prejudice all future suggestions. But either Westminster mismanaged its case, or else satisfactory partition of so mixed a population is impossible, for it failed to convert either the Jews or the Arabs to its way of thinking.

So far as the Jews were concerned, the share of territory awarded in the Commission's map was distinctly favourable. The best part of rural Palestine was to be theirs in full sovereignty, open to Jewish immigration on any scale that they wished, and certainly on a scale greater than would be possible in any state run jointly with the Arabs. They were torn by doubt as to whether to accept the offer, but, after anxious debate, decided to turn down 'Zionism without Zion'.

The Arabs stood to lose more by the plan. They would have seen all their richest orange groves and their hills of Galilee pass into Jewish hands, and even the generous money offers included in the scheme could not compensate them for the loss of 'face' involved. Moreover, the Report reduced them to despair, for they argued with some reason that the Jews, once having seen the offending map, would never accept less than the 1937 proposal. The British Government, its dilemma as complete as ever, is left to the gloomy reflection that Solomon's judgement, though so famous, was never carried out.

Where men of experience have tried and failed to find a remedy, a student may well hesitate to make suggestions, but destructive criticism alone is of so little use that there is excuse for offering a view.

There are three interests to be considered when weighing a solution for Palestine—not only those of the Jews and Arabs, but also those of Great Britain, who, however much she may be to blame for what has happened, is the party who will ultimately suffer the recriminations which are bound to come from all parts of the world. For interest in the solution of the Palestine problem is not confined to Jews and Arabs; it is also displayed by the many foreign states who actively support one side or other either because their people are Moslems or because they wish to rid themselves of their Jews.

Great Britain's biggest interest in the matter is to secure a peaceful Palestine; from the point of view of her imperial security, this consideration now outweighs her original interest in oil outlets and strategic bases. Therefore she cannot afford to impose a solution against the will of both parties; therefore it seems that she would be wise to abandon the much reviled partition plan. On the other hand, she cannot continue to uphold the present abnormal situation, in which she must protect a colonizing people, many of whom have never attempted to make themselves acceptable to the population whom they found in possession. The fact that they are not obliged to do so, because a mandatory is there to handle the Arab if he becomes vindictive, has bred a form of irresponsibility in the Palestinian Jews.

What is Great Britain to do? Her problem is vastly aggravated by the rising tide of anti-Semitism in Europe, yet Europe is not the only place where Jewish lives are exposed to risk. Jewish as well as British security all over the Moslem world forbids that she should go on allowing large numbers of Jews to pour into the mandate as at present constituted. One course, however, remains open to her. She, who was the giver of the National Home promise, and is the party upon whom falls the responsibility for its success or failure, is the party who is entitled to define it. She will enjoy no peace in the Middle East until she does so in terms more explicit than those which she used when she merely stated that she had never meant to support the establishment of a 'wholly Jewish Palestine'.

This solution, which involves limiting Jewish numbers to a percentage of the Arab population, presents several drawbacks, the first and worst of which is that it fails to recognize the worth of the average Palestinian Jew compared with the unworth of the average Palestinian Arab. The second is that it constitutes a surrender to Arab violence, but that now seems unavoidable unless Great Britain is prepared to antagonize all the Moslem friends whose goodwill means so much to her imperial security. The third is that the necessary percentage can only be achieved by holding frequent and complicated censuses, but to do so is not thought impossible by Englishmen on the spot, and the process, though expensive, would cost less than the constant dispatch of armed forces to Palestine. A last drawback to the solution is that it would subject the British Government to pressure not only from powerful Jewish elements in London, but from several foreign governments, among them that of the United States, which has strong Jewish sympathies, and—ironically enough—those of Germany, Poland, and other countries who favour a Jewish Palestine because it provides them with an excuse for anti-Semitism.

But drawbacks of similar dimensions beset Great Britain whichever way she turns. She is in a predicament from which she cannot escape unscathed. Her first consideration is therefore for her own imperial well-being, and, as things stand, the solution which seems to bode her least harm is one which decreases the break-neck pace sought by the Zionists, and forces the Jews already in Palestine to expend less energy upon increasing their numbers and more on creating their own security. Whether, at the same time, she tries to relieve the Jews' tragic plight by offering them a Palestinian Preparatory Home in some other part of the British Empire—a place in which to sift and winnow their tens of thousands and to pick of their best for the Holy Land—is a matter for serious consultation with the Jewish leaders in England and America, for experience is proving that to offer the Jews unlimited sanctuary is to increase the tempo of anti-Jewish movements in Europe, since it enables governments to expel Jews with a clear conscience. Jewish as well as British leaders are in a grave dilemma.

Thus, as far as the British position in the Mediterranean is concerned, definition of the limits of the National Home seems a wise course to contemplate. Talks with the more thoughtful Arab leaders still give grounds for belief that the Arab masses, once relieved of their fear of being outnumbered, could be brought to welcome so great a mercy and to settle down, and there is some hope that, given a new atmosphere in which Arab fears were removed, and in which Jews had more time and thought to spare for making themselves acceptable, Great Britain might once more see a chance of fulfilling her triple promise. Not until then can she hope to establish the provincial autonomy which might in the end lead either to a federated state, or to a partition proposed from below instead of imposed from above.

Out of four Mediterranean territories, therefore, only one presents Great Britain with any real difficulty, but that one offers a problem so formidable as to endanger her reputation, not only in the Mediterranean, but in more than half the countries in the world. In Gibraltar, Malta, and Cyprus, goodwill is something tangible which her money can help to buy; in Palestine, it is elusive and unobtainable until her Government is ready to admit that the problem has surpassed the stage at which it can be solved by mere administration, and until she summons the courage to handle a political problem in a political way. In the pass to which Palestine has brought her, unequivocal definition of her intentions seems to be the only means of recapturing the reputation she has already lost. Come what may in the way of recriminations, she will at least occasion a certain respect if she ceases to beat about the bush, and presents the world with a policy which is frankly based upon that soundest and best-understood of all aims—the improvement of her own security.

7. *Summary: Why remain in the Mediterranean?*

'The Mediterranean—main artery of the British Empire.' This familiar tag, sadly overworked at political meetings, is in fact a little misleading, for the metaphor implies life-blood, and therefore a channel of vital supply. To Great Britain, the Mediterranean is not this, for she can do without the commercial route if need be; indeed, she is more and more easily able to do so as modern invention lessens the distance by the ocean routes which she can use instead.

Her chief reason for maintaining her Mediterranean strength is in order to increase her voice in the councils of

Europe, and to uphold her prestige in a belt of territory where 'face' counts—namely, in the desert region which she must cross in her day-to-day contact with her eastern Dominions and India, and which is also one of the world's great oil areas.

Her second reason is strategic. In the event of war, her fortresses in the Mediterranean increase her mobility for purposes of imperial defence. They also enable her to get at her adversary in an area where he is highly vulnerable—in the Grand Canal running from Gibraltar to Aden, where the U-boats of twenty years ago and the pirate submarines of to-day have successfully demonstrated that defence is difficult and attack easy. Her third reason is commercial; as one of the world's greatest traders, she finds that it pays to advertise along one of the world's main highways.

Here are three motives for remaining in the Mediterranean. Some Englishmen like to add a fourth, which is that Great Britain is bound by duty to the peoples who inhabit her Mediterranean dependencies. But examination proves that this theory does not everywhere apply. Were Great Britain to abandon the Mediterranean, the Arabs of Palestine would be delighted to see her go. The Cypriot Greeks, too, would vote joyfully for union with Greece, provided that they could do so without losing the protection of British arms; on the other hand, they would regret their vote if they woke to find that the British forces had sailed away, and left them exposed to annexation by Turkey or Italy. With the Maltese, her relation is different, both because of their loyalty, and because they came voluntarily into the British Empire. No doubt Great Britain's feelings towards them weigh less with her than does her need of their island as a base, but this does not alter the fact that many Maltese have worked actively on her behalf against alien influence, and that (judging by precedents in Ethiopia and Austria) she would be playing them a shabby trick were she to leave them to the mercies of a newcomer. Towards one people, however, moral duty is her first consideration—namely, towards the Palestinian Jews.

When the British begin to talk of the moral obligations of empire, foreigners always hide a smile, seeing in the statement but another example of the perfidy of Albion. Thus, when the Englishman asserts that British forces remain in the Mediterranean partly because Great Britain is committed to 400,000 Jews settled under her guarantee in the midst of an inimical Arab world, the foreigner replies: 'Thou hypocrite!' He contends that she is thinking not of moral duty but of dissatisfaction in Lombard Street, and of the havoc which the wrath of the great Jewish financial houses could wreak in the City. There is some truth in the allegation, but, at the same time, the man who makes it is failing to give the British people their due. Any suggestion that the Jewish National Home in Palestine should be left to sink or swim would cause a feeling of revulsion among large numbers of Englishmen; already outraged at the treatment which a great race is receiving in certain states of Europe they would be loth to countenance any action which exposed more Jews to oppression, or which smacked of deserting the Jewish people in one of the black moments of its history.

To sum up, then: Diplomatic influence, imperial strategy, national prosperity, a sense of obligation to the Jews. These reasons, in order of importance, help to explain why Great Britain is 'quitting nothing' in the Mediterranean. All but one are highly material, for material reasons are undeniably at the bottom of every nation's imperialism. But to strike a solely material note is to give a false idea of the qualities which make the strength of a successful empire. However self-interested the original motives for which Great Britain grabbed her colonies, her subsequent handling of them, and in particular the work of the man on the spot, often provide a record of disinterested service. Palestine is a blot on her escutcheon, and her handling of Cyprus is not a very creditable performance, but penetrate a little farther and you will gain a more just impression of her Empire as a whole. When you see the Sudan, or Transjordan, or the mark which she has left in Egypt, you realize that a Cromer or a Macmichael could not have won the name he has made had British material interests been his only inspiration.

To say this is to make no unique claim for Great Britain; the same applies, in the French Empire, to the work of a man like Lyautey. Nor is it to deny that material motives usually underly a government's imperial policy. Great Britain could abandon her Mediterranean dependencies without causing bodily harm to any of their inhabitants except the Jews and, no doubt, those Maltese who have worked openly in her interests. She does not do so, partly from the instincts that prompt the holding of possessions and the finishing of a job once begun, but chiefly because her presence there affords her standing and influence in Europe and Asia, and enables her to do the buying and selling upon which depends the high standard of living to which her people have become accustomed in their over-populated British Isles.

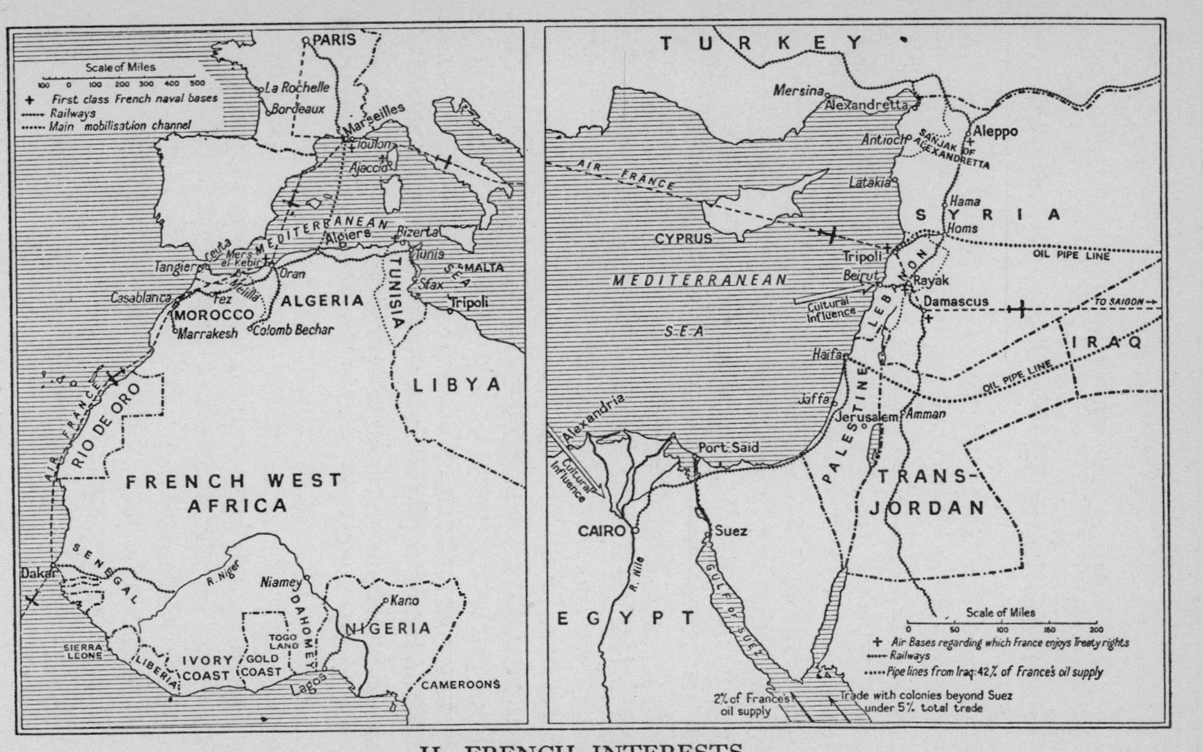

II. FRENCH INTERESTS

a. In the Western Basin. *b.* In the Eastern Basin.

CHAPTER III

FRENCH INTERESTS

1. *Mediterranean Strategy through French Eyes*

FRANCE sees the Mediterranean from a different angle because the French are not empire-minded. Of course there are exceptions to so general a statement. Men like Bugeaud, Jules Ferry, Gallieni, or Lyautey spent themselves in creating a greater France, but they laboured without the support which an interested British public gave to Disraeli, Roberts, or Salisbury. Marshal Lyautey had his countrymen's measure when he said: 'C'est presqu'à l'insu de la métropole, en s'en défendant comme d'une œuvre à peine avouable, que les grands coloniaux ont donné à leur pays cet admirable domaine d'outre-mer.' Thus, where an Englishman, visualizing imperial communications, thinks of outgoing ships, a Frenchman sees incoming traffic; where England and Italy christen their air lines Imperial Airways or *Linea del Impero*, the French lines, however far afield, are always *Air France*.

This habit of thinking in terms of the home country causes Frenchmen to see all international situations in the light of home defence, and, since their eastern frontier has been invaded twice within living memory, home defence means defence against Germany. They ponder and calculate how to match forty million Frenchmen against over seventy million Germans—how to equalize their falling birth-rate with the stable rate achieved by the Nazis. They see all Mediterranean problems from this standpoint. In any crisis, their thoughts fly at once to Algeria, Tunisia, and Morocco, firstly, because over a quarter of their serving army is stationed there, and secondly, because the three North African territories are not only the nearest but the most populated of their overseas possessions, and offer the greatest possibilities of both white and native recruitment.

Films and novels so often depict French North Africa as a desert manned by black troops and the Foreign Legion that the real nature of the garrisons is forgotten. In real life, they include whole divisions of European troops—not only the white regiments of the *Armée d'Afrique* (the *Chasseurs d'Afrique*, and the *Zouaves*), but also nearly a fifth of the *Armée de France*.

Moreover, the number of Frenchmen that North Africa can yield upon general mobilization surprises any one who does not know Algeria, and how like it is to Languedoc or Provence. The explanation of the likeness is that nearly a million Frenchmen migrated there, that Algeria is not a colony, but an integral part of the home country, and that France, to make it so, peopled it officially and artifically with men of her own flesh and blood. In the event of war, therefore, she expects to call up Algerians as quickly and easily as she calls up Bretons or Savoyards.

Besides these white reserves, she looks to North Africa for Moslem man-power also. The Frenchman-in-the-street is apt to overrate this native resource. He knows that there are fourteen million Moslems in North Africa. He is accustomed to the sight of Arab or Berber troops strolling cheerfully in the garrison towns of France, and he naturally deduces that the stock is willing and plentiful. He remembers that Moslem troops fought beside him in the trenches, and he asks from time to time why military service is not enforced in Algeria, where it exists in principle, and why it is not instituted in Tunisia and Morocco, where the basis of recruitment is voluntary. His voice is almost plaintive: 'Comment pourrions-nous négliger ce moyen de compenser le déséquilibre de la natalité française vis-à-vis de l'Allemagne?'[1] But, to come down to facts, he cherishes extravagant hopes. In the opinion of

[1] Article in the *Revue des Deux Mondes*, May 1, 1933.

most experts, the safety limit is reached when the French army numbers one native soldier to every three Frenchmen. This being so, native reinforcements can never raise forty million Frenchmen to the level of seventy million Germans without exceeding the margin of safety. Perhaps happily for the nation's peace of mind, few Frenchmen have done this revealing proportion sum.

Their optimism has been shaken, however, by another revelation—that of the Spanish civil war and the assistance which one side has received from Rome and Berlin. They have realized that, supposing the enemy were not only Germany, but also Italy or Spain, or both, they might be called upon to man fronts not only in Europe but in Africa. The fact that reinforcements travelled from south to north in 1870 and 1914 is no proof that one-way-traffic will prevail in the next war also.

In 1938, France's strategic problem is not as simple as it used to be. Her old Mediterranean defences, which date back to the days of the Triple Alliance, were all on her eastern flank, running from Toulon to Corsica and on to Biserta in Tunisia. She was able to leave her west flank unguarded, thanks to a long-standing Spanish policy by which she had secured a friendly or at least a neutral Spain. She needed no troops in the Pyrenees and no ships off the Balearic Isles. But General Franco's revolution destroyed this comfortable situation. France's support of the Spanish Left was not all prompted by ideology. She wanted it to win for the more material, personal reason that a victory won by the Right, thanks to German and Italian support, portended the establishment of a pincer-grip on her highway to North Africa. Smitten with new fear, she began to lay new plans, among them the construction of a naval base on her undefended western flank.

Mers-el-Kebir, which is five miles to the west of Oran, looked little enough like a naval harbour in January 1937, when its foundation-stone had just been laid on the shore of a rocky little bay. But, though bases are not built in a day, this one was said to promise quick results, because it possessed a great natural breakwater a few feet below the surface—an asset which was invisible in the ruffled winter sea.

At the same time, lest the triangle Toulon–Mers-el-Kebir–Biserta should prove an inadequate defence for her mobilization channel, France must, like Great Britain, envisage plans for an alternative route. In her case, these plans are well advanced.

The events of the Spanish civil war were not her first reminder that the Mediterranean route left something to be desired. The Germans had shaken her confidence during the World War, not only with their submarines, but on one memorable occasion with their surface ships. On August 4, 1914, the *Goeben* and the *Breslau*, trapped inside the Mediterranean, had bombarded the Algerian ports of Philippeville and Bone. This brusque warning of their presence and their power caused the naval authorities to suggest to Marshal Joffre that all troopships should await naval escort. Had the Marshal accepted their suggestion, the Moroccan Division could not have been flung in at the eleventh hour to turn the Battle of the Marne.

With this narrow shave fresh in mind, the French General Staff laid its plans for an alternative route in the years just after the War. Morocco, being on the Atlantic, provided the safety-valve, and a scheme was produced whereby troops should be transported by road and rail to Moroccan ports, and thence shipped on a slower but safer ocean journey to Bordeaux or La Rochelle.

The railway running along the north of French Africa was built at enormous expense to the state, and was completed in 1934. Whether it offers an alternative route of value an amateur hesitates to say; but it certainly does not *look* a national mainstay. It is of uniform gauge from Tunis to Casablanca—where a magnificent port awaits the troop-trains—but it is single track for most of its length, and though the line is now being doubled on the busier stretches, even the most triumphant organization could not dispatch trains at speed if a heavy traffic in empties were returning the other way. At present, the non-stop journey takes two days and two nights. Moreover, the line, together with the ribbon of tarred road which runs beside it, lies for almost the whole of its length within bombing radius of foreign aerodromes. In the east, it can be attacked from the Italian bases in Sicily and Sardinia; in the west, where it runs through the narrow Taza corridor between the Atlas and the Riff mountains, it is within fifty miles of the Spanish Moroccan base at Melilla. A bridge bombed here or a culvert there anywhere along a thousand miles of line could cause considerable confusion and delay.

These elaborate French plans for defence and evasion of danger affect the western Mediterranean only, but in the eastern basin, too, France's strategic policy is governed by her obsession regarding her German frontier. Her concentration of energy upon the Maginot line has caused her to write off the eastern Mediterranean as relatively unimportant, and to take few steps to consolidate her position there by means of armaments. Despite the fact that it is her channel of communication with her allies in eastern Europe, that the whole Levant exudes French culture, that France is the largest foreign investor there, and that she now relies on the pipe-line from Iraq for over 40 per cent. of her oil, she possesses no naval base east of Biserta. Indeed, one school of French military thought considers her Syrian venture to be so futile a waste of men and money that it draws maps of her Mediterranean interests without even marking Syria and states that French interests are 'wholly concentrated' in the west.[1]

[1] See an article in the military magazine *Armée Moderne* for July 1937.

An opposition school of strategists, led by the great General Weygand, deplores her failure to turn her Syrian mandate to strategic account. France, they say, is vulnerable in that she has no Malta, no Leros, no harbour as good as Haifa from which to defend her many interests in the eastern basin. So far, the government has listened in silence to their strictures, but, though silent, it is not deaf to their argument, as is proved by several acts of policy since the War. In 1920 it cut the port of Tripoli off Moslem Syria and included it in the more friendly Christian Lebanon. Some ten years later it arranged for the building of a branch of the oil pipe-line from Iraq to that port. In 1936, when it embarked on the slow process of bringing its mandates to an end, it signed different treaties with Syria and the Lebanon. By the Syrian treaty, France was to withdraw her garrisons within five years from the date of ratification, retaining nothing except a twenty-five-year tenancy of two air bases; by that with the Lebanon, she was to maintain protective forces in the territory for an unspecified period. Within the letter of the second treaty, a French base at Tripoli, safe inside the accommodating Lebanon and enjoying the enormous advantage of a local oil supply, could pass muster as Lebanese national defence.

But though this loop-hole has been left open, no move has been made to start building the base. All the funds available for such a purpose are being poured into Mers-el-Kebir. Despite the vehemence of General Weygand, France's strategic planning in the Mediterranean is still based on the firm conviction that she must concentrate her money and energy in the west, and that, so long as she has a British ally looking after common interests at Suez, a stronghold in the eastern Mediterranean is not vital to her position as a power.

2. *Syria: Liability or Asset?*

Syria has not fulfilled her strategic promise, but strategy was not France's only motive in acquiring the mandate. Another was sentiment; yet another, the 'protection of our interests in the Near East'. This last description was nebulous, but so was the protection that Syrian garrisons could afford. They had their hands full with local management, and the outside interests were left to fend for themselves.

From a business standpoint, France's chief interests in the eastern Mediterranean are her communications with the Far East, her investment and her Levant trade.

As regards Far Eastern traffic, Syria has provided her with a convenient halt for air liners, and with an imperial wireless station on the way to her eastern colonies, but no one can claim that it has affected her shipping or trade through the Suez Canal.

The amount of French shipping plying on the Suez route is small for so great a maritime power. French ships come fifth on the list of canal returns—below those of Great Britain and Italy, the Netherlands and Germany—and the goods they carry represent but 6 per cent. of the volume of Canal-borne trade. Yet the route is more important to France than these figures would imply, for ships of all nations carry her goods, and a high percentage of the Suez traffic calls at Marseilles.

She uses the Canal for much the same purposes as does Great Britain. If anything, she is able to dispense with it more easily, because less of her empire lies beyond it and because she is far less dependent than the United Kingdom upon supplies of oil from Iran. Though she is less vocal on the subject than are Great Britain and Italy, the Canal's greatest significance to her is its strategic convenience for imperial policing and defence; it is her short cut to several of her colonies, of which the most important are Indo-China and Madagascar. But her presence in Syria has affected none of these things. Such of her Canal business as is not transacted in Paris is managed under the green domes of the Suez Canal Building at Port Said.

Nor has her Syrian venture vastly benefited her Levant trade. It has somewhat increased her trade with Syria itself, for, though the Open Door prevails in mandated territories, mandatory powers, when they introduce officials and soldiers, shipping and air connexions, usually also introduce the habit of buying and selling in their home country. But elsewhere in the Levant the proportion of French trade has fallen considerably since the War; where France used to be second only to Germany, she is now fifth or sixth on the list.[1]

As a buyer, she only finds the eastern Mediterranean essential for one commodity—her oil from the Black Sea countries and Iraq, which between them supply about 55 per cent. of her needs. Egyptian cotton and Russian timber could be replaced from elsewhere, and most of her other purchases in the Levant are made to balance her sales. As a seller, she has lost many former customers. Her losses are often due to factors which have affected all western industrial exporters—the rise of local industries, competition from Japanese goods, and, above all, the currency restrictions which have enabled the countries adopting them to transact business at abnormal prices—but France suffered even more severely than the sterling and dollar countries owing to her long retention of the gold standard. Between 1932 and 1935 she lost ground which she will take years to regain.

Again, in the matter of France's third Near Eastern interest—her investment—the French forces in Syria cannot claim to have played a very protective role. For four centuries France had known a much more stalwart

[1] See table on p. 253.

protector—the Capitulations under whose wing she had been the leading investor in the Ottoman Empire and in Egypt. Once deprived of this bulwark, her capital was, like every one else's, exposed to the buffets of local nationalism.

The first country in which she met this fate was the new Turkey. Before the War, her vast interests in the Ottoman Empire had included the lion's share of the public debt as well as innumerable and very profitable concessions. In 1914, French capital in Turkey was said to represent 53 per cent. of the total great-power investment there, as against German and British commitments representing 33 per cent. and 14 per cent. respectively. But post-War history shows that no amount of watchfulness exercised from Syria could keep these interests intact. France could but acquiesce when Kemalist Turkey abolished the Capitulations, repurchased the concessions, took over the railways and the coasting trade, set up its own industries, and promoted its own banking and insurance companies.

The outlook in Egypt is only less unsettled because the bulk of the French capital there enjoys a special guarantee. A French estimate made at the time of the 1937 Capitulations Conference placed the total French investment in Egypt at 26 milliard francs,[1] of which 17 milliards represent French holdings in the Suez Canal Company. This vast sum, which is a monument to the faith of the Frenchmen who financed de Lesseps, is watched over by an office in Paris. Its bulwark is the international utility of the Company's concession, and, until that concession expires in 1968, it is a gilt-edged security safe in the hands of a rich and powerful French organization. Less is heard of the Canal's French management than of the British soldiers who defend its banks, but in fact those Frenchmen are a colony of importance. So French are they, and so strongly

[1] Out of a total foreign investment of 50 milliard francs, which at the then rate of exchange equals £500 millions; cf. p. 30 above.

have they imposed their personality on the neighbourhood, that the Egyptians of Ismailia are said to count their cash not in piastres but in *sous*.

The remaining 9 milliards of French money in Egypt were until lately protected by the Capitulations. Its distribution is easier to describe than is that of its British counterpart, for it is as concentrated as the British investment is diffuse. It is devoted to the ventures undertaken before the British occupation; it antedates the cotton boom, and there is little French money in the cotton trade. Apart from the French share of the public debt, it is chiefly employed in the water, gas, and light services introduced in the 'fifties and 'sixties, in the sugar industry, and, above all, in land and mortgage companies. The French *Crédit Foncier* alone represents one-third of the total capital invested in joint-stock companies in Egypt.

With the abolition of the Egyptian Capitulations, the French holders of these interests saw themselves threatened with the fate of their fellows in Turkey. They hated the Anglo-Egyptian treaty; they considered that Great Britain, seized with panic during the Italo-Ethiopian dispute, had sold their rights in the interests of British imperial security. Their influence accounts for the stubborn fight for the retention of privileges which France put up during the 1937 Capitulations Conference at Montreux.

In fact, therefore, the only place in which a French Syria can claim to have protected French investment is in the ex-Turkish territories which became League mandates, and, even here, Palestine must be excluded, for there are no French business interests there. French Jews are seldom Zionists, and almost all the French citizens in the Holy Land are either members of religious orders or else elderly Jews from Algeria who have gone to Jerusalem to die. On the other hand, in France's own mandates and in Iraq, the existence of a French government in Syria and the Lebanon has contributed somewhat to the security of French capital. Above all, it has added to the security of the pipe-line. French oil interests own a $23\frac{3}{4}$ per cent. share of the capital of the Iraq Petroleum Company and, had it not been for French influence in the Lebanon, the Company might have been more hesitant about forking the pipe and placing one terminal at Tripoli. It might also have spent less upon oil prospection in Syria itself.

Apart from the oil interest, however, France's presence in Syria has not promoted any increase of French capital in the territory; her investment there is little larger than it was before the War. The total, then as now, is well under 1 milliard francs, of which about one-tenth is concentrated in the railways. The only new concern of importance is the bank of issue—the *Banque de Syrie et du Grand Liban*—which was founded in 1919 with a nominal capital of $25\frac{1}{2}$ million francs. Compared with the stake in Egypt, the figures are insignificant.

France's diffidence over investment in Syria is unlike her usual habit of pouring money into her overseas possessions, but the contrast is explained by political events. Syria under mandate underwent two long periods of insecurity, and new capital was not forthcoming because investors were nervous as to the future. They had seen men and money expended on the conquest of Cilicia, and then—in 1922—the cession of Cilicia to Turkey. For years they were nervous lest Syria should go the same way, and they were scarcely reassured when, in 1925, French troops were defeated by rebel Syrians and France had to resort to bombarding Damascus. Their doubts were not set at rest until 1927, when the French Government told them categorically that it had no intention of abandoning its mandate. During the six years of peace which followed, they indulged in a little wary capital expansion, but their old sensitiveness revived as soon as the termination of the mandate loomed ahead. Even in the French heyday they had found difficulty in collecting their interest, and they feared worse once an independent Syrian Government controlled their destiny. They began to reduce their commitments. One of the biggest investors, the *Crédit Foncier d'Algérie et de Tunisie*, ceased to offer long-term credits, and the *Banque de Syrie et du Grand Liban*, when negotiating its first agreement with a purely Syrian government, asked high rates of interest in anticipation of scanty security.

Weighed in the balance, therefore, France's Syrian venture is found wanting not only as a strategic but as a material asset. Except for a certain security afforded to her oil interest, and the advantage of possessing a half-way-house for air and wireless communications and a potential naval and air base, she has seen little or no return for the 17 milliard francs she is said to have spent on pacifying and policing the territory.

There remains her third reason for taking over Syria—her historic link with the Christian populations of the Levant.

Sentimentalists like to think that her presence in Syria has reinforced her cultural influence all over the Near East, and up to a point it has done so. The very presence of a French state so near at hand constitutes a link with France for the French teachers in schools everywhere from the Bosphorus to Egypt and the Persian Gulf. Priests, *pères*, and *sœurs* of all the religious orders, as well as masters and mistresses employed by the *Alliance Israélite* and *Mission Laïque*, look to Beirut as a substitute for home, and spend their holidays there if they cannot afford the fare to Marseilles. They enjoy for a week or so the French atmosphere created by a French government and a large French colony. They come back, tell travellers' tales in class, and fire their pupils with some of the warmth they feel. Moreover, Beirut is venerable from a more strictly intellectual point of view, for it is the seat of the great Jesuit *Université Saint-Joseph*, which is the apex of French education and culture in the Near East.

'To predominate in the realm of ideas; to have dominion over their minds and souls; such is our aim. Others may surpass us in the fields of business or arms; all we ask, at all times, is the welcome that comes from the heart.'[1] Here is the explanation of the French atmosphere which still pervades the Levant, even though French political predominance ceased nearly seventy years ago. The very disinterestedness of the French men and women who laboured there did their country a lasting service. If their work enabled France to reap a material advantage, they were patriots and were therefore glad, but this was not their primary purpose. Between 1870 and the War, the majority of Frenchmen on the spot strove for the improvement of learning, and worked without thought of gain.

Seen from afar—from a French school in Smyrna or Bagdad—Beirut still shines with this untarnished lustre. But seen from Syria itself the shine is dimmed, for, as soon as France was metamorphosed from a remote goddess into an earthly creature who taxed and policed and punished, she became far less popular than she had been before the War. Of course her cultural influence increased; the French language, for instance, made strides all over the territory. Of course she brought certain benefits; most Syrians, however anti-French, will admit that she did them a good turn in establishing internal security, and many will also acknowledge that she built roads, increased trade, gave them a good land registration system, and showed them how to organize a civil service. But these admissions can only be extracted at the cost of listening to a long list of grievances. In all other matters France is a robber and an oppressor.

To some extent this reaction was inevitable. No people likes a foreign ruler. Moreover, carping is inborn in the

[1] Maurice Barrès, *Enquête aux pays du Levant*, vol. i, p. 5

Syrian. He has a scant sense of gratitude and an infinite capacity for complaint—characteristics both of which are at least two thousand years old, for the Pharisees carped at healing on the Sabbath, and nine of the ten lepers ran off without a word of thanks. On the other hand, part of the anti-French feeling is the fault of French policy. France treated the Syrians firmly, and at times even harshly, but they brush aside old resentment on this score in order to save their breath for their main indictment, which is that of cupidity. France made her great mistake in Syria when she failed to go on looking disinterested. Moslems and Christians alike interpreted all her early acts as devices for filling French pockets at their expense. Some of their accusations were justified, others were misrepresentations of her policy, but the stories contained enough truth to cause even her Christian protagonists to turn against her. In 1927 the Maronite Patriarch complained of the avarice of French officials, and of what he politely called their 'preoccupation with their personal affairs'.

A Syrian or Lebanese, spinning out his stories with little cups of coffee, can cap one with another as untiringly as any Scheherazad. The themes have local variants; the sore points are not always the same in Damascus as in Aleppo or Beirut; in particular, the theory that the Turkish days were the good old days is upheld lustily in the south, but with diminishing vigour as you travel towards the northern frontier, where Turkey, meddling in the Sanjak of Alexandretta, has become a pressing reality.

But in all parts of the country three refrains recur with dreary monotony.

The first is the tale of the *coopérative militaire*. France introduced this general emporium when she first introduced her troops, doing so in order to keep the price of necessities within the limits of their pay. The same form of duty-free shop—the N.A.A.F.I., or Navy, Army, and

Air Force Institutes—exists in most British garrison colonies. But the privilege was abused in Syria. Soldiers' wives bought goods at the *coopérative* not only for themselves but for all their civilian friends. Syrian shopkeepers resented and still remember the queue of friends and friends' friends which was capable of stretching to the farthest limits of the French community.

The second tale is the tale of the Turkish gold. When France established a Syrian currency based on the franc, she called in the supplies of Turkish coin which were still circulating in the country, and replaced them with new paper money. Many Syrian savers held on to their gold, which they had never entrusted to a bank but kept in a secret place known neither to their wives nor their heirs. But those who had bank accounts considered themselves robbed when the cash which they had deposited in gold was paid out in paper. The robbery assumed graver proportions when the French franc was devalued and the Syrian paper money depreciated with it. In some countries a devaluation process might pass unnoticed by local buyers and sellers: not so in Syria, for there price quotations in Turkish gold pounds still prevail. House rents, for instance, are always quoted in gold, and so are the prices of eggs, meat, and vegetables in the markets on the edge of the desert, for the Bedouin buyers and sellers in the bazaars of Aleppo or Damascus know no other medium of exchange. The devaluation was noticed at once by every shopper and tenant, all of whom earned wages in paper, and who were suddenly compelled to pay more of that paper for the same object. (The converse of this argument, which is that hoarders of gold were at a corresponding advantage, is set aside or politely forgotten, for no man talks of his gold.) The conviction that France was draining Syria of gold was enhanced by a decree of 1923 ordaining that no one but the French *Banque de Syrie* could export gold from the country. In vain do French bankers argue that Syrians cannot understand the gold movements underlying international banking, that banks buy gold when gold is cheap, and that when gold prices are favourable there is often more gold in Syria than ever went out of it. To the Syrian, gold is essentially one of those 'things that you can touch or see'; it is something solid for which a banker's mumbo-jumbo is no substitute. He feels that he is being robbed by every device known to the grasping west; he has the last word on the subject when he points out that France pays salaries in paper but levies fines in gold.

The stories of the gold and the *coopérative militaire* are known to everybody. The third story, which concerns the guarantees secured for the interest on certain French loans, is current only among educated men. Their grievance is that France abused her position as mandatory power in order to enable her nationals to recoup the losses they had suffered in Turkey during the War. Between 1920 and 1925, the French companies who had many years earlier invested their money in Syrian railways, water, trams, and electric light, induced the French Government to secure for them guarantees of interest from the Syrian authorities. The agreements were signed on behalf of the companies by their French directors, and on behalf of Syria by the French officials in charge of the different districts. They provided for agreeably large dividends; for instance, the electric light company in a small town like Aleppo was to pay 8 per cent. The railway agreement rankles most in the Syrian mind, for in order to suit the powerful Parisian *Régie Générale des Chemins de Fer*, which is the biggest French investor in Syria, a pre-War guarantee applying to the busiest railway was extended to cover other uneconomic lines, among them the fantastic rack-and-pinion railway which climbs the Lebanon range, and which takes seven hours to wind its way over the pass which a lorry can cross in two. The Syrians hotly resented these decisions taken in their name; they saw no reason why their government should dip its hand into its pocket in order to complete the handsome dividends expected by French speculators. In their annoyance they forget to offset against these interest payments the convenience of possessing trams and water and light. They show their resentment by omitting to fulfil the guarantees.

And so on. Story follows story, each in the same vein. The gossip is endless, and is so endlessly repeated that it causes Syrians to see all foreign activities in the same light. For instance, the Iraq Petroleum Company has treated Syria well; it paid a good price for the strip of land through which the pipe-line runs; it employed Syrians to lay the pipe, and it still employs the handful of them necessary to maintain and guard it; yet they do nothing but complain that Syria gets no more than 'the smell of the oil'.

France is responsible for striking a wrong note. For the sake of a five-franc profit, she has repeatedly lost fifty or even five hundred francs' worth of goodwill. She has established a reputation for self-interest which western nations will not easily live down.

Sentimental considerations, therefore, do not right France's Syrian balance-sheet. She has won as little moral gain as material reward; she has next to nothing to show for the energy she has expended in Syria, for she has registered a net loss not only of cash but of friendship.

To do her justice, however, a distinction must be drawn between the feelings she evokes in Moslem Syria and in the Christian Lebanon.

In the Lebanon she is at least tolerated. Many Lebanese Moslems are anti-French, but a Lebanese Christian will talk lovingly of Paris, and often speaks French better than Arabic because he uses the French language in his home. His French tastes are no new development; they are the outcome of an ancient link between France and the Maronite Christians which dates back to the Crusades, and which was never entirely broken even after Saladin drove the last French kings from Jerusalem. Moreover, from 1536, when Francis I secured the first Capitulations from the Sultan, she began to exercise an influence on Levantine politics which she retained until her defeat by Prussia in 1870, when the birth of the *revanche* idea called for the concentration of all her energies in the west. But even then she did not lose her place in Maronite hearts, for she had won new veneration during an incident of 1860.

In that year, the Druses and Moslems of Syria rose and murdered their Christian neighbours. All Europe was deeply affected, and Austria, Great Britain, France, Prussia, Russia, the Netherlands, Sardinia, and Greece sent vessels of war to Beirut. But the French, singing '*Partant pour la Syrie*', were the only nation who felt sufficiently moved to try conclusions with the Ottoman Empire, and the force which they landed to protect their old friends the Maronites landed alone. 'I need hardly say,' reported the British consul, 'that the occupation is viewed with the utmost aversion by the Mahometans. A scowl is visible on their faces as the troops march past, and their general manner is irritable and sullen. On the other hand, the Christians are overjoyed.' The Lebanese have not forgotten this incident nor its outcome—the establishment in 1861 of an autonomous Christian sanctuary in the hills behind Beirut. Since then they have faced west, not east. They are nervous of the fanatical Moslem world which is seething in the spacious deserts at their back, and they know their dependence on a strong western protector. Had France contrived to look a little more disinterested during her time as mandatory, she might in the Lebanon have retained most of her old popularity. As it is, the days when a French consul was received with a 'sparkling tumult'[1] of salvoes and rose-water are dead and gone, and many Lebanese say they would prefer an international guarantee of independence to a French protector.

In Syria proper, on the other hand, the Mahometan scowl of 1860 has deepened during the years of the mandate. France is actively disliked. She is reviled almost as freely as are the British in Palestine. Apart from her niggardliness, she is looked upon, first, as the tyrant who undid T. E. Lawrence's work and expelled the Arab king Feisal from his rightful seat at Damascus; secondly, as the bully who banished the Syrian leaders for the whole decade after the 1925 rebellion, and thirdly, as the butcher who carved slices off Syria, first, in order to add Tripoli to the Lebanon, and next, in order to appease the Turkish appetite. The new Syria, strutting confidently towards independence, suffered a humiliating loss of 'face' in 1937, when France and Turkey reached agreement over her head about internationalizing the Syrian Sanjak of Alexandretta. Loss of Moslem sympathy in Syria is one of the heaviest items on the debit side of France's account, for Islam is a well-known sounding-box, and hatred incurred in a great religious centre like Damascus is disadvantageous to a power which has fourteen million Moslem subjects in North Africa.

3. *North Africa: Non-Military Interests*

To return to France's more cherished interests in the western basin.

The military importance of North African man-power is so well known that most Frenchmen, if button-holed and questioned in the streets of Paris, would answer that it is the only reason why the north-south route is the basis of all French Mediterranean planning. Just as to the average Englishman the Mediterranean means the route

[1] Maurice Barrès, writing in 1914.

to India, so to the average Frenchman it means the mobilization channel, and nothing more. He is inclined to leave out of account three or four other good reasons why communications with North Africa must be maintained.

The reason which is vital, if France is to retain her position as a first-class power, is that Algeria is the keystone of her whole African empire—of the vast territory which stretches from the Atlantic to Tunis, and from the Mediterranean to Senegal, the Congo, and the Sudan. Yet Algeria is seldom seen in this light in Paris, firstly, because the French are unaccustomed to thinking in imperial terms, and secondly, because the territory only took on this significance at a very recent date. Imperially speaking, it was not born great; it achieved greatness with the development of modern communications.

For decades it was no more than a coastal foothold—that thin strip of land between the Atlas and the sea which had never survived for long under one ruler, so fragile for very length that it always seemed fated to snap in the middle. At either end, too, it tapered to nothing, for it was separated from Tunisia and Morocco by wide no-man's-lands of hilly country, where the habit of intercommunication had been forgotten ever since the conquering Arabs, after sweeping through to the Atlantic, had allowed the Roman aqueducts to fall into disrepair, and had let their goats eat the trees under which men used to ride from Tunis to Fez. Thus, although the natives of Algeria talked the same languages, ate the same food, and worshipped the same God as their brothers in Tunisia and Morocco, they knew little and cared less about the happenings next door.

Frenchmen caught the same exclusive habits; they thought and planned in local grooves, and the three administrations—Algeria under the Ministry of the Interior, and Tunis and Morocco under the Ministry of Foreign

Affairs—led separate, parochial lives. They preferred to ignore one another and to deal directly with France. The lengths to which they used to carry these narrow notions are almost unbelievable for three territories under the same flag. For instance, when iron ore was discovered on the eastern border of Algeria, the mining concession delivered in 1901 raised the problem of carriage to the sea. The obvious port was Biserta, through the building of a link with the Tunisian railway system. But the ore was Algerian, and Algeria therefore held that the handling of its export was her perquisite. The result was a twenty-year delay; the mine was not worked until 1921, when the Algerian authorities settled the matter by building an expensive line to a port within their own territory. This singular history of the uneconomic Tebessa railway is not the only story of its kind.

Moreover, neither Frenchmen nor Moslems conceived that their lands adjoined tropical Africa. They were cut off from the south by the Atlas, a great double barrier split into two ranges by a forbidding steppe-like plateau, and beyond that was the Sahara—a frontier more effective than any sea. In fact, Algeria was to all intents and purposes an island until a very few years ago.

Even modern invention, with its good trains and comfortable buses, did not at once fill the role of a link with the neighbouring territories. The railway from Algiers, running east to Tunis and west to the Moroccan ports on the Atlantic, was completed in 1934, but for years the long-distance travellers were almost all people from Europe—a handful of business men and a small cargo of tourists. An air service which was opened between Algiers and Tunis was abandoned for lack of passengers.

Curiously, the far less practicable southern link across the Sahara made more appeal to the French imagination. Mr. Gladstone had dubbed the desert 'enough sand for the French cock to scratch in', but the handful of men who conquered it saw it in another light—as the link between white and black Africa.

The Trans-Saharan railway for which they had laboured was seriously considered in the years just after the War. It was discussed by the *Conseil Supérieur de la Defense Nationale*, and advocated as an improvement upon the 'slow and insecure' Atlantic route for obtaining Sudanese troops to 'defend the soil of the home country'. Slow the Atlantic route might be; the connexions between French Equatorial Africa and the sea were and still are bad. But in using the word 'insecure' to describe the Atlantic in contrast to the Mediterranean, the committee made the habitual French assumption that the enemy would be a non-Mediterranean power. However, the railway was to afford more than man-power; its advocates grew lyrical about its other possibilities. It was to open up the 'even more valuable resources derived from the vegetable oils and fats produced in French West Africa'; the Niger was to become as fruitful as the Nile; an area the size of France was crying out for development, and would yield not only fats but cotton, rice, and even perhaps rubber, once a little money was spent on irrigation. The northbound trains would be loaded with all the materials most needed by French industry; those southbound would carry imperial unity and the benefits of civilization. Between seasons, thanks to conveniently alternating harvest periods, the empty trucks would run at their famous capacity of 'HOMMES 40', and would solve at a blow the labour shortage on the Niger and the seasonal unemployment problem in Algeria.

These flights of fancy came to nothing because the line was considered too expensive, not only to build, but to maintain. Experts still argue and disagree about the project, but, even to the amateur who travels in the Sahara, one main difficulty is obvious. On the morning after the mildest night of sand-wind, every small stone, tuft, and excrescence is built up with ripple upon ripple of fine sand. Thus road has for the moment beaten rail traffic, and motor-buses ply the route with success. Two companies dispatch comfortable weekly services from one side to the other of that vast waste space—one from the railway terminus at Colomb-Bechar to Niamey on the Niger, and the other direct from Algiers to the railhead at Kano in Nigeria.

Like the east-west railway, these north-south communications have till now been the prerogative of the rich, but in both cases the traffic runs so smoothly in both directions that it is beginning to create a new mentality. The through railway-carriage from Tunis to Casablanca, and the blue bus labelled for a destination near the Equator, which climbs the Rue Michelet at Algiers, between them symbolize a metamorphosis which opens a new chapter in French African history.

In the first place, contacts are rapidly increasing between Algeria, Tunisia, and Morocco. The three territories are still under different ministries, but, ever since the great Colonial Conference of 1934–5 laid stress on their unity, their administrators have met the cabinet ministers concerned in a *Haut-Comité Méditerranéan* for joint discussion of their problems. Since 1937, too, the co-ordinating process has been quickened by the establishment of a permanent secretariat attached to the Prime Minister's office. A sign of the times is the ease with which officials are summoned by air to extraordinary meetings. This new mobility—mental as well as physical —applies not only to Frenchmen but to Moslems. In 1936 the visit to Tunis of a party of politicians from Algeria was cited as a wonder. In 1937 the contacts were increasing steadily; their progress was evident in the simultaneous unrest which pervaded the three territories in the autumn of the year. Moreover, travel is no longer an essential preliminary to co-operation; the new day has dawned when a sheik buys a wireless set and discovers how easily he can make a trunk call.

In time these connexions will spread southwards. The Sahara is not yet a regular air-route; for greater safety, flyers bound for the Cape still prefer to use the Air France itinerary via Dakar, or the Imperial Airways' detour via the Nile. But, for those who doubt that trans-Saharan traffic is on the increase, three milestones serve to measure an impressive advance: in 1900, the Fourreau-Lamy mission, marching inland from Algiers, rose from the dead when it achieved its meeting at Lake Chad with fellow-expeditions from the Congo and the Niger, for nothing had been heard of its fortunes for over a year. In 1922, a Haardt-Citroen expedition made news when it performed the same journey by car. In 1937, a companion in the Trans-Saharan bus asks if you are 'getting out at Tamanrasset or going on to the Niger' almost as casually as he would ask about Clapham Junction and Waterloo.

The pace is quickening, and, as it develops, Algeria increases in importance. As the nearest point to France, it becomes the distributor and receiver of everything from news and ideas to passengers and merchandise. Its security becomes vital to the stability of the rest of the empire. 'S'il n'y avait plus d'Algérie française, il n'y aurait plus d'Afrique française.' France is waking to the fact that a stone which used to lie idle is becoming the headstone of the corner.

The second tie with North Africa is a tie of flesh and blood. The million Frenchmen who crossed the Mediterranean are *Français de France* who, thanks to proximity, have kept contact with home friends and home politics. Moreover, the tie goes deeper than mere relationship. It is more profound because the planting of North Africa with Frenchmen was an artificial process which, being deliberate, has created a national responsibility.

In this, as in almost all human affairs, Algeria differs from Tunisia and Morocco. In the first place, it was conquered much earlier; the French first disembarked there in 1830, in order to vindicate their honour in a dispute during which the Turkish Dey had struck the French consul with a fly-switch, and they have had over a hundred years in which to strike national root. Secondly, the political positions are different. Algeria was conquered by force, peopled with Frenchmen, assimilated to France and included within the French republic. Tunisia and Morocco are protectorates, in which French officials 'advise' a native ruler. They were taken over in order to buttress Algeria—Tunis in 1881, Morocco in 1912—but in neither case did France adopt an assimilation policy. Moreover, since she upheld the local ruler, her colonists in each territory settled on a footing different from that of their neighbours in Algeria. Not only were they much less numerous, but they had not the same rights. Apart from a little official colonization attempted after the World War, the French landowners in Tunisia and Morocco are a planter class, who have emigrated not for national reasons, but to pay a dividend or to make a pile. They see new-comers as competitors, not auxiliaries. The difference between them and the Algerian farmer can be summed up in a word. If you ask an Algerian where he comes from, he says: 'Je suis d'Alger', or 'Je suis d'Oran'. Colonists in Tunisia or Morocco reply: 'Je suis de Poitiers', or 'Je suis de la Charente Inférieure'. The one finds it natural to live and die in Africa; the others are exiles who mean to end their days in France.

France's intimate concern is, therefore, for the Algerian colonist, and his history is a feather in her cap, for, once launched, he never looked back. The pioneers suffered hardships of which there is still evidence in the fortress architecture of the older farms. Some were ex-soldiers planted with instructions never to plough without their gun; others were down-and-outs from France, arriving without a penny, tempted over by the offer of a free passage, food and shelter, land, tools, building materials, and a few head of cattle. But, whatever their origin, after ten years nothing would move them—neither Arab raids, nor deathly malaria, nor yet liberal proposals for indemnity when the government decided that the outposts were too costly to defend. They were making money and preferred to hold out.

Security once assured, the original stock was replenished in a steady stream, with now and then a tidal wave—malcontents after the 1848 revolution, Alsace-Lorrainers who opted for France after 1870, southern French peasants moving in search of fresh fields after phylloxera had ravaged their vineyards in the 'eighties. From 1870 onwards the movement became a national crusade; free land was only given on condition of residence upon it. But this was no deterrent. By 1900 the outlook was promising enough to eliminate the element of risk; the free concessions died out because a richer and better class of farmer was ready to buy his land.

This process is checked only when agricultural price-levels defeat the weaker farmers. Many succumbed during the slump of the nineteen-thirties, sold their land to sturdier rivals, and, despite government assistance, began to move back towards the towns. But, though the link with the land is diminishing, the ground already covered is so extensive that the change makes no visible difference. The north Algerian landscape is still a testimony to the effort of a century. All over the wine-growing districts, peasants with Provençal accents drive ploughs between the vines. The village squares with their church, their *mairie*, and their players at *quilles* might be anywhere south of Lyons. A notice in Arabic is a rarity. The weekly holiday is on Sunday, not Friday, and an Arab crossing the street, swathed in his dirty white, looks out of place. In fact, so long as you remain north of the Atlas, you are not in the Dark Continent, but in France.

One flaw mars the Frenchness of the race of colonists, and that is their mixed origin. Until lately unimportant, it is now attracting the attention of French pessimists, who see in it a threat to Algerian unity. When France peopled Canada, she had men to spare, but by the time she needed a fresh relay for Algeria, her birth-rate was decreasing and she was short of human material. She therefore had recourse to foreign recruits; Spaniards from Andalusia, Italians from Sicily, Greeks and Maltese filled the gaps in her ranks. She found them easily assimilable; coming from weak states and overcrowded homes, they felt no strong national tie. They were flattered when a great nation offered them her nationality, and they accepted the rights she pressed upon them. This position, say the pessimists, is now changing. The states from which they came are becoming important and alluring; Fascist Italy, in particular, is setting out to win back her grandchildren. The struggle is a game of nuts-of-May, with heredity pulling one way and environment the other, and, when the ex-Spaniards of western Algeria began shipping volunteers and sending money to General Franco, the protagonists of heredity prophesied the beginning of the end. But on the whole the balance is in France's favour. She does not look upon non-French colonists as foreigners, and they usually return the compliment. Moreover, after two or three generations of living, voting, drinking, holidaying, and marrying with Frenchmen, they have evolved a new breed—an Algerian type, with all the sturdiness of a mongrel, and as vigorous as the race born of similar parents in the United States.

And once an Algerian stock is evolved, all Algerians, whatever their origin, have the same significance for Frenchmen. They are the brothers who were pushed out into the cold to do a job, and who made a job of it, and to whom France is therefore bound by gratitude as well as by pride.

Frenchmen also set store by North Africa for an economic reason—the belief that it can provide them with resources which they lack in France. So far as essentials are concerned, the theory is almost unfounded, because the three North African territories are incurably Mediterranean, and chiefly produce commodities which French soil already amply supplies. The majority of their exports are foodstuffs; as in Pliny's day, 'the glory of the land is in its harvests'. But France is that rarity in Europe, an industrial state which can go far towards feeding itself; unlike Great Britain, she has preserved a balance between industry and agriculture. Her deficiencies, and they are many, are all in industrial raw materials. To mention only the most important: she has no rubber or cotton, and, of minerals, no petroleum, tin, or copper and not enough lead, zinc, or coal. North Africa, being near at hand, could play a big role if it could fill these major gaps, but it does not. In order of value, its three leading exports are wine, phosphates, and wheat, and all but the second are coals to Newcastle in France.

But the idea of a self-sufficient empire is attractive, and a modern politician has only to mention it to raise an easy cheer. As part of the general world movement towards autarchy, France is making an effort to encourage North Africa to supplement home deficiencies. *Économie complémentaire* is its name, and it can do a good deal to improve the position in regard to non-essential commodities.

Much of North Africa's duplication of French products could have been avoided with a little planning, but forethought was never exercised. Domitian forbade the extension of African vineyards, but French peasants do not read Domitian. They had always planted vines, and knew how to plant vines, so they planted vines again when they reached Algeria and Tunisia. The brake was only applied in Morocco. The spread of their vineyards is an impressive sight, but it has caused much bad blood in France. Stormy scenes take place when the home wine-growers accuse the Algero-Tunisians of succumbing to the influence of cheap labour and low taxes, and indulging in 'planting hysteria' which spells ruin for the whole trade; they call it 'driving us to a second Sedan'. The Marseilles shipowners, foreseeing losses in the carrying trade, join the North African camp, and each side deluges the other with spitfire pamphlets. The Government has lately paid bonuses for the uprooting of vines and the planting of other crops, but the growers are conservative, and, since in good years they can sell all their produce, the feud smoulders on.

Wheat, which is often mentioned in the same breath as wine, does not present at all the same problem. A Moslem may not drink alcohol, but hard wheat is his staple food; therefore, in contrast to wine, wheat finds a large local market, which will be larger if native purchasing power increases, for the average North African Moslem is undernourished. Moreover, the wheat which grows in France is the soft wheat used for bread, and North Africa can contribute the hard wheat which French manufacturers need for making macaroni and like foods.

On the other hand, two or three great and obvious possibilities of fulfilling national needs have been ignored for half a century, and are only now being stimulated, thanks to the *économie complémentaire* campaign. The first is the production of citrus—oranges and grape-fruit—which France imports from foreign countries in quantities worth about 450 million francs per year. To give an idea of the possibilities: between 1905 and 1935 the area of Algeria under vineyards increased by 225,000 hectares; over the same period, the area under citrus increased by 6,000 hectares only. The contrast is partly due to the fact that a vine produces in three years, an orange tree only in six, and that many emigrants could not afford to wait. But it is also due to a less reputable influence. France buys her oranges from Spain, and any suggestion that she should cease to do so raises an outcry from the powerful French metallurgical industry, which relies on the orange trade to provide payment for its Spanish sales.

Wool production is another undeveloped possibility. The North African sheep-raising industry is almost all in native hands, and, since it is run as in the days when Jacob served Laban, it produces tough hides and skimpy fleeces. If Frenchmen had sunk less money in vineyards, and had had the courage to break new ground in the cattle-raising areas, Algerian railways might be paying their way as steadily as do the Australian lines, and France would undoubtedly be less dependent upon wool supplies from the other side of the world. Silk and hemp production, too, only awaited a few men of enterprise. France imports both in large quantities, and, since Italy and Spain can grow them, there is no reason why the similar soil of North Africa should not do so.

But until now none of these things has been forthcoming. The supplementing of home produce has been confined to early fruits and vegetables—which ripen in Morocco a fortnight before Algeria, and in Algeria a fortnight before the south of France—and to a few more genuinely southern products—dates from the desert oases, and palm fibre, alfa grass, and cork. None of these, however, is a vital commodity, and France now talks of more ambitious schemes, particularly in southern Morocco. She need not strain after the vegetable oils, for she can obtain them in quantities from her colonies farther south, but plans are in hand for cotton, jute, and sisal, and optimists even mention rubber.

An excursion into the ethics of *économie complémentaire* is out of place in a chapter whose business is merely to record that the campaign is in progress, but the conception of rubber, which is essentially tropical, in connexion with invigorating, windy Morocco is so incongruous as to warrant a digression. Just as a Londoner who can afford a hothouse can grow bananas, so France if she can afford to irrigate the Moroccan desert can grow jute or cotton; the drawback is that to grow them is more expensive than to buy them from the normal purveyor—the London fruiterer in the first case, India or Egypt in the second. Such is the effect of the self-sufficiency bacillus. The Ottawa Agreements—their real nature disguised in a drapery of Union Jacks—set a fashion which now hypnotizes other empires. France conformed to that fashion. The process was a Just-so Story; like Yellow Dog Dingo, she HAD to. And so she is constrained to throw bad money after good in North Africa, to spend inordinately on producing fancy crops, and to root up vines whose fruits Northern Europe would enjoy in order to ruin a Spaniard, a Palestinian, or a Chinaman by planting oranges and breeding silkworms instead. In an age of rationalization, the procedure is unbelievably irrational, particularly as total self-sufficiency is impossible, since the world's natural resources are so unevenly distributed that we are all inevitably dependent upon general trade. But subject to this important reservation, France's *économie complémentaire* organization, especially in Morocco, is efficiently run and planned.

As contributors to French self-sufficiency, North Africa's minerals are rather more precious than her vegetable products, for one or two of them fill important gaps. They are a new or newly rediscovered asset, for they had lain untouched through the thirteen centuries since the Arab invasion; for some reason, Islam is not a mining creed. Moreover, even after the change of master, prospectors dallied and hung back. The French are not, like the British, a speculative nation ready to hazard their savings in some colony at sight of a mining company prospectus, nor do they encourage foreign investment in their Empire. Thus, only under state management has there been a real drive—that which is now in progress in Morocco—in search of the materials which, if discovered, would be an invaluable asset in war.

The wharves of Algiers, Tunis, or Casablanca give a good idea of present resources. Immense white piles looking like cream-coloured chalk are phosphates. Exported all over the world for fertilizers, they now share the glory with the harvests, for the three territories between them produce between 40 and 50 per cent. of the world supply. A smaller red pile is iron ore, not wanted in France. The black stacks of coal at Algiers look promising, but are misleading; they come from Wales, and are waiting in bond to be shipped as fuel, for Algiers, being half-way between the northern European ports and the Suez Canal, is one of the four great Mediterranean coaling-stations. The other minerals are hidden in discreet little bags; there are not many, as yet.

Apart from their phosphates and their iron ore, Algeria and Tunisia have little to offer; they supply a modicum of lead and zinc, but from mines which only pay their way when prices are high. Algeria produces coal at Kenadsa, in the south of the department of Oran, but the amount extracted is so small that it is exhausted by the time it has fuelled the engine which draws it to the coast.

It is to Morocco that France pins her hopes, encouraged by its likeness to the mining areas of southern Spain. Apart from phosphates, manganese is her richest find. The discovery is a national asset, because the iron ore of Lorraine has next to no manganese content, and manganese, as an ingredient of steel, is essential to the French metallurgical industry. France is therefore a large-scale importer, and if, as is estimated, the Moroccan deposits can supply two-thirds of her needs, she can reduce her present dependence on sources in India, China, and Brazil. But this and other discoveries in the way of lead, cobalt, and molybdenum would pale to insignificance could she but find petroleum in workable quantities. The search is diligent, for there are tantalizing signs of its presence; on one occasion a very fountain spouted forth, and provided some impressive photographs, only to expend itself in that first fine flush, and peter out. Up till now, the Eiffel Tower-like erections which mark borings in the coastal hills represent the faith, but not the exploit, of the state petroleum company.

Even this most cursory survey of North Africa's capacity as a producer shows that France could live satisfactorily without North African supplies. She would suffer only minor inconvenience if war in the Mediterranean were to cut her off from the southern shore, for she could trade with Morocco via the Atlantic, and dispense with Algerian and Tunisian produce. She would be deprived of an important market, but, were a war in progress, her exporters would no doubt be busy elsewhere.

The suffering would be experienced in another quarter. France could dispense with Algeria, but Algeria and Tunisia could not dispense with France. Even during the World War, when Mediterranean traffic, though reduced, was possible, the territories were pinched for lack of fuel. They would not face starvation, for they can feed themselves in essentials, but their modern, westernized economy would crack beneath the strain. They would be deprived of their staple income—that derived from the sale of wine and phosphates—and their industries and communications could not live without coal and oil. Their Moslem face would change little; more camels would be mustered for caravans, more women would work oil presses, more donkeys would turn grindstones in a never-ending round. But their European face would wither and fade. Abandoned buses and silent factories would demonstrate a truth which seems eternal—that the Barbary Coast depends for prosperity upon contact with Europe, whether Rome two thousand years ago or France to-day.

A final reason for prizing North Africa is the instinct to hold on to a possession that has been bought not only with money but with blood.

France's casualties in her North African campaigns look trifling beside the figures to which modern slaughter has accustomed us; she lost only 6,500 men, for instance, during her twenty-five-year conquest of Morocco. But her expeditions so often possessed dramatic qualities that their significance is out of proportion to their size. Sometimes they provide stories famous in French history, like the epic of Colonel Flatters and his men who were murdered by the Touaregs in 1881; more often, the heroes are lesser known—commemorated only on the frequent small monuments by the Algerian roadside which mark the site of a skirmish, or in the streets named after le Caporal this and le Capitaine that which are so common in Oran and Algiers. The story began in 1830; the final campaign in the south Moroccan desert did not end until 1934. The present map of North Africa is therefore the outcome of sustained effort, and France values a prize so hardly won.

The money spent on the expeditions is another consideration; the total cost of conquest must have been high. The financial details of the Algerian campaigns are lost in the dusty records of the last century, and the Tunisian adventure was an occupation—a cheaper victory, but the conquest of Morocco alone is known to have cost some 13 milliard francs. Moreover, in all three territories the state bore much of the cost of equipment; it settled colonists, drained marshes, made reservoirs, and it built harbours, railways, and roads. In hard years, too, it was often compelled to put its hand still deeper into its pocket, making sometimes a direct contribution to an unbalanced budget, but more often helping farmers by means of debt redemption or by offering easy-term loans.

To these vast sums must be added the money contributed by the private investor, coming not only from great business houses like the *Crédit Foncier*, or from the *Banque de Paris et des Pays Bas* which financed Morocco, but also out of the stockings of thrifty peasant families, brought over in the pocket of some emigrant brother or son. The total is impossible to compute, just as there is no calculating the sums which settlements like Maryland or Virginia cost their founders, but, between the three territories, it must run into three or four or even five scores of milliards—a sum which dwarfs even France's Egyptian investment.

What return has the nation seen for this mass of capital? Are the territories overloaded with debt, or have they succeeded in making good?

The boom which swept Algeria between 1920 and 1931 proved that, when world conditions are favourable, France can count upon a respectable Algerian dividend. The territory is her best customer, and French shipping, secure in a monopoly, profits largely by the carrying trade involved. Goods travelling to or from Algeria represent 35 per cent. of the exports and 10 per cent. of the imports of the port of Marseilles, and the import figure is thus small simply because Algeria's chief product—her wine—usually travels via the Atlantic to Rouen, because it is bound for the Paris market. Moreover, even in bad years the territory can hold its own; it enjoys a customs union with France which enormously benefits it, and which enabled it to live through the world economic crisis in a condition less stricken than that of most young agrarian states.

The investment in Tunisia is less gilt-edged. The territory is poorer, because its Mediterranean regions are smaller. The last slopes of the Atlas slide into the sea a little way south of Tunis, and beyond that it is flat and waterless, and hopelessly dependent upon rain. Moreover, Tunis is not, as is Algiers, either a distributing centre or a coaling-station. Tucked out of the way in its sheltered gulf, it is off the beaten track of Mediterranean communications. It is not even on any great air route, and it enjoys no entrepôt trade. Lastly, Tunisia is highly susceptible to world conditions, because its customs arrangements with France are less beneficial than those of Algeria. 'Such prosperity as it can expect to enjoy', drily remarks a British consular report, 'can only result if the country is administered on modest lines.'

Morocco is, of the three territories, the land of promise, and no expense has been spared to make it so. The spending was lavish from the start. When the French cabinet of 1912 discussed the appointment of the right commander for the newly acquired territory, M. Briand is reported to have said: 'I vote for Lyautey, for I believe him to be the man for the job; but let us be under no illusion; he will cost us a pretty penny.' He knew his man. Marshal Lyautey's vision, conviction, and driving power between them turned Morocco into the pride of the French Empire, but the expenditure involved was great. Lyautey spent on two accounts. The first was in order to promote economic development; in 1919, upon completion of the first stage of Casablanca's great harbour, he spoke of the 'thousands of kilometres of railway, thousands of horse-power, thousands of kilowatts' which must send life coursing through the port, and, like a magnet, he set about attracting the funds for their construction. Secondly, he spent upon the look of the territory. Arguing that France's innovations must be worthy of the race which built the Alhambra, he devoted thought and money to the lay-out of the modern Moroccan towns. His critics condemn his extravagance, and his over-expenditure on *constructions de prestige*, but those who doubt the soundness of his psychology should compare Moroccan comment on the unpretentious beauty of the government buildings at Rabat with Arab comment on their dingy counterparts at Jerusalem.

Including the cost of conquest, the French investment in Morocco is said to have exceeded 30 milliard francs, and if so, there is no denying that the return for the outlay is, so far, small, that Morocco bears too heavy a burden of debt, and that during the crisis years only an unlimited overdraft with the French treasury kept its payments balanced and its currency stable. But this unsound position is not altogether France's fault; it is due to a stroke of misfortune that Frenchmen could not possibly foresee. In 1930 and 1931, just as France had finished spending on equipment, just as exports were rising and profits beginning to show, a calamitous fall in world prices cut off all hope of dividends; the territory was like a prize bloom nipped by the frost on the night before the flower-show. Some enterprises died; others were able to hang on, but, to avoid the collapse of all its hopes, the French Government was obliged to take over larger shares than it had intended in enterprises of national importance.

All young countries were blighted by the crisis, but Morocco was an especial sufferer; it was particularly susceptible, owing partly to the abnormal spending which had preceded the catastrophe, but partly also to a crippling customs position. Under the Act of Algeciras, which dates back to 1906, and to a truce declared between the powers who were at that time scrambling for Moroccan concessions, the Sultan's government must apply a uniform tariff to the goods of all countries. That Act is still in force. Like the Open Door arrangement in the mandated territories, it was intended to benefit the Moroccans, but, again like the Open Door arrangement, it is a handicap once the world starts practising economic nationalism, for it deprives the territory of a weapon which is necessary in the hard-bargaining process to which foreign trade is reduced. For lack of the right to raise its tariffs, Morocco competes at a disadvantage, for it has no means of preventing the dumping of goods by unscrupulous states who take no Moroccan wares in return. For instance, the dumping of Japanese rubber shoes at three francs a pair temporarily wrecked the famous Moroccan trade in leather slippers, while Japan could not be forced to make purchases to compensate for the damage she had done.

But the outlook, though dark, is not hopeless. Given a revision of the Act of Algeciras, or, better still, a return to freer world trade, Morocco's wheels would go round and her ports grow busy, and her economy live up to expectations. Indeed, France's Moroccan outlay might one day prove more repaying than that in Algeria, for even the most pessimistic critics of the lavish spending there admit that the investment promises good dividends.

On balance, then, France finds North Africa economically dependent upon her in bad years, though in good years an economic asset. Of the three territories, Tunisia will always be the economic weakling, but, as Morocco advances to Algeria's stage of development, the other two territories should prove a bulwark to the mother-country, not only as a market but as a source of supply.

Moreover, economic gain was not the only end which France sought. Strategic motives also prompted her steady expansion on the other side of the Mediterranean, and from a strategic and imperial point of view she has done well. Possession of her three North African territories consolidates her position, not only imperially but in Europe, and she can feel that she has expended neither her men nor her money in vain.

4. *The Moral Hold on French North Africa*

But the winning of North Africa was only half the battle. The power who has it must hold it, and in so doing, France is confronted with problems arising out of Arab nationalisms and independence movements of the type already encountered in Egypt and Syria. She shares the experience common to all powers who rule large and lively native populations, when those populations suddenly learn western ways by means of photographs and interviewers, wireless and the cinema. She finds that her security depends not on strength alone, but on her skill in humouring and cajoling the fourteen million Moslems whom she controls.

This task takes a different form in each of her three North African territories, for, though in many aspects they are a unity, from the human point of view they are still a trinity, and their different characteristics demand different handling.

The Algerians are the unique problem. They stand in a relation to Europe which is different not only from that of their two neighbours, but from all the rest of Islam. A hundred years of day-to-day contact with Frenchmen have bred intimacy and emulation. They want to be like France. The educated class wears French clothes, and drinks in cafés with French friends. You hear veiled Arab women talking French together in the tram; you even see a middle-class Moslem of Algiers taking his evening stroll with a wife on his arm.

The French imparted these habits without effort, partly because of their willingness to rub shoulders with an African race, but partly also because of the early date at which they did so. When other colonies were being run as profit-making concerns where the white man supervised while the native laboured, Algeria was undergoing experiences which are common enough nowadays, when we are all bred on ideas of trusteeship and equality, but which were rare privileges then. As long ago as 1865 the Algerian Moslems were accorded the favour of acquiring French nationality without abandoning what is called their 'personal status'—that is, they became French subjects while retaining Islamic laws and customs. What is more, if they gave up those laws and customs, and accepted the French Civil Code instead, they could obtain French citizenship, and all the rights of a born Frenchman. To quote the decree in full:

'The Moslem native population is hereby declared to be French. It will nevertheless remain subject to Moslem law. Its members may be admitted to service in the army and navy. They are eligible for public office, and for civil employment in Algeria. Upon request, they may be accorded the privileges of French citizenship; in such case they are subject to the civil and political law of France.'

In 1870, assimilation progressed a stage farther. By another decree the Algerian Jews, who had in the course of centuries become almost indistinguishable from Arabs except in matters of dress and religion, were out of hand granted full French citizenship in order to secure their support in the Franco-Prussian war. During the past seventy-five years, therefore, Frenchmen, Jews, and Moslems in Algeria have frequently been pounded in the same crucible, and the modern Algerian, with his ambitions centred on France, is the result of the process.

This rare blend would not have been so smoothly achieved but for one other important characteristic in which Algeria differs from its neighbours—namely, its lack of a culture and an aristocracy. In contrast to Tunisia and Morocco, it is poor in art and architecture, and its French conquerors had not to contend with the prejudices of a ruling class entrenched in cities of learning like Tunis or Fez. They packed the piratical Turkish upper class back to Turkey; they fought and killed or captured a few tribal leaders inland, and they stepped unchallenged into the lead. In Algeria, you do not meet princely sheiks of classic pattern until you come to the Southern Territories—that is, the Sahara—which were conquered much later than the north, which are run under army management, and which are no longer part of France; and even there, the few examples that survive are disappointingly modernized, and run their card-indexed tribes through telephones boasting several switches. Thus, the leading Moslem class to-day is a creation of French policy, is French-educated, and cherishes a wish to be French. France's modern problem in the territory is that she has given birth to a potential Frankenstein—a growing child whose desires are beginning to clash with those of the million Frenchmen whom she has also planted in the area—a prodigy who wishes to be more closely associated with France than the European Algerians will allow. Such, in a word, is the native vote problem upon which hangs French popularity in the territory.

In 1930, the year of Algeria's centenary, the goodwill and speech-making which accompanied the celebrations led the French Government to make a promise to the Moslem population. Amid general agreement, it decided that their loyalty deserved recognition, and that, owing to the advanced stage of development of the educated class, an extension of the native vote for the French Parliament was the obvious gesture to make.

As things stood at the time of the promise, Algeria sent ten deputies to Paris, who were elected by a voting public consisting of the Europeans, the Jews, and such Moslems as had abandoned their personal status—this last a surprisingly small group of no more than 2,000, for, though many educated Algerians no longer practise their faith, they are as loth to cut adrift from Islam as is the Englishman who 'has no use for religion' but, nevertheless, would not dream of being married or buried except by the Church. France's centenary promise therefore necessitated the extension of voting rights to a class of individuals who would be subject to Moslem and not to French law.

The difficulties and procrastinations which followed, and which leave the voting situation unchanged at the beginning of 1938, have all arisen out of a cleavage of opinion as to the form which that extension should take.

The European population—the generic term for which is the colonists, *les colons*—realizes that so long as the native vote is confined to educated men, European will for some years yet outnumber Moslem voters, but it envisages a day when education will become more widespread and when the position will be the other way about. Though the *colons* are divided in political colour into the countless pastel shades of the French parties, their left wing automatically swings half-right, and they present a united front as soon as any question of the native vote arises. Through the mouth of their leading spokesman—a picturesque figure who is mayor of Oran and who enjoys the distinction of being an unfrocked *abbé*—they are almost unanimous in demanding that the Moslems shall vote for their own deputies and in separate constituencies.

The Moslems will not hear of this. They argue that a handful of Moslem deputies would be a museum piece in the Paris Chamber, and that since they fight for France, and pay taxes on the same footing as the Europeans, they have a right to vote in the same constituencies.

A number of draft bills embodying these rival theses were drawn up for presentation to the French Chamber, but no government gave time or thought to the matter until M. Blum assumed office in 1936, by which time the Algerian Moslems were growing restive. The Blum government took a vigorous step forward. It gave its blessing to a draft proposed by a senator called Maurice Viollette—an ex-Governor General of Algeria who had in his day been most unpopular with the *colons*. The *projet Viollette* favoured the Moslem view that the voting should take place in joint constituencies, but it demanded such high educational qualifications for voters that, at the time when the draft was published, only some 20,000 Moslems were eligible, whereas the *colon* franchise numbers about a quarter of a million.

The bill had a mixed reception in Algeria. Europeans with left-wing views admitted that the educational qualifications were a safeguard for years to come, but the majority of the *colons* were in no two minds about it. They saw in it the thin end of a wedge whose other end was of incalculable dimensions, and they therefore opposed it bitterly. The Moslems hesitated before they pronounced their view. The proposal was not all they had hoped for, but a few far-sighted leaders agreed that it was preferable to a much wider franchise for native constituencies, since, produced to infinity, it offered a Utopia in which several million Moslems would be able to vote for the French parliament. They sensibly decided that it was idle to try and wring more out of France in the circumstances, and they persuaded all factions to support it. The violence of the *colon* opposition convinced the illiterate class that the proposal must be for the native good, and the Moslem community achieved a degree of unanimity unprecedented in Algerian history.

This situation places the French Government in an unenviable dilemma. If it gives way to the pressure of the Moslems, it causes a loss of 'face' among the Europeans who have fought the draft. On the other hand, if it fails to offer the Moslems the minimum which is embodied in the *projet Viollette* it runs the risk of alienating their loyalty and causing them to turn separatist and Arab nationalist.

The danger of this last is more acute than might be imagined from the first part of this chapter, for, although the Algerian Moslems have so far been described as if they spoke with one voice, and though they are at one over the question of the vote, they are in fact a motley crowd.

They fall into three main groups. The first is that of the *Évolués* or Developed Ones, the very name of whose party flatters the vanity of recruits. These are the type of whom a description has been given; Francophile, and well educated, either at Algiers University or in France, they are many of them more reflective and less self-confident than their counterparts in other Arab countries. They are a group the size of which any visitor is fatally prone to over-estimate, because they include the journalists and politicians to whose offices he has easy access. In fact, however, though they are vocal and influential, their numbers are small. But they make an appeal which is rich in externals, in that they stand for the western machinery of life with its comforts and dazzling inventions, and they have, therefore, a large potential following in the shape of the town worker, who, though he is seldom able to read, has learnt the rudiments of politics and mob tactics from French fellow workers whom he overhears discussing the methods of parties and strikers in Paris.

At the same time, the *Évolués* have not abandoned the possibility of using Islam as a rallying cry. Though most of them have long ceased to attend the mosque or to pray daily, they still call themselves practising Moslems, and in an emergency could raise the standard of religion and make a far wider appeal than they could compass by means of political slogans. To those who assert that Bolshevism is rife in North Africa—a theory that is propagated in Italy—the answer is that when any Algerian crowd is called upon to give a salute, you see a considerable sprinkling of clenched fists; you also see arms raised in the Fascist greeting. But if the occasion is one which arouses emotion—for instance, the funeral of a victim of a political riot—the majority of both factions change their gesture to that of the uplifted fore-finger, in token that there is no God but Allah.

This predominance of religion over politics is not surprising, for the other two groups which make up the Algerian population, and which between them far outnumber the *Évolués* and their town-bred disciples, are both profoundly and primarily religious. The more organized is that of the *Ulema*, whose name, which means 'sages', stands for Koranic learning, and who preach a puritan revival not unlike that of Ibn Saud and his Wahhabis in Arabia. The *Ulema* constitute a political force through the clubs and newspapers which they run in order to combat social vices and perversions of the true faith, but their chief significance, so far as French security is concerned, is that they derive their impetus from the east. Their movement is a product of the Islamic Congress held at Jerusalem in 1931, and their head-quarters are not at Algiers but farther east, at Constantine, where the breezes from Cairo and Mecca first strike Algeria.

The *Évolués* and the *Ulema* both preach a forward policy. The third and far the largest section of the Algerian population is a die-hard, standstill element which is led by the *marabouts* or holy men of the perverted form of Islam generally practised in the territory. Since modern notions tend to reduce the *marabout*'s influence, his aim is to let things be, and, though the more up-to-date *marabouts* sometimes meet in congress, it is misleading to call them a party, for they are in fact unorganized, individualistic, and parochial. Politically speaking, however, they can be important, for each is the mentor of his tribe or village, and between them they therefore control the type which makes up the vast majority of the population of Algeria. For the French polish of the *Évolués* is not typical of the people as a whole. At least four out of the six million Moslem inhabitants are illiterate, slow-moving, and unable to speak French. They know little of politics and still less of the vote, and think only in terms of to-morrow's food and drink for themselves and their beasts. To them, France means the police, and the administrator who sometimes distributes seed loans, or even free food, in bad years. The French are an institution; no one can remember when they were not there.

The object of this description of the Algerian scene is to show that, if France were to thwart the European ambitions of the political leaders, and if those leaders were to retaliate by throwing off their Parisian trappings and preaching an anti-western crusade, they would have no difficulty in rallying a large Islamic following, in preaching separatism or any other form of nationalist movement, and in undermining France's security to a degree that she would find inconvenient, not to say damaging.

On the other hand, France enjoys several safeguards against a unified movement of this kind. The first is the strength of her army in North Africa; so long as she is at peace in Europe, the very presence of her troops spells quiet in Algeria. The second safeguard is the divergence of view which prevails among the Moslems. The unity with which they support the *projet Viollette* is only skin deep. No two men could be farther apart in outlook than the dapper, bustling *Évolué*, who pours you out an apéritif and tells you with a laugh that he is almost ashamed of his Arabic, and the grave, dignified *Ulema*, dressed in the green of the Prophet, who tells you through his interpreter that he has preached at Mecca, and who begs you to excuse him for a few moments during your interview because it is the hour of prayer.

For the present, a third and still more adequate safeguard against a united Moslem rising in Algeria is the lack of intercourse between district and district. As you travel about, the different parts of the territory might be so many different planets; a few hours in the bus brings you into another world.

The biggest bar to unity is that of language. Thirty per cent. of the Moslems of Algeria are Berbers of Mediterranean race, who live in districts unconquered by the invading Arabs, and who, though they accepted Islam, rejected Arabic, and talk their native Berber to this day. Stories of the innumerable gulfs which separate district from district would fill volumes, but the best illustration is perhaps that provided by a description of the largest and most remarkable tribe, the Kabyles of Great Kabylia.

The Kabyles are Berbers, and you know it as soon as you enter their territory, for when, only seventy miles from Algiers, your bus climbs into their mountains, you find an atmosphere which is the very antithesis of everything Arab, because it is busy. All the Kabyles are working industriously, the men at lordly, the women at menial jobs. Decency forbids that the latter should stop and speak with a stranger, but the men are welcoming and discursive, and almost all speak good French. They have learnt it easily and well because they are born with a strong business sense, and because their native Berber, being unwritten, does not carry them far. Moreover, they need it in order to earn extra substance, for over-population is the problem of their tribe. Their villages, strung along the hill-tops and clinging to the precipitous slopes, disgorge unbelievable crowds on market day, but, though the hillsides are cultivated wherever they are not too steep, they cannot support a tribe of 800,000 in an area so small that it is more thickly peopled than Holland—the most densely populated country in Europe.

The Kabyles, who are resourceful and thrifty, therefore keep their families alive by migrating, sometimes going singly and peddling their way for a few months through the villages of northern Europe, more often leaving in groups to work for a year or two in French factories.

There are always some thousands in the Michelin works at Clermont-Ferrand.

The Berbers are distinct from the Arabs in one other important respect besides their language and their character. Though they were converted to the religion of the invaders, they adopted its customs but not its law. Thus a Kabyle is a follower of the Prophet, but rules his women and marries and divorces them according to Berber, not Moslem, rites, and of these customs he is extremely proud. The French have found him more assimilable than the Arab because his Berber nature is more like their own, but they have not weaned him from his individuality. He says of European habits: 'Cela ne se fait pas chez nous.'

The single example of the Kabyles serves to show that in any anti-French rising in Algeria, the insurrectionists would find it difficult to secure the unanimous support of the country-side, and that Islam is the only rallying cry that is sure of making a universal appeal. But this state of affairs will disappear with time. As education spreads and communications improve, the inflammability of the Algerian population will increase. The voice of restless, dissatisfied leaders has till lately been confined to the towns, but its sound is spreading outwards, like the rings on a pond. And France's problems are spreading with it.

Almost immediately on arrival in Algeria, I met one of the high French officials exercising control over Moslem affairs. He spoke wisely of British difficulties in Palestine, and then added: 'Ah—vous aussi vous avez votre projet Viollette.' At the time, I thought his comment almost incongruous. Knowing next to nothing of Algerian affairs, I decided that his outlook must be warped by perpetual concentration on Algeria, and that he had lost his sense of proportion. But I was wrong. The dilemma that confronts the French in Algeria—torn as they are between the fears of the *colons*, on one side, and the hopes of the Moslems, on the other—is of the same nature as the Palestine problem, and threatens to assume something of the same dimensions. In each case, a Moslem and a non-Moslem population present the ruling power with rival claims which are hopelessly irreconcilable. In each case, that power has to decide between claims each of which has right and reason on its side.

In both Tunisia and Morocco France's problem is less formidable than that in Algeria because less out of the ordinary; both are protectorates undergoing a process already experienced in Iraq, Egypt, and Syria. In each a native ruler is 'advised' by Frenchmen; in each case the Moslems are working for independence; in each case, realizing their weakness, they are working for it under French protection. Both territories want a 'treaty' on the Egyptian model; in both the word possesses the fetish value which it enjoys among the Arabs of Palestine. Here, however, their likeness ends. France's problem differs in each, firstly, because of their different geographical positions, and, secondly, because they are at different stages of development.

Tunisia turns her back on Algeria and her face to the east. Her low east coast is strewn with the remains of eight or nine invasions—so many monuments to her accessibility. Not one Tunisian in a hundred has followed the vicissitudes of the *projet Viollette*, but all are genuinely interested in news from Egypt, or from anywhere in the Arab world. The high officials round the Bey often belong to Turkish or Syrian families; the professors at the Zitouna mosque—one of the great universities of Islam—are in touch with Mecca, and a travelled, lettered bourgeoisie keeps up connexions with Oriental friends. The eastern tastes of the less educated classes strike your ear and eye as you walk through the bazaars. Wireless sets are relaying Cairo; photographs of King Farouk are on sale, and Egyptian newspapers—which Tunisia imports at the rate of several tons a month—are being read aloud to the smokers in the cafés.

Morocco, on the other hand, faces the Atlantic; all its ports are on its western shore. The sounds which come from Cairo therefore come faintly, while its ocean coastline gives it a sense of freedom and assurance. Tunisia is only eighty miles from Sicily; it houses an Italian colony of ninety-five thousand, and cannot forget for a moment that, if it throws off the yoke of one European power, another will snap it up. Moroccans do not see such obvious signs of this menace. They have forgotten the scrambles and struggles which took place before the War, and are consequently more jaunty and self-assured.

The differing stages of development of the two territories are due to the different dates at which they were conquered—dates which are discernible from the deck of the ship in which you arrive. For the architecture of modern Tunis is in the taste of the eighteen-eighties and 'nineties; the cathedral on the hill above Carthage is reminiscent of the fussy outline of the old Trocadero. The sky-scrapers of Casablanca, on the other hand, are streamlined, severe, and post-War. This difference of vintage extends to the Moslems to whom you have introductions. The French-educated class in Tunisia includes older men and staider intelligences. The Moroccans who have received a French education, and who lead the independence movement, are men who were still of school age when the protectorate was declared in 1912. Since France did not concentrate on the spread of education until after the World War, most of them are under thirty.

In 1937 and 1938, tumult and shouting, punctuated by occasional riots, marred the peace in both territories, but, of the two, Tunisia seems the more likely to give the French immediate trouble. 'La Tunisie, c'est notre point noir', admits the Frenchman-on-the-spot, adding, in order to preserve the international balance, 'comme la Palestine c'est le vôtre'.

Several factors combine to create this unease in Tunisia, not the least of which is foreign—namely, the influence of events in Egypt; but the majority of its causes are indigenous, and are due either to the nature of the Tunisians or to the behaviour of the French.

For one thing, as soon as unrest germinates it spreads rapidly all over the territory, for, in contrast to conditions in Algeria and Morocco, news in Tunisia travels fast and far, both because the territory is relatively small, and because the bulk of its population is concentrated in the watered north and along the friendly east coast. Here, where contacts are incessant, unity of thought prevails in spite of local differences of race and character. For instance, the people of the port of Sfax, in the south, are as unlike the rest of the Tunisians as the Kabyles are unlike the rest of the Algerians, yet a Sfaxian shares the political views of the capital. The average Tunisian lives in the north in an atmosphere of lazy sufficiency. Secure in the knowledge that his fruit will ripen anyway, he sits by his door, and sells his crop to the passer-by rather than trudge round the town in search of a better price. The Sfaxian is all the opposite. He travels far after markets, and bargains for them with an acumen believed to be due to his Phoenician ancestry. He is no less energetic as a manual labourer. Generations ago he discovered that; though he lived in a desert, he could make it blossom by planting olive-trees at great intervals and ploughing incessantly in the sand between them, because if the roots had room to spread the trees prospered on dew. The result of his labours is the most singular sight in all Tunisia—the Sfax olive forest with its trees marshalled row on row like well-drilled soldiers, stretching for fifty miles into the Sahara. Yet, in spite of his un-Arab ways, he is of one mind with the people of Tunis because of the ease with which their ideas reach him by road and rail along the flat coast. Conveniently for the townsman who preaches politics, only the southern oases are isolated and out of earshot. Tunisia, therefore, boasts an awakening peasantry, which Algeria and Morocco do not.

The ease with which the populace can be rallied is enhanced by the dominance of the town of Tunis, which has swelled, under the combined influence of climate and snobbery, into a head too big for its body. Within fifty miles of its gates, the Atlas ends and the inland plains begin, and from there onwards life is at the mercy of a scanty rainfall; half-nomadic peasants sow every year and reap once in four. Hope must spring eternal, because some tattered families stay and persevere, but in the second and third famine years others inevitably move towards the capital in search of work and food.

And in that capital they find discontent. As in Egypt, the Sudan, India, and everywhere where literacy is rare, a man who can read and write is above manual labour, and a candidate for the learned professions. Tunis is the door to these; therefore it is the goal of every countryman, while no townsman wants to leave it. Moreover, France has aggravated this tendency by her educational policy. She imported from Algeria the system which turns Arabs into Frenchmen, and, spending her money on quality rather than quantity, gives a *lycée* education to every boy passing through school. The Arab boy who has learnt about 'notre ancêtre Vercingetorix', and knows and produces proudly for you the fact that Madame de Staël was *née* Germaine Necker, sets out for Tunis as soon as he has finished his schooling. As a result, the capital teems with educated unemployed, who will not defile themselves by touching work less dignified than that of a doctor, a lawyer, or a civil servant, and who, failing to find room in these overstocked professions, turn their disgruntled minds to politics. White-collar unemployment has more effect upon general opinion in Tunisia than in any other territory in the world.

The party run by these educated Moslems during their long hours of leisure is called the *Destour*, which means Constitution, and since 1920, when it first published its aims in a book called *Tunisie Martyre*, it has cultivated a growing resentment against the French and an increasing desire to be free. Its sentiments are widely shared for the reasons already stated, but also because it enjoys an impressionable audience. The Tunisian is like the Irishman, born 'agin' the government and easily roused. He is quick and witty, but he thrives best on complaint. Put a question to a *Destourien* and you evoke an able monologue, but every word of his criticism is destructive. After a time, your inevitable reaction is: 'Yes, but what do you *want*?' His answer, just as inevitable, is: 'It is for the government to propose. Our role is to say whether we think its proposals are right or wrong.' He never pursues his reasoning to its logical conclusion—namely, that would-be leaders of an independent government need practice in constructive thinking.

He levels all this complaint against France. Islam is venerable and unquestioned, and the critical faculty which he has learnt in the French school is directed, undiluted, against the west from which it came. Moreover, he gains many adherents because some of his grumbling is justified; France would face less resentment in Tunisia had she avoided some of her administrative mistakes.

Of these, the most blatant has been her excessive importation of Frenchmen for employment in the public services, despite the fact that she has simultaneously educated Tunisians on lines that qualify them for most of the posts. Frenchmen pervade those services from highest to lowest; there are 6,000 of them in civil employment as opposed to 4,000 Tunisians; they even drive trams and deliver letters. All the bitterness of *Destour* feeling on the subject is brought out in the cartoons in the local newspapers. A typical drawing shows a Tunisian swimming for his life after a boat full of Frenchmen, who call to him: 'How can we take you aboard? Can't you see the boat is full?'

The cartoons concentrate on two other grievances. The first is unequal pay for equal work. After Tunisians have been educated as class-mates of French boys and have passed the same examinations at the *lycée*, they resent differential treatment at a later stage of life. The second is French colonization. The *colons* officially planted since the War have been settled upon land to which Arab tribes consider that they have a right. This situation might have been accepted had the new-comers been successful, and thereby brought employment and financial benefits to Tunisians, but they have not. The French gave preference to colonists on grounds of War service rather than of experience, and, in the enthusiasm of the post-War boom, installed the families on uneconomically small holdings. As a result, few of them have made good, and both *Destourien* and peasant can point to the misuse of land which they consider should be in their own more deserving hands.

Unfortunately for France, the French population, instead of acting as a national advertisement, makes matters worse because it shows a poor spirit. The civil service is too big, and is badly paid, while many of the small *colons* are failures. Mentally out of sorts, the French, too, take refuge in politics. They reproduce the polemics of all the splinter parties at home, and their bickerings are listened to with interest by the *Destour*, but lower France in Tunisian esteem. The ill impression thus created is heightened by the changes of policy and personnel which take place with every change in the French Government. France's custom of distributing colonial governorships as rewards for party merit causes reversals of policy which are more unsettling to a people politically awake, like the Tunisians, than to a remote or backward colony.

In this gloomy atmosphere, the *Destourien* habit of grumbling has become ingrained. All their country's ills are not France's fault, but, from the world economic crisis downwards, they lay everything at the French door. They have reached an unreasoning frame of mind, and grumble over action which, if examined, is for their own good. For instance, they grumbled when the French proposed to spend more money on teaching the rudiments of agriculture, and less on the higher education of peasants—a change designed to reduce the white-collar unemployment from which they suffer. Their minds are vitiated by constant complaint. What is France to do? Palliatives are useless, because the discontent always outstrips them. Only some radical change of policy, sufficiently unexpected to leave the Tunisians breathless and mute, can clear the air.

That change is obviously a 'treaty', provided the offer is made before the word loses the glamour with which it has been endowed by events in Egypt and Syria. But several difficulties stand in the way of a treaty for Tunis. The stage of development of the territory is not one of them. Tunisia is just as ready for independence as is Syria; the difference between them is that France is more loth to loosen her grip on the first than on the second because of its greater strategic importance. The stumbling-blocks lie elsewhere. The first is the presence of the 6,000 French civil servants. Tunisia is poor, and cannot pay to rid herself of the incubus, as Egypt paid the British in 1922, and while France is in her present financial plight, no French government is anxious to ask the French nation to shoulder the cost of withdrawing its nationals. A second and greater obstacle is the belief that an independent Tunisia would pervert Algeria. Until the question of the *projet*

Viollette is settled, points cannot be conceded to the *Destour*. A final difficulty is the fact that a third party—Italy—enjoys treaty rights in the territory.

As if France's Moslem problem were not enough, she also has to cater for an Italian population in Tunisia, almost equal in numbers to her own.

Italian settlement there dates back to long before the beginning of the protectorate. During the overflow of population which took place in the nineteenth century, many southern Italians found that they could make a living within a bare eighty miles of the coast of Sicily. As is usual with Italians who migrate, the majority preferred town life, and settled in Tunis itself, but about 30 per cent. took up agriculture, and began to grow wine on Cape Bon in country which looks very like their own. They arrived in such numbers that enthusiasts in Italy began to talk of a second conquest of Carthage, and poets to compare King Victor Emmanuel to Scipio. This idyll was shattered by Bismarck. His hint that 'the Tunisian pear was ripe', given to France at the Congress of Berlin, led to the French occupation in 1881, and created Italian ill feeling which subsists to this day.

The Franco-Italian quarrel over Tunis waxes and wanes with the strength of Italy's international position. At first it was acute, but it abated after 1896, when the Italian defeat by the Ethiopians at Adowa disenchanted the Italian people with the idea of overseas adventures. Thereupon the French magnanimously allowed Italy to establish direct relations with the Bey of Tunis, and to secure for her nationals the right to settle in Tunisia while retaining their Italian citizenship and Italian schools. The inflow of Italians during the next twenty years woke France to the alarming realization that the Italian community might one day outnumber her own to an extent with which she could not compete. She therefore took a step which caused a fresh outburst of Italian bitterness. In 1918, just as the

Italians were entering on their post-War crisis, she denounced the 1896 agreement upon pretext of economic necessity. She then set about increasing the French population of Tunisia by adopting an aggressive naturalization policy. She put obstacles in the way of foreign schools; she taxed contracts signed by non-French citizens; she adopted a differential salary-scale for French and non-French civil servants; she promised fathers who became naturalized that their sons in government employment would become eligible for the French expatriation bonus—equivalent to a 25 per cent. rise in salary. The pressure was not unsuccessful. The Italian community—at that time more than half-illiterate—had no very strong nationalist feelings, and fell to temptation. In 1921 only 6 per cent. of the population of Tunisia applied for naturalization; five years later the percentage had risen to 21.

But there the process reached its zenith. Very naturally, it piqued Fascist pride, and as soon as Signor Mussolini was firmly established at home, he began to snatch the brands from the burning. He offered rival inducements to remain Italian; he engaged France in a tug-of-war.

A general atmosphere of antagonism and stalemate in Tunis kept both French and Italian tempers on edge until 1935. In January of that year the Duce decided to settle the account. The Walwal incident on the Abyssinian frontier had happened a month before, and he needed an ally before pursuing his plans for conquest in Africa. Tunisia played the unflattering role of a pawn in his game of diplomatic chess with Monsieur Laval—a match in which he was to prove the better player. The Laval-Mussolini agreements of January 7, 1935 (which looked so favourable to France, but turned out to be so favourable to Italy, when they secured French connivance during the Ethiopian campaign), settled the Tunisian question in terms which seemed much to the French advantage.

Italian schools were to become subject to French legislation, and Italian subjects were automatically and compulsorily to become French; but these most un-Fascist concessions were subject to one important reservation—a respite till 1945 in the case of the schools, till 1965 in the case of the nationals. Italian behaviour in Tunis since the day when the agreement was signed points to the conclusion that, when the Duce appended his signature, he reasoned that much might happen before 1945, whereas the immediate matter in hand was Ethiopia. Italy continues to inspire her Tunisian community with enthusiasm for Fascism and their native land, and cannot be said to be preparing their minds for a forthcoming change of nationality.

Though France has to contend in Tunisia with two nationalisms—one Arab, one Italian—the double problem is not as formidable as it sounds. The two minuses make a plus. Both communities dislike French rule, but their ambitions clash, and they can never make common cause. The Italians cannot capture Tunisian support so long as they rule Libya on authoritarian lines, for the Tunisians have enjoyed more liberty under the French Left than under the French Right, and therefore hold democratic views. Moreover, they have not forgotten the harsh treatment of the Senussi during the subjection of Cyrenaica; they shake their heads at the thought of Italian protection. They enjoyed a joke when the Duce, making his great 'protector of Islam' speech in Libya in the spring of 1937, received the gift of a so-called sword of Islam and flourished a straight, cross-hilted Christian sword. 'He must have forged it for himself,' they said, 'for the sword of Islam is curved.' Further, they fear the Italians because of the talk of expansion with which the Duce stimulates enthusiasm from his balcony in Rome. They know their weakness; they share all Egypt's apprehensions, and since the day when Italy converted words into deeds and conquered

Ethiopia, they have talked less of independence and more of autonomy within the French Empire.

In Morocco, though the setting is different from that in Tunisia, the problems are many of them the same. For the time being, however, the handling of the younger territory seems to present the easier task for France, because its population is less developed, and therefore less at one. But this state of affairs is passing, and, ultimately, Morocco threatens to become the more capricious and difficult to manage. It is a richer country than Tunisia, a sounder economic unit and more capable of standing alone. Moreover, the Moroccan is a nobler animal than the Tunisian. Lastly, no foreign menace is as yet sufficiently obvious to cause him to cling to France for fear of falling into worse hands. Germany seems remote, and is far more of a bogy in French than in Moroccan eyes; Italy is looking eastwards; Great Britain is sated; Spain is weakened by war. So long as these conditions prevail in Europe, Morocco, once grown to years of discretion, will cease to feel the need of a protector.

But for the time being—the reservation must be repeated—the territory has not reached this stage. Indeed, France has perhaps less to fear from unrest in Morocco than elsewhere in North Africa, because of the disunity which still prevails there.

Being the extremity of the great wave of the Arab invasion, it contrived to remain more than half Berber, and, though the two stocks often mix, Moroccan Arabs and Moroccan Berbers are still a divided people. Their languages, customs, and characteristics are different; they live in different regions; Islam has up till now been their only bond. The Berbers are a mountain race, and speak their own tongue over a great crescent running from the Riff mountains in the north, round the whole sweep of the Atlas, and back towards the Atlantic in the south, near Agadir. The Arabs belong to the plains. The difference between the two is much the same as that between Scottish highlander and lowlander in the days of Montrose. Arabic is the language of the coast, of the Sultan, and of Islam, but it is spoken by a bare third of the inhabitants. It is gaining ground because it is the language of government, and because it is written, which Berber is not, but it is seldom well taught, and few Moroccans can speak it correctly or write it well.

Another dividing line is that between town and country. Perhaps a million people live in the towns, or near enough to them to feel their influence; the other five million, as in Algeria, think of nothing but the harvest and their daily bread.

There is yet another subdivision, for the towns in their turn are exclusive and hold apart. Before the occupation, the Sultan had four capitals—Marrakesh, Meknes, Rabat, and Fez. Meknes has since dropped out of the running, but its place has been taken by the modern port of Casablanca, and these four chief cities still lead separate lives. Fez is the strongest in spirit. It is reserved and secret, and inside its high walls a great mosque which is a Moslem university, and a powerful, well-organized *bourgeoisie*, breed wilful, confident young politicians. Fez is grey and Mediterranean, and looks as serene as Oxford. Marrakesh, three hundred miles to the south, is all the contrary—red and African, gaping and ingenuous, with little or no culture except among a few feudal families, and with a life which hums like a fair. Whoever named it the 'mother of villages' named it well. Casablanca and Rabat are different again: the former busy in a modern industrial way, and with a population which is a proletariat in embryo; the latter more sedate, as becomes a seat of government which contains a large class of relatively well-paid civil servants.

Good communications are a new development in Morocco and, though cheap to Europeans, are not yet widely used by the Moroccans, so that intercourse between these different groups is only beginning. Unity of political thought is still, therefore, a long way off.

Inevitably, these divisions extend to politics. The Moroccan independence movement was originally a single party, but was never as unanimous as is the *Destour*. The young men who led it, almost all of whom lived in Fez, were divided even on fundamentals. Half were French-trained, knew French better than Arabic and, thanks to visits to Paris, had hastily assimilated the traditions of the French parties of the Left. The other half had been educated in the Moslem university, spoke no French, and desired a national development along Islamic lines. The result was a confusion of thought over the ultimate end in view, and disagreement in the matter of newspapers, organization, and even policy. A split was inevitable in a party which was trying to combine democracy and Islam, but which had produced no brain capable of thinking out the conflict between the two, and evolving a clear-cut policy. The party's official programme, which was published in 1934 with the confident title of *Plan de Réformes Marocaines*, was glib and mature in appearance owing to French help with the drafting. But it was not a work of reflection, and when the rival factions finally broke into two parties in 1937, the new groups—one lay, the other religious—had little time to clear up the prevailing confusion of thought before they and their newspapers were banned as a result of the disturbances which broke out in the autumn of the year.

For lack of a party programme which appeals to all, Moroccan malcontents rally support by means of slogans couched in general terms. They have several themes at their disposal. One, of course, is Islam. Another is hatred of the Jews. Morocco is the home not only of eastern Jews who spread along North Africa at the time of the Dispersion, but also of a later influx of exiles from Spain, and both types are despised and disliked, partly out of age-old prejudice, but partly also out of pique and jealousy. Formerly the under-dog, the Jew is now more prosperous than many Moslems because, being more adaptable, he has been quicker to adopt French standards and business methods.

These two potential rallying cries are common to all the North African dependencies, including Libya. A third slogan adopted by the young Moroccans is interesting because it is unique, and because it throws light upon the national character. They have copied Herr Hitler in making a national appeal on the strength of the greatness of their race. They write articles on the splendour of their past; they extol the 'proverbial, not to say terrifying bravery' which is in their blood; they invest the Sultan with the magnificence and renown which befits the leader of such a people. They represent him as their *Führer*. When communications become easier and they are able to bring this conception to the ears of a wider audience, it promises to be a powerful weapon in their hands, for it is capable of uniting all factions.

The French have so far been able to hold these nationalist emotions in check. They have found the task relatively easy, because of their greater force of arms, because of the divided nature of the population, and—last but not least—because they have ruled well. Morocco represents the apex of their imperial achievement—run by a corps of officials who are proud of their work, contented, well paid, and versed in the traditions of service which are inspired by a great mind like that of a Lyautey or a Cromer. The *Corps du Contrôle Civil* in Morocco manifests the spirit to which reference has already been made in writing of the best British administrations; its peer is that in the Sudan. Fired by Marshal Lyautey's genius, it administers the country in the name not of France but of the *Maghzen*—the Sultan's government—and is at pains to leave Moroccan customs and religion inviolate. Even the tourist, landing for a day from his cruising liner, cannot fail to see the chief symbol of this conception—the building of the French towns outside the old Moroccan cities, which still lead their lives as if Europe had never intruded on their privacy.

Le Maréchal (Lyautey needs no surname in Morocco) left the territory in 1926, and seeds of discontent began to germinate once his magnetic personality was gone. A leader who had won such popularity with the Moroccans was a difficult man to replace. The Riff war, which was dragging on between Abd-el-Krim and the Spaniards in the mountains to the north, began to lower the prestige of Europeans. Moreover, Lyautey's successors made mistakes. Ignoring the lessons which they could have learnt by studying Tunisia, they took steps which were later to provide the young Moroccans with two grievances. They began to import civil servants from France, and to settle ex-service men on Moroccan land. Further, they were unsubtle in their native policy. In the interests of her own security, France had always stimulated the exclusive habits of the different towns and districts. She provided the Berbers with separate schools and did not encourage them to learn Arabic; she endowed Marrakesh with a college in order that its young men should not learn sedition in the more revolutionary atmosphere of Fez. Under Lyautey, the French had wisely practised this policy in silence, but in 1930 their love of precision got the better of them, and they must needs put it on paper. A decree of that year, the *Dahir Berbère*, laid down separate treatment for the Berbers; notably, it subjected them to French jurisdiction in penal matters. The Berbers themselves raised little objection, since the *Dahir* tallied with their customary law, but the measure loosed the tongue of opposition in Fez. It was labelled an attack on Moslem personal status, and an attempt to deflect the Berbers from Islam. It became the pretext for an Islamic revival which was also anti-French. Young Arabs wore Berber turbans in token of national unity; they acclaimed the Sultan as their only ruler, and boycotted French tobacco. The blaze died down in time, but the *Dahir* awoke sentiments which have been cherished ever since, which have been encouraged by left-wing enthusiasts both in France and Spain, and which are growing more coherent as the years go by.

This increasing resentment against western control—a symptom common to every Moslem territory except Algeria—is stimulated by social discontents, not all of which are due to French policy. Some are economic ills caused by the crisis in international trade, and should disappear as conditions improve or as the administration take steps to relieve want. But other grievances are less curable—among them the rise of the Jews in the social scale, and a second rather curious complaint. In the days before the protectorate, tenure of government office changed hands with the frequent changes at court. Men of all classes enjoyed a chance of rising in a night from the bottom to the top. 'He was a bookbinder, and very poor,' wrote the British Consul in 1857, 'but no sooner did he get the Sultan's letter than he assumed the reins of power well and with the dignity of a grandee.' Consuls write no such dramatic reports nowadays, for the French destroyed this exciting atmosphere. They crystallized the position of those who happened to be on the crest of the wave in 1912. Only death could remove these lucky few; the Grand Vizier of the period was still in office in 1937, aged eighty-five. Aspiring families, when they realized why climbing conditions had deteriorated, began to nurse a grievance against France. An older generation of Moroccans, who in former years admired France in the person of Lyautey, and deplored the new fangled notions of its sons in the new political parties, is beginning to feel that, all things considered, there is much to be said for independence.

These are Arab sentiments; the Berber chieftains of the Atlas entertain similar views, but for another reason. Far from sighing for posts at the Sultan's court, they resent France because her conquest subjected them to his government.

The voice of opposition, therefore, is as yet a confused noise, but when it becomes coherent, the Morocco of a not very distant future is likely to create difficulties for France, and promises to be more troublesome than Tunisia because the Moroccans are capable of putting up a stouter resistance. Not only are they more numerous—five millions as opposed to two; they are also more spirited owing to their mixed blood and their triumphant past. They belong to a race of men who have been conquerors and creators, who have left their mark all over Spain, and who have produced a great art. Though they have been through a period of eclipse, their former vitality is not dead. They are reserved and aloof by comparison with eager, plodding Algerians and quick, carping Tunisians, but they possess a latent vigour. 'Le Marocain c'est un lion; l'Algérien c'est un homme; le Tunisien c'est une femme.' The aptness of the comment is illustrated in the titles of the two rival national programmes: proud *Plan de Réformes Marocaines*, plaintive *Tunisie Martyre*.

Morocco, too, is beginning to murmur the magic word 'treaty', and when that murmur swells to a clamour France may find herself in a predicament. Self-confident Moroccans will not lightly take no for an answer, whereas France will have difficulty in saying yes for some years to come. For one thing, 'eldest first' is a principle which she is bound to apply in North Africa. She cannot promote Morocco before Tunisia; she cannot promote Tunisia before she settles the native vote question in Algeria. For another, Morocco is not ready for self-government; too many of its would-be politicians have scrambled through a cursory education; most of them boast no higher title than that of '(failed) B.A.' In 1937, only one Moroccan in all the protectorate had qualified in the technical examinations required for the exercise of the learned professions. The territory is at least twenty years behind Tunisia in intellectual development.

Up till now, France has been able to hush talk of independence, and to stave off the day by living on the reserve of goodwill established by Marshal Lyautey and his methods. But that reserve is dwindling, and when it is exhausted she will be faced with a perplexing problem, namely, how to rein in Moroccan impatience during the years which she will need in order to educate the territory up to the Tunisian level.

The picture drawn in this chapter may sound gloomy, but, in fact, up till now France's imperial venture in her three North African territories must be counted a success. Despite unrest in the Moslem world, and despite the numbers, the education, and the consequent strength of her Moslem subjects, none of the three is anxious for separatism. On the contrary, Algeria's present aim is to draw closer to her western ruler, while Tunisia and Morocco, although they have toyed with the theories of a separatist organization called the *Étoile Nord-Africaine*, offered no resistance when it was banned in 1936, and both aspire to self-government under French auspices.

Whether France can keep these sentiments alive probably depends more on her solution of the Algerian vote question than on any other single factor. If the Algerian Moslems were to remain loyal and contented, she could safely satisfy Tunisia, and later Morocco, with 'treaties', and retain the African shore of the western Mediterranean within her orbit. But if her policy in Algeria should prove a failure, another Arab invasion—this time, an invasion of ideas—will surge through the territories as relentlessly as did the last, and will render her task as complicated as that of Great Britain in India or Palestine.

5. *Summary: The French Position*

The most striking feature of a map of France's interests in the Mediterranean, therefore, is the unbalance between their importance in the eastern and the western basin. In the former she has many concerns, but is wholly dependent upon her alliance with Great Britain for their security. In the latter, she has staked her all, and needs to dominate not only economically but strategically.

Though her North African territories are unanimous in their desire for change, and are growing more restive as the years go by, their unrest does not yet disturb her equanimity. Her army is a safeguard against a general rising; a return to better economic conditions would lull much of the resentment against her, and, in any case, her strength for a little time to come lies in the lack of cohesion between the three territories.

Would this situation continue were she at war in Europe? That depends upon her handling of the territories, and upon developments in the Islamic world. But suppose a general war were to break out, her reputation among her Moslem subjects is such that she might well divide their loyalties if she were to offer them good pay in a powerful army. Many of them would fight for her for the same reason as the Spanish Moroccans fought for General Franco—namely, for money and in the hope of booty. In North Africa, as everywhere on earth, hard cash and display of might are two exceedingly persuasive arguments, and, so long as her north-south communications are not cut, she has little reason to fear a cataclysm until the Moslem world is more at one.

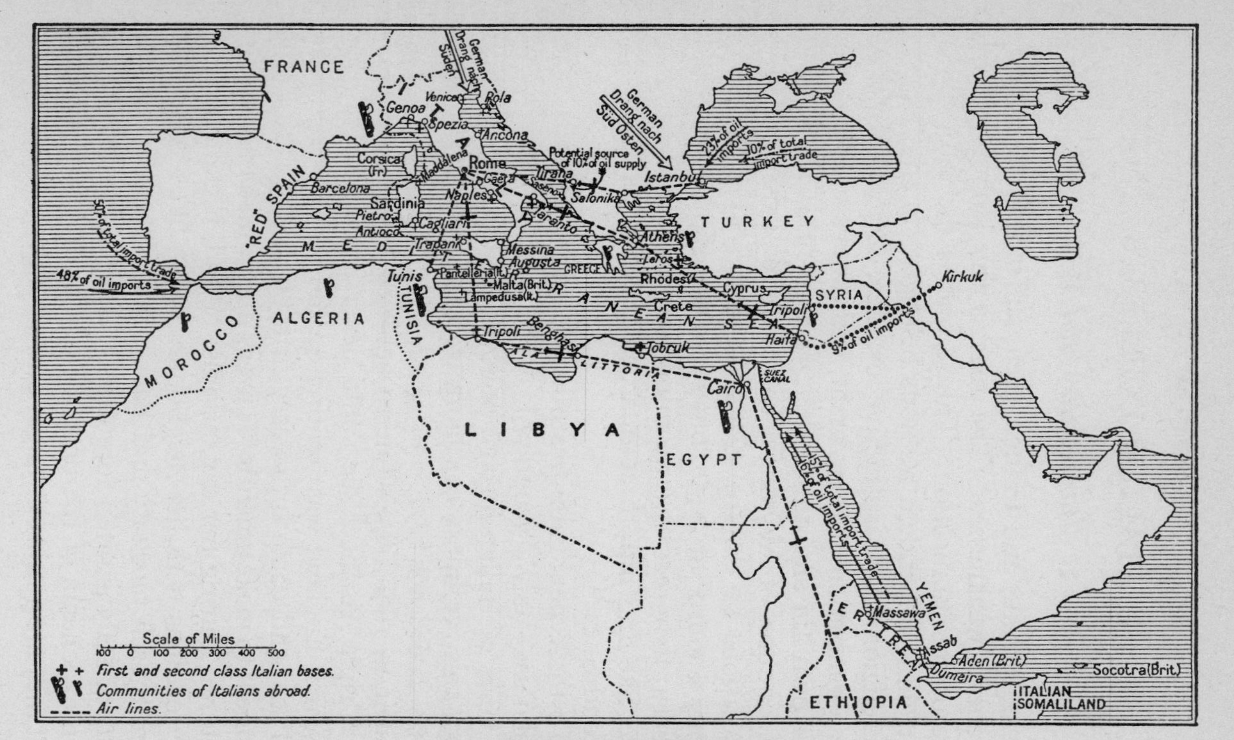

III. ITALIAN INTERESTS

CHAPTER IV

ITALIAN INTERESTS

1. *Vulnerability and War*

GREAT BRITAIN and France, then, suffer from two Mediterranean weaknesses. The first is the length of their lines of communication. The second is the difficulty of controlling dependent millions belonging to another race and religion whose instinctive loyalties, deep in the primitive organization of their brain, will always be devoted to their own kin and not to their foreign ruler. Italy, with the conquest of Abyssinia, has come to share both these tribulations of empire. Most Italians see in their new colony a source of pride, but some also see in it cause for anxiety; they read two meanings into the statement: 'We have, like England, three-quarters of our colonial interests beyond Suez.'[1]

To these new liabilities must be added another, older weakness—Italy's geographical position. Looking down the years of Italian foreign policy since the unification in 1870, this weakness has hampered her again and again. It has forced her to sit on the fence; to tell Germany and Austria in 1896 that, while recognizing her obligations to the Triple Alliance, she could never participate in a war in which England was fighting on the other side; to wait and see, and come into every firm of allies as the junior partner; to make amends for every fling with a conciliatory gesture. During her expansionist period, it explains why her relations with her neighbours swing like a pendulum from breach to treaty and back again. Yet the vulnerability of Italy is often forgotten. Dictators are the champion exponents of the doctrine of Coué. They proclaim that they are getting stronger and stronger. They say it so

[1] Article in *Gerarchia*, May 1937.

loud and clear that, besides raising the morale of their own people, they hypnotize others. For instance, Signor Mussolini sometimes hypnotizes Englishmen into arguing in terms of British weakness in the Mediterranean, and disregarding the weakness of Italy.

To compare their respective Mediterranean positions point by point: some strategists hold that Italy is at an advantage in that she is at home in the Mediterranean, with her national resources lying just behind her bases. Others reply that this factor is no longer the benefit it used to be, since it means that a civil population is easily exposed to the terror of air raids. For welcome lack of experience, there is no solution to this argument; it is a form of the long-drawn-out controversy as to the respective strengths of the power of defence and the power of attack. But other factors are more measurable. Italy suffers a liability in that she has 2,500 miles of national coast-line to defend, not to mention the two large islands of Sardinia and Sicily. Further, whereas only some 20 per cent. of Great Britain's trade is sea-borne through the Mediterranean, the Italian percentage is 86. In some matters the two powers are on a par. Both have fortress colonies to maintain; Rhodes and Leros have points in common with Cyprus and Malta, Pantelleria with Gibraltar. All can inflict damage, but all can be cut off. Each power enjoys more bases in one important area—Italy in the central, Great Britain in the eastern Mediterranean. Each has investments in Mediterranean countries; Great Britain's are greater in amount, but Italy's represent a larger proportion of her total investment abroad. Both powers have Mediterranean shipping interests; Great Britain's are bigger on the Suez route, Italy's in the Levant. Both run Mediterranean air lines. Moreover, Italy has to think of large communities of Italians abroad, consisting partly of colonists from the old republics and duchies, but mainly of emigrants who left home during the efflux of the nineteenth and early twentieth centuries. Italy is at an advantage in having a smaller and more manageable Moslem population under her rule; the Libyan Arabs are fewer than the Palestinians, are less developed, and are not yet in contact with the sympathetic and well-informed allies on their frontiers. But Great Britain enjoys a far greater advantage; she possesses an alternative route for supplies, whereas Italy does not. The positions are alike, but on balance Italy's is the more unlucky.

These weaknesses caused Italy little anxiety during the long years of Anglo-Italian friendship, but they became prominent as soon as she became class-conscious, and sought an empire. Fascist foreign policy has striven to overcome them. So far, it has done so with considerable success.

Signor Mussolini is often called an opportunist, but the label is not quite right. An opportunist is a man of no fixed principles or plan, who acts according to the needs of the moment. This is not true of Italian policy, which is calculated and planned. It contains only one element of opportunism—the seizure of the right moment and the right ally for executing the plan. This cannot be denied by any one who reads the speeches made by the Duce over the last ten years. Four extracts speak for themselves:

In 1925:

'Every nation with a vital capacity for progress is compelled by its own qualities to develop its own productive forces and its thought, to increase its pacific and economic penetration in the world, and to expand beyond its own confines its power and its intellectual and moral prestige.'

Later:

'The precise, fundamental and paramount duty of Fascist Italy is that of putting in a state of preparedness all her armed forces on land, sea, and in the air. We must be in a position at a given moment to mobilize five million men, and we must be in a position to arm them. Our Navy must be reinforced, and our air force—in which I have growing faith—must be so numerous and so powerful that the roar of its engines will drown any other noise in the peninsula, and the span of its wings hide the sun from our country. We shall be in a position then—to-morrow—when, between 1935 and 1940, we shall find ourselves at a point which I would call a crucial point in European history—we shall be in a position to make our voice felt, and at last to see our rights recognized.'

Surprisingly, the date is still only May 1927. By 1929 the tone is firmer, surer:

'To-day we can say, without exaggeration and with a quiet conviction, that Italy is heard and respected, and we can add that, with the continuance of the Fascist régime, the Italy of to-morrow will be still more respected and, if necessary, feared.'

In 1935, the Duce squares France, and successfully achieves his first expansionist *coup*. In 1936:

'I hold out a great olive branch to the world. This olive branch springs from an immense force of eight million bayonets, well sharpened and thrust from intrepid young hearts.'

Read in the light of the Abyssinian success, these extracts reveal a highly developed power to plan. They teach the lesson that the Duce's words should never be lightly set aside. The last is no lullaby, for Birnam Wood once came to Dunsinane.

To return to the Mediterranean. As soon as Italy starts to override her weakness, her ideal becomes *mare nostrum*. Owing to her geographical position, she cannot command except by preventing others from commanding. So she corrects her physical disability by means of her naval policy. Through all the bitter years of her naval rivalry with France, she claims parity, while France holds out for superiority because she has an Atlantic seaboard to defend. Italy gains her point, and then decides to excel in agility. She can afford to build racers, since she need not consider ocean-going endurance. She maintains a superiority in light, high-speed vessels. She builds a swift, efficient air-fleet. She reaches a point when she can challenge not only France, but Great Britain. She then strengthens her position by establishing herself at the southern end of the Red Sea.

But no measures that she can take, no amount of invention, or storage, or production of substitutes can wholly cure her greatest weakness: her dependence upon seaborne trade and her consequent vulnerability in face of blockade.

Reflective Italians know this spectre, and recognize it when they see it peeping out of speeches, slogans, and newspaper articles exhorting the nation to self-sufficiency. But the mass of the people is less perceptive; it hears the exhortation but not the warning when the Duce launches one of his eloquent appeals:

> 'Italy is an island. Bit by bit Italians must acquire an insular mentality, for this is the only way to place in their proper light questions of the nation's defence. If for others the Mediterranean is a route, for us it is life itself.'

The self-sufficiency campaign stimulated by this and other speeches has so fired the public imagination that the nation has forgotten its weakness. Most Italians, bereft of their sense of proportion by the half-truths told in the newspapers, brush aside any suggestion of vulnerability. They read of the manufacture of textiles from hemp, petroleum by hydrogenation, and paper from cellulose, and they are encouraged to extravagant conclusions by films showing the opening of a sumptuous new coal-mining city, but never mentioning how scanty are its reserves compared with Italy's needs, or by photographs of cotton in Ethiopia which bear no hint of the years which must pass, and the millions which must be spent, before the nation can reduce a tithe of its vast import from the

United States. They watch an exhibit machine which swallows milk at one end and disgorges wool at the other, and their imagination scampers far ahead of reality. 'Can I help?' says the foreign supplier in a cartoon of 1937. 'No, thanks!' replies Italia. 'No porters wanted; I've enough muscle for the job,' and she strides on under a load of her own wheat, petroleum, cotton, wool, coal, iron, copper, and so on. Italians, attracted by this vision, forbear to notice that imports are unreduced, that shops still display the old-fashioned wares, and that if a customer asks for best quality goods, English cloth or German tools are produced with a flourish out of a bottom drawer.

Much of this self-confidence can be ascribed to the failure of sanctions. Sanctions are a disastrous policy unless they are applied with a determination to uphold the law, and therefore in full. Applied as a half-measure, they not only goad and stimulate the culprit state; they also tend to awaken in its people a profound illusion. In the eyes of Italians, their nation emerged victorious from a trial of strength with fifty-two others, has proved its might, and is capable of doing so again. They forget that the curtailment applied only to certain categories of war material, and that, however sincere the fifty-two votes at Geneva, a newly devised machinery was in many cases defectively applied. They remember the victory; they finger samples of substitutes, and they are ready to snap their fingers at the risks of blockade.

In reality, Italy's position is still weak. She can derive one comfort from her sanctions experience, which is the knowledge that her people have a magnificent capacity for tightening their belts. Further, she has been able to reduce the proportion of one or two imports, notably cotton, by dint of her search for substitutes, but unless she makes discoveries as revolutionary as was that of rayon, a large-scale reduction of her raw material imports must be a matter of years. Though Fascism has worked wonders with her fuel problem by developing hydro-electric power and though it has wrung the maximum out of her resources by its highly competent organization of industry, it cannot invent a magic touchstone which will provide the other forms of fuel, nor can it create metals. In fact, were she faced with the stern test of a naval blockade, no amount of national courage could wholly cure her ills.

She would not be short of food. She supplies her own wheat if the harvest is good, and in a bad year she could make up her deficit with supplies received overland from Central Europe. She grows enough sugar for her needs, and she has plenty of fruit, vegetables, and dairy produce. She is less well off for meat, but even here she could make shift. At worst, she could survive by killing off immoderate numbers of cattle, and no such expedient would be necessary provided her continental neighbours were allies, or at least neutral. The foodstuffs she would lack are fish and coffee, both of which she imports in quantities from beyond Gibraltar, but neither of them is essential, and deprived of them, she would not starve.

Her weakness lies elsewhere—in industrial raw materials. Of the metals, she can provide her own lead, zinc, and bauxite—the ore which yields aluminium—and about half her manganese. She also furnishes about half her own iron, thanks to careful use of scrap, and she stores an adequate nickel reserve in her coinage. But she is totally deficient in tin and copper, and to these must be added five important non-metallic materials which she must buy abroad—all her petroleum, cotton, and rubber, and most of her wool and coal. These last are so important to her that between them they represent over 30 per cent. of her total import trade—a percentage which, despite success with substitutes, was still as high as ever in 1937.

A naval blockade, however, would not deprive her of all these essentials. She has one advantage over an island in that she has nine railway lines through or round the

Alps, and, within the limits of the traffic which they can carry, she can provision herself with coal, iron ore, and copper from continental sources. But most of her petroleum and cotton, and all her rubber and tin, must always arrive by sea, and lack of the first, which is nowadays the most prominent of all war needs, would paralyse her fighting power. Moreover, she can be victimized with ease, because, except for the rising amounts which she purchases from Albania and from the Iraq Petroleum Company's pipe-line, all her oil comes through the Dardanelles, the Straits of Gibraltar, and the Suez Canal. The respective proportions via each route vary enormously from year to year,[1] but at present, an enemy enjoying control at or near the bottle-necks could turn off nearly 90 per cent. of her supply as by a tap.

So her strategic planning must include the question of stocks. Before she can fight a war with a naval power she must lay in vast reserves of oil, and, since the sources of petroleum are few and its movements easily traceable, inquisitive neighbours have some guide to her intentions.

A cursory glance at her trade returns for 1937 gives the impression that she is preparing for just such a siege. The value of her imports is nearly double that of 1934—which, being the last year undisturbed by war or sanctions, is the only valid basis of comparison—and most of the materials which account for the increase are the metals and fuel she would lack were she to go to war. But a closer scrutiny of the figures to a great extent allays misgiving. Firstly, the value figures (which are usually those quoted) are misleading because they are shown in lire, and the lira underwent a 40 per cent. devaluation during the period under review; reckoned by volume, the figures for the two years in question present less of a contrast. Secondly, imports of wheat are largely responsible for the increase, as the Italian harvest of 1936 was a failure; and

[1] For the difference between 1934 and 1937, see table on p. 251.

thirdly, many of the abnormal purchases represent the re-establishment of industrial reserves which were depleted to far below normal during the Ethiopian war. Whether this last explanation accounts for Italy's increasing purchases of petroleum, whether normal consumption is increasing, or whether stocks are being laid in for other purposes, the 1938 figures may help to show.

The stocking of granaries and petroleum-tanks against a rainy day calls for heavy expenditure of foreign exchange, and here Italy's strategic problem takes on another form; it becomes a question of capacity to pay. She is not a rich country. For years she has lived from hand to mouth as far as her international payments are concerned, importing more than she exports and righting the balance by means of shipping receipts, tourist traffic, and remittances sent home by the ten million Italians who live and work outside Italy. At no time has she funds to spare for the establishment of extraordinary stocks. Moreover, in 1938 her position is worse than usual. Her credit is bad, for she has acquired, since the Ethiopian war, a reputation for being a dilatory payer. Her emigrants in the Americas have ceased to send home money, partly because of local restrictions, but as often as not because they hesitate to invest, as they used to do, in Italian mortgages or insurance policies, lest some government decree should deprive them of their savings by forbidding the export of moneys from Italy. Her shipping services are efficient and busy, and she is making the most of her two invisible exports—her sunshine and her antiquities—by offering endless facilities to tourists, but these two items alone cannot right her balance of payments, much less provide a surplus for the purchase of war stocks.

Yet she is still buying raw materials in quantities for which her exports do not pay. How does she do it? The jugglings of Fascist financiers baffle even the experts. 'Why not a Swiss admiralty,' says the Roman cynic, 'since we have a Ministry of Finance?' Among the mystic workings of the Italian experiment in an unbalanced budget, two facts only are clear. The first is that Italy is piling up a huge internal debt, the second, that to make foreign purchases, she is living on reserves, like the lizard which feeds itself by consuming its own tail. Foreign balances, wedding rings, and church plate have been devoured; business houses have suffered a capital levy; no one knows whence the next meal will come.

This situation, which would cost an Englishman his sleep, is luckily less disturbing to an Italian, who has not the same veneration for all that is fireproof and seaworthy. Blessedly unstarched by sun and the all-pervading sirocco, he usually enjoys the state of mind which so quickly infected the Anglican bishop in Norman Douglas's *South Wind*—readiness to relegate any event to the rank of the unimportant. He takes pleasure in the beauty of his new Italy, and forgets to wonder who put up the funds and whether it pays its way.

But to return to Italy's position in a naval war. Her weakness does not end at the problem of stocks and payment for stocks; even if she could store her needs and defend her coasts, she would still suffer from one great liability, which is that unless Great Britain and Egypt were her allies, or were neutral, she would run the risk of almost total severance from her new empire, for communication could only be maintained by aerial dashes across the Sudan. For this reason she is concerning herself with the question of Ethiopian self-sufficiency; but the process will take years—perhaps a generation—and meanwhile a war would throw her into the predicament which faced Germany and the German colonies in 1914.

In short, since she is a young empire and an impecunious country, peace in the Mediterranean seems to be her chief requirement, and a naval war an adventure she can ill afford.

2. *Strength Within the Sea*

'Italy has been great in the Mediterranean. I want her to become so again.' The speaker is the Duce, seated on horseback, addressing ranks of Italians and a crowd of Arabs at Tripoli. The date is twelve years ago—1926.

A step towards this end is the establishment of outposts —not among allies, who might waver and be drawn into some other orbit, but among dependents, of whose defection there is less risk. Italy has four such outposts in the Mediterranean—Albania, Pantelleria, the Dodecanese Islands, and Libya. During the Spanish struggle, she was suspected of hoping for a fifth in the Balearic Isles.

Her security in these outposts offers in Albania a contrast, in Pantelleria and the Dodecanese a likeness to situations already described in British and French possessions. Her position in Libya, like that of any westerner among Moslems, is more difficult to assess and catalogue.

If Italy's aim is to achieve Mediterranean greatness, her opening move is to make herself queen of the Adriatic. By so doing, she gains two advantages. She secures half her long coastline against attack from the sea. She also ensures the security of the port of Trieste, and so increases her standing among the central European countries who use it for their south and east-bound trade.

Mastery of the Adriatic was one of the bribes offered to her by the Allies to induce her to desert the Central Powers. The Secret Treaty of London of 1915 promised her most of the Austro-Hungarian coast, and protection over an 'autonomous neutral state' of Albania. But when the time came for peacemaking, the Serbs and Croats of Dalmatia had declared against their Austrian masters, and —except for one or two islands and the small town of Zara—Italy saw the coveted coast pass to Yugoslavia. Moreover, the Albanians, grasping at the new League of

Nations as a guarantee of independence, also shouldered the Italians into the sea. Italy, in her chagrin, forgot to count one blessing—the elimination of the Austro-Hungarian navy from the Adriatic. This, though seldom mentioned, is one of the chief advantages she derived out of the World War.

The rise of Yugoslavia meant that Italy, instead of occupying the queenly position she had been led to expect, was obliged to be mannerly to a new and quite important neighbour. She had to steer a difficult course between neighbourliness and expansion, and her relations with the Yugoslavs are the best example of her pendulum policy: breach—treaty, breach—treaty, breach—treaty. The details belong rather to European than to Mediterranean history; they lead into the maze of France's anti-German alliance policy. So far as the Mediterranean is concerned, the swing is so constant that the latest movement is the only one of current interest. At the moment it is an Italo-Yugoslav treaty of friendship signed in March 1937, repairing the breach caused by Yugoslavia's application of sanctions during the Italo-Abyssinian dispute.

During the longest breach, which lasted from 1926 until 1934, Italy won a round in the Adriatic by buying influence in Albania.

Albania, who was poor and down-at-heel, possessed one marketable asset—her strategic position. The Albanian mountains command the forty-five mile width of the Straits of Otranto which is the exit from the Adriatic Sea. They are high and dominating, as opposed to the low Italian coast across the water, whose level line on the horizon looks as flat as a Dutch dyke. Albania also possesses one good deep land-locked harbour—Valona—directly opposite the narrows, and another, better placed for combating Yugoslav influence, but too shallow for convenience, at Durazzo.

With these strategic assets in mind, both Italy and

Yugoslavia sought Albanian friendship. Italy won, because she jingled the heavier purse. The sound was too much for a small and backward country with an ambitious king, and Italo-Albanian treaties of friendship and military alliance were signed in 1926 and 1927. The flow of money had begun a year earlier, when Italy secured the concession for establishing an Albanian National Bank at the price of a 50 million gold franc loan. She seldom received any interest payments on her capital, but the money was not all lost to her, for she managed to direct large sums into the pockets of the Italian firms employed to execute the public works on which the loan was spent.

The belief is common in Europe that this money was expended solely for Italy's benefit and that it turned Albania into a virtual Italian colony, but no one who visits the country could continue to hold this view. The funds went to deepen Durazzo harbour for naval purposes, to build roads which have a strategic significance, and to set up public buildings which would provide convenient barracks in the event of war, but up till now all these innovations have served Albania rather than Italy. The roads and harbour have increased national trade and communications, while the business-like ministries at Tirana add to the Government's efficiency and enhance its prestige. Albania has had something for nothing, for King Zog and his ministers have contrived to pay Italy little or no interest, yet at the same time to evade political bondage. They vote faithfully with Italy on points which do not directly affect them (for instance, over sanctions, the Nyon Agreement, or the League of Nations resolution regarding the war in Spain), but where home affairs are concerned they keep their distance. Whenever they enter into agreements with the Italians, the clauses which seem to see swiftest execution are those which bring most benefit to Albania.

Nevertheless, Italy seems to find the investment

repaying, for she has several times made refresher loans. In 1931, when Albanian pockets were empty and enthusiasms flagging, she made an agreement on unusual terms; she was to pay yearly instalments of 10 million gold francs, and Albania was to repay either 'on its own initiative' or when Albanian revenues reached 50 million gold francs per year (the present average revenue is under 30 million francs). But only two of the promised instalments were ever paid, and neither of them in full, for an Italo-Albanian quarrel in 1933 cut short Italian generosity. This was not resumed until 1935, when—perhaps as a thankoffering for the Albanian vote regarding sanctions—a small payment of 3 million gold francs caused King Zog to send a special aide-de-camp to Rome with a letter of thanks, and to publish an address of loyalty to Italy in the leading Albanian newspaper. These acts were the prelude to a new series of agreements made in March 1936, which cancelled the 1931 arrangement, and substituted for it loans amounting in all to 25 million gold francs, lent at little or no interest, to be paid to Albania between 1936 and 1942. Italy is therefore faithful to her methods, though she must realize by now that she is lending to a race of spenders, not savers—to men who have lived for so long among the hazards of Turkish taxing raids, Balkan wars, and family blood feuds that their instinct is, sensibly enough, to spend while they may. At the time of the new agreement in 1936, Albania already owed Italy 280 million gold francs—a figure which even her own finance minister described as 'astronomical'.

Did Italy expect a more profitable return for her money than she has yet seen? This is an open question. At one time she thought of planting colonists in Albania; indeed, once or twice the Albanians talked of offering land to settlers in place of paying interest in cash. But large-scale Italian colonization is out of the question, because Albanian pride jibs at alienating national soil.

Italy also hoped that the Albanian mountains would yield minerals, and here, perhaps, is the secret of her munificence. As far as metals are concerned, Albania is disappointing. Her rocks are a geologist's delight, for numberless specimens exist, but a prospector's despair, for the quantities are almost always too small to be worth working. Her copper and chrome ore, which are the most valuable finds so far, are neither of them very promising speculations; nor are the best deposits in Italian hands. But among the Italian concessions, one promises good results, and that one yields petroleum. Reference has already been made to Italy's dependence upon oil from beyond the Mediterranean bottle-necks. The Albanian oil is of very poor quality; indeed, a concession to work it was for this reason abandoned by the Anglo-Iranian Oil Company. But to Italy its strategic convenience is such that, however poor, it is worth working; she had sunk some 180 million lire in Albanian wells by 1936. She seems to be doing creditably, for the investment is scheduled to pay its way when the oil output reaches 350,000 tons per year, and the company hopes to be able to ship 300,000 tons yearly to Italy by 1940. The estimated figure for Italy's present oil consumption—3 million tons a year—gives an idea of the value of the Albanian supply.

Apart from this oil resource, Italy's chief return for her stake is strategic. She has a well-placed ally on the Balkan side of the Straits of Otranto, on the construction of whose roads and fortifications and bridges she can rely, because she built them herself. Can she also rely on the man-power?

The Albanians are a race of character, and Italy, when she tries to give orders, has once or twice found them stubborn and intractable. For instance, in 1933 she demanded increased rights for Italian schools, and an increased number of Italian officers in the Albanian army. She chose her moment badly, for the world crisis had just caused her to abate her money payments. Albania refused the demand, stating that it was not compatible with national independence. Again, in 1934 an Italian squadron sailed into Durazzo harbour without warning, behaving as if it were in home waters. Sighting twenty-two ships, an astonished harbour-master clapped his glass to his eye and decided that he must have mistaken the date of a foreign visit which was due some weeks later. But the ships which drew in were clearly Italian, and they settled at anchor pending payment of some of the overdue interest. Once more the Albanians rebelled. Their pride was roused, and the Italians found themselves explaining that the telegram announcing their arrival had gone astray.

Each time a brush occurs, Albania flirts with Yugoslavia and talks of joining the Balkan Pact, but each time, Italy clinks the money bags; so far, she has never clinked in vain. The important point, however, is neither the amount nor the method of payment, but the nature of the concessions which go with it, and, since the quarrel of 1933, these have been less mortifying than in earlier years. For instance, under the 1936 agreements, Italy no longer enjoys a military mission in Albania, and, though she still maintains advisers in most government offices, Albanian ministers now have a right to disregard their advice. The agreements read as if the Italians have learnt that they have more to gain by beguiling than by bullying the Albanian people.

If this change of tone is permanent, Italy stands to strengthen her position in Albania and win a spontaneous ally. If not, her security there depends upon ceaseless largesse. She has a strong hold upon King Zog, both because she finances him, and because her support protects him against his rivals, who know that revolt would bring Italian intervention 'to preserve the *status quo*', and that the last state would be worse than the first. But, until she shows consistency in her new tactics, and chooses advisers and officials who will pursue them, her hold on the Albanian population as a whole is doubtful. Albanians —especially the mountain peoples of the north—never forget their benefactors, but they draw a distinction between selfless benefactors and benefactors who serve them with an ulterior motive. In the former class they place people like Mr. Aubrey Herbert, who helped them to independence, or the Rockefeller Foundation, which is draining their malarial marshes. So far, they have placed the Italians in the latter; they enjoy the moments when they assert their independence, and see no shame in meeting insincerity with insincerity.

Italy's Albanian investment is therefore speculative. Her policy there cannot be counted a success or failure until the day when the alliance is put to the test; for, bribe as a nation may, it cannot be sure, nowadays, of any one who is not of its own flesh and blood.

Italy has a more dependable stronghold in an island which she inherited as part of the kingdom of Naples and the two Sicilies. A year or two ago, Pantelleria's fancy name was unknown except to connoisseurs of muscatel grapes. But in 1935, the Italians, fearing a naval war, conned the map, discovered their rock, and decided to make use of its strategic advantages—its commanding height of 2,500 feet, its position in the narrow channel between Tunisia and Sicily, and its lake offering possibilities for an air base. It has no natural harbours; its anchorages are bad and exposed; but Italians have overcome worse technical difficulties. They began to fortify it, and forbade foreign aeroplanes to fly over the area.

As a fortress, the island shares one merit with Gibraltar. There is no local dissidence to consider. Its owner need waste no time and energy on courting the loyalty of the inhabitants. He has it already. He is king of the castle, with nothing to think of but strategy. His busy progress is evident in the string of bright lights, high and low on the mountain, which come out as the boat to Tunis passes at dusk.

Albania is a foreign state; Pantelleria is national soil. The twelve islands of the Dodecanese, on the other hand, are colonies, and here we meet Italy face to face with the standard colonial problem—the handling of a population whom she has endowed with Italian nationality, but who are of foreign flesh and blood.

Her position in the Dodecanese is much like that of the British in Cyprus. The population she rules is considerably smaller, but it is composed of the same elements—a majority of Greeks and a percentage of Turks. In Rhodes, there are in addition a few thousand Spanish Jews. As in Cyprus, local sentiment is incurably Greek. As in Cyprus, outward visible signs of this sentiment are not allowed. Since the Italians are more strict than the British, the longing for Greece is more secret; but its existence is nevertheless discernible. I saw it light up the face and conversation of a villager when he was asked the way by a foreign visitor who spoke modern Greek.

Those who doubt such slender evidence will find the past full of better indications. The feelings which were expressed by the islanders upon liberation from Turkey in 1912, and again at the Peace Conference in 1919, do not vanish in a few years.

Under Turkey, the Dodecanese enjoyed the pleasant name of the Privileged Isles. But, in spite of privileges, they felt Greek, and joined in the War of Greek Independence. They hated the Turks, and welcomed the Italians in 1911 as 'Christian liberators'; but they wanted to be liberated into the arms of Greece, not Italy. The Balkan Wars were in progress, and a Greek as well as an Italian fleet was roving round freeing islands from the

Turkish yoke. Inspired by these activities, a conference of the island leaders held at Patmos in 1912 asked for the establishment of an 'Aegean State' and proclaimed the 'permanent wish of the Aegean Islanders to be united with their mother-country, Greece'.

Disappointment was to follow. Until the World War, the islands were occupied by the Italians, but remained, like Cyprus, under Turkish sovereignty. Italy failed to acquire them outright because Great Britain and France, fearing the establishment of an unfriendly base so near the Suez Canal, encouraged Greek aspirations and put spokes in the Italian wheel.

In the War years the islands, now far from privileged, were bandied about during the struggle for Italian support. The British and French ate their pre-War words, for Greek feelings were a trifle in comparison with war needs. They offered the Dodecanese to Italy in full sovereignty in the Secret Treaty of London. Modern history affords few better examples of generosity with other people's property.

But the islanders hoped on. At the Peace Conference, they again raised their voice, repeating their 'unalterable and centuries-old aspiration to unite with Greece'. This time, their cry was heard. Greece was represented by M. Venizelos—'shrewd, tireless . . . speaking in fluent French and with an engaging appearance of frankness'[1]—and was in the ascendant; thus, though Greek and Italian ideas about the future of the islands were very different, a compromise was reached in the Venizelos-Tittoni agreement of 1919. Sovereignty was to pass to Greece except in Rhodes, where a plebiscite was to take place 'if and when Great Britain ceded Cyprus'. The last words look as if Greece was in the ascendant indeed. The islanders began to envisage a bright future.

Their hopes were dashed by that 'staggering surprise

[1] House and Seymour, *What Really Happened at Paris*, p. 191.

for all'[1]—the fall of M. Venizelos in the Greek elections of 1920, rejected by his countrymen because they could not accept his repressive internal policy. The Allies, deeply committed to M. Venizelos, felt no obligation towards his successor, King Constantine, to whom the old label 'pro-German' still clung. France and Italy tested the wind and sensed Mustapha Kemal—at the time a dissident leader in Turkey—as the coming man. Italy, by fraternizing with him, secured a promise of the Dodecanese. She received them when he came into power and signed the Peace Treaty of Lausanne. As things turned out, the Greek electors of 1920 had handed her their islands on a platter.

Throughout these transactions, the islanders were the losers. To-day they are, like the Cypriots, sentimental and not wholly resigned to their fate.

Every colonial power cherishes the dream that its own colonial inhabitants are more contented than those of other people. The English believe it of the Cypriots as opposed to the Dodecanese islanders; the Italians hold the opposite view. A judgement on this point seems to depend upon whether personal liberties are ranked above or below economic benefits.

The Cypriots enjoy more liberty. They receive their basic education in their own language. In church, their priests preach more freely than can a priest in Rhodes. They do not cast a cautious look over their shoulder before they utter a confidence. Moreover, they are not obliged to go through certain tiresome motions of subservience which are enforced in the Dodecanese. For instance, the people of Rhodes must salute the Italian flag when it is hoisted and lowered at the morning and evening gun. 'Not interesting', said my Turkish chauffeur.

Freedom is precious, but every one does not rate it above prosperity, particularly in the Levant. The Italians

[1] Mr. Winston Churchill in *The World Crisis: The Aftermath*, p. 387.

make a rival appeal in the greater flow of money which their enterprise has brought into the major islands of the Dodecanese, especially Leros and Rhodes. Italian garrisons are there, with pay to spend. Excellent shipping and air services bring tourists. A first-class hotel tempts them to stay. Their money goes largely into Italian pockets, but a proportion filters through to local guides and taxi-drivers and shop-keepers, and to the purveyors and producers of food and drink. Further, local labour—masons, bricklayers, builders, gardeners—is being employed on the transformation of Rhodes into an almost over-tidy city.

This chapter is not concerned with the cost of Italy's policy to the Italian state, but with the effect of that policy upon the Dodecanese islanders. When the boat in which you are travelling (which is always Italian) calls at a Cyprus port, only the spartan English disembark, for only they will brave the beef-and-horseradish fare of the Cypriot hotels, and only a keen sightseer thinks the crumbling churches of Famagusta worth a walk ankle-deep in thistles and sand. The big spenders—the rich Levantines from Egypt and Syria—are all going on to Rhodes. They explain that they cannot afford Nice this year, and their wealthy backs disappear into the pink-and-white portals of the Hôtel des Roses. The reader may find the second picture less attractive, but some of the islanders like it better.

Comparing Rhodes and Cyprus, then, Great Britain wins on psychology, Italy on material attractions. In other ways, their respective territories share many of the same experiences. Both would prefer to belong to Greece, though neither may say so. Both are taxed by a foreigner, though here the Dodecanese islanders seem to be the more content, for they cherish no old grudge like that about the Cyprus Tribute; Rhodes and Cos pay taxes considerably less heavy than those levied in Italy, and the other islands are still 'privileged', and contribute no more than is necessary for their own administration. Both colonies possess a cultured class which sees all good administrative appointments given to the ruling nation. Here, on the other hand, the Cypriots are better off in that Great Britain has imported far fewer officials, merchants, and workers from home. Strategically, there is little to choose between the possessions. One is to the Dardanelles as the other is to the Suez Canal. Italy owns the better natural harbour—at Porto Lakki in Leros—but her bases are closer to a foreign coast; the steep hills of Turkey frown on Rhodes, whereas from Cyprus the shore of Asia Minor is only visible on a clear day. Equally equipped, the two fortresses would represent a stalemate. The chief contrast between them lies in the initial *coup d'œil*, and in a matter which is internationally important—the very different reputation which their respective rulers enjoy in neighbouring countries.

In Turkey, the fact that Cyprus was once Turkish is almost forgotten, whereas the fact that the Dodecanese belong geographically to Anatolia is a grievance which is anything but minimized by the strength and proximity of Italy's fortifications. In Greece, though Great Britain's handiwork in Cyprus is deplored, that of Italy in the Dodecanese is reviled. Hatred of Italian rule is kept alive, not only in Athens but in the great Greek colony of Alexandria, by the bitter tongues of some tens of thousands of Dodecanesian Greeks who live in exile, and whose vituperation points two reassuring morals—the first, that money cannot buy everything, the second, that freedom of thought is still a valued prize.

Libya is the most important of the Italian outposts, for Italy, as she strives for *mare nostrum* and for the creation of an empire beyond Suez, must seek good relations with the Moslem world, and her actions in her Moslem colony can make or mar her progress. She claims that she is more secure in Libya than is any other power in a Moslem dependency. She is probably right, for no one else governs a population so small, so cowed, and so efficiently cut off by nature (as well as by its ruler) from foreign news and supplies.

Italian Libya has always been invested with a certain mystery. Few visitors go there. For years it was on the way to nowhere, for the caravan route from the Sudan to Europe, on which it lies, was no longer a beaten track. The only boats and aeroplanes which served it came from Italy and went back again. Young men in agencies pursed their lips and searched in obscure drawers if you asked them for a boat via the Libyan ports from Tunis to Alexandria.

Since the Ethiopian campaign, however, it has been thrust on to the map. A through air line—the *Linea del Impero*—now calls there on its way from Italy to Egypt and Italian East Africa, and a thoroughfare, tarred and well built, runs from the Tunisian to the Egyptian border. The road is advertised as a tourist route, but Tunisia and Egypt do not keep it up to standard at either end. Neither the French nor the Egyptians have so far attached enough importance to 'tourism' in the area to spend so lavishly upon it, and the Tunisian main road degenerates into a track before it reaches the frontier, while the route on the Egyptian side is hardly even that. The tourist who leaves the tarmac on the border of Libya does not meet a road again until he gets half-way to Alexandria.

So Libya remains unvisited—a piece of the map known to be poor, without minerals, without much water, without many inhabitants—a slice of territory which imagination depicts as limitless, useless, and yellow.

Actually, it is in parts a country of character, or rather, two countries of two characters, for Tripolitana and Cyrenaica are separate, cleft in two by the 650 kilometres of dreary waste round the great bay of Sidra—an abomination of desolation which must be one of the most marked natural and human frontiers in the world.

Tripolitana, in the west, looks like Sfax in southern Tunisia. Its light sandy soil blows about in the same little clouds; it needs as little water. To any one who knows the prosperity of Sfax, its future obviously lies in dry farming, and in the cultivation of hardy, thirstless olives. Actually, Tripolitana is richer than is Sfax in underground water supplies—'dead water', say the Arabs, as opposed to 'living water', which flows—but it is not so rich as to render pumping economic in the quantities required for growing irrigated crops on a large scale.

Cyrenaica is very different. Its small area of good land looks like Greece. It breaks into red and black soil and—in one place—into forested valleys. It is not so hot as Tripoli, nor so prone to exasperating, exhausting siroccos. Apart from the fact that its clay demands far more water than is at present available, it is a richer proposition than its neighbour. It offers a future for cattle-raising, and for some products which Italy does not yield.

Nevertheless, Tripolitana has one immense advantage. Its best land is near its port and chief marketing town. In Cyrenaica, the tolerable land only begins some 150 kilometres from Benghazi, and the good area is as much as 250 kilometres away over uninhabited, marketless country. Seen from the air, the town of Tripoli is satisfactorily girt with labour and produce; Benghazi, on the edge of a desert, looks neat but overdressed.

Man, as well as nature, kept the territories separate. Tripoli was Phoenician, and, like all Phoenician colonies, was used not for settlement but for exchange and mart. The ruins of Leptis Magna speak for the traffic on the old route to the south, which fell into disuse with the opening up of Africa, its merchandise diverting to the Nile railway, Port Sudan, and the Nigerian line from Kano to Lagos.

Cyrenaica, on the other hand, was Greek, and planted with Greeks. Cyrene was a flourishing centre of Greek learning to whose taste and culture the Cyrenaic Venus, now in the baths of Diocletian in Rome, is an abiding memorial. When Roman unity collapsed, the two territories remained separate, living back to back; Tripoli belonged to the Western, Cyrenaica to the Eastern Empire. The Arab invasions swept over the rift between them, but joined them only to destroy. What the first invasion left standing, the even more destructive wave in the eleventh century laid waste. Sand obliterated the remains, and no one, till the Italians came, attempted to re-enliven so derelict a scene.

Italy conquered Libya in 1911–12 purely for political and strategic reasons. 'We knew it was no Eden . . . we went in there simply in order to be able to breathe freely in the Mediterranean—to avoid being stifled amidst the possessions and naval bases of France and Great Britain.'[1] The success of her strategy was demonstrated in 1935, when the presence of Italian troops in Libya caused the British and Egyptians to mass men and aeroplanes in the western desert of Egypt.

Conquest of Libya therefore achieved its object, but it was an an expensive venture, if only because it had to be performed twice. The first conquest, before the World War, was blood spilt in vain, for when Italy joined the Allies, the Turks and Germans armed the Bedouin, who drove the Italians to the sea. Reconquest began in 1922. Tripolitana, though three times as populous as Cyrenaica, surrendered far more easily. It was pacified by 1925, whereas the 180,000 Bedouin in Cyrenaica held out until 1932. They were at an advantage in their wooded valleys and remote oases, and they were buoyed up by the fervour of the Senussi—the desert fraternity which exercises influence through its preaching of a purified form of Islam.

[1] Ambrosini, *I Problemi del Mediterraneo*, Rome, 1937, p. 23.

Devout, independent, desperate—these people took even less kindly to the Italians than they had to their old masters, the Turks. The Senussi gave no quarter. The Italians brutally retaliated. They sealed the wells. They shut surrendered tribes into concentration camps, and let their animals die for lack of pasture.[1] They shot or hanged any surrendered Arab who fed or spoke with a 'rebel'. They perpetrated cruel deaths, of which I have met witnesses, but which are best not described. They seem to have grown nervy and berserk. They gained for themselves a reputation for colonial bullying which they will take years to live down.

No sooner was the conquest account settled than new bills began to come in for policing the vast desert areas of the colony. But the strategic gain was accounted worth the outlay, and Rome contributed, and still contributes, two-thirds of the revenue of Tripolitana and three-quarters of that of Cyrenaica. Nothing that the territory promises to produce is likely to counterbalance the money swallowed by the desert.

Italy laboured manfully, however, to derive benefits other than strategic from her new land. The story of the conquest explains why, despite Cyrenaica's greater promise, she has so far achieved more success in Tripolitana.

Like the French in Algeria and Tunisia, she wavered for some years between orthodox economic development and a policy of planting colonists. In Tripolitana, at any rate, the two do not go together. Olives demand little labour, but produce no crop for fifteen years. Olive cultivation, therefore, needs a few men equipped with enough of their own or other people's capital to be able to carry

[1] Some figures given in M. Jean Despois' detached and excellent book, *La Colonisation Italienne en Libye*, indicate the waste of animal life, which the Italians are now trying to repair:

	Sheep	*Goats*	*Oxen*	*Camels*	*Horses*
1926	800,000	70,000	10,000	75,000	14,000
1933	98,000	25,000	8,000	2,600	1,000

on until the time for harvest. This problem suits France but embarrasses Italy. France has no men to spare but has money to spend. Italy has the men, but they are penniless. Italian periodicals of the nineteen-twenties are full of articles deploring the hesitancy of the private investor.

In 1928 the state made up its mind. It would plant surplus Italians in Libya regardless of expense. It would itself provide the capital. Colonization has therefore gone ahead, sometimes successfully, sometimes not, but at an exorbitant price where smallholders are concerned. Not even the Jews in Palestine have aided colonists on such a scale. The French expert on colonization who has made the only unbiased study of the subject calculates that, without that aid, at least nine-tenths of the colonists would have been bankrupt by 1934.[1] But despite the outlay, the number of settlers on the land is still low. An article in an Italian magazine for May 1937 gives the total number of Italian holdings in Tripolitana in 1936 as 841, providing a livelihood for 7,746 individuals, and records that these settlements make labour for a further 2,862 persons employed in experimental stations, hydraulic works, and so forth. The same article gives the number of Italians who live by agriculture in Cyrenaica as 2,672. The total—some 13,000 only—is a drop in the ocean by comparison with Italy's mounting population, which is at present increasing at the rate of a quarter of a million per year.[2]

Once the Ethiopian venture began, little progress was made with Libyan colonization. The struggle for a bigger and better colony elsewhere deflected thought, money, and energy into another channel, and Libyan effort was wholly concentrated upon finishing the great strategic

[1] M. Jean Despois, *op. cit.*

[2] These figures from *La Conquista della Terra* for May 1937 are given because they are slightly more generous and much more complete than those given in the official Year Book of the Italian colonies.

road from east to west. Many Libyan farmers felt that they were being neglected, and, indeed, a study of Italian colonial magazines for the period confirms their view. From 1935 onwards Libya is scarcely mentioned; now and then it is even used for purposes of unfavourable comparison, while the superlatives are all reserved for Ethiopia. But Libya is not to be left on one side. The Duce, paying it the honour of a visit in the spring of 1937, assured its inhabitants that the state had no intention of deserting an old love for a new—that Italy was ready to maintain both. Since the Italian capitalist does not willingly speculate in colonies, the task must fall to the state. The question is: do the coffers contain enough for two such absorbent colonies?

And now to add up the Libyan balance sheet.

Strategically, the colony represents an asset. In a good harvest year, it seems to be able to feed an army in the staple foodstuffs. Troops stationed there can threaten Egypt or Tunisia, while ships and aeroplanes based on Tobruk command the 200-mile channel between Cyrenaica and Crete. Italy strengthens her garrison there whenever she wants to exercise pressure on some rival. She did so in 1935, over sanctions; she did so again in the autumn of 1937. At the same time, her colony is secure, for its desert wastes are scarcely worth attack.

Financially, Libya represents a loss. Short of a miracle —for instance, the discovery of minerals—production can never hope to pay for policing and colonization.

From the point of view of settlement, it represents a technical success; each administrator can show you road-building, well-boring, or planting that constitutes a triumph of mind over matter. The economic triumph is less assured. Cyrenaica may in time produce foodstuffs which Italy lacks, but Tripoli, like Algeria, is incurably Mediterranean and seems bound to concentrate on products in which Italy abounds, and which are inferior in quality to the home produce. 'I could do ten times more with the money in Sicily,' says the Libyan farmer, but to the state, this consideration is beside the point.

Last and most delicate question: How does her Libyan policy affect Italy's position round the shores of *mare nostrum*? A western power which takes upon itself a Moslem colony enters into a new relation with the rest of the Moslem world—with that belt of Moslem peoples who divide Italy from Italian East Africa just as they divide Great Britain from India.

Italy is aware that she must walk delicately. Since completing the Libyan conquest, she has set about effacing her reputation for brutality. In 1937, she was buying sheep in Tunisia in order to replenish Arab herds; she was tempting fugitives back from the western desert of Egypt with money offers; she was currying favour by the public flogging of two Jews in Tripoli, and the Duce, during his visit, was declaring himself the protector of Islam.

On the other hand, her colonization policy will here and there hamper her courtship, for the planting of colonists will automatically absorb the emergency grazing-grounds of Bedouin herdsmen. This is already a problem in Tunisia; it threatens in Cyrenaica, where droughts devastate the land, and where the fertile Jebel Akhdar—already earmarked for colonization—is the standby of Arab flocks in two years out of every three. Even Italian experts are pointing out in guarded language that if the state continues to plant colonists it will stifle Cyrenaica's greatest economic possibility, namely, sheep-raising.[1] Further, some critics feel that competition from imported Italian labour is bound to breed discontent among Arab peasants. On this point, the shepherded visitor can form no judgement; his Italian chauffeur (provided free with the car he

[1] See articles in *Rassegna Economica dell' Africa Italiana* for July and August 1937.

hires) vaunts the advantages of planting a peasantry which mixes with the native peoples, and indeed, the Arab families living round some of the Italian settlements look less pinched than their counterparts in some other Arab countries. What they have lost in freedom, they have gained in daily bread. If they grumble as they eat it (as, being Arabs, they are bound to do), they grumble without purpose, because there is no one left to direct their energies. A noticeable difference between the cities of Libya and those of the rest of north Africa is the absence of the *effendi* type. You do not see in Tripoli the sight so familiar in Tunis or Fez—an Arab notable, in his lovely clothes, taking a stately walk through the bazaars and gravely acknowledging the reverences of the passers by. He has disappeared from Libya—ruined, dead, or in exile—and only a humbler class is left—a class which has always served, and which is at the moment serving a new master who is in many ways no worse than the old.

In Libya, therefore, the Italian position seems strong. The Arabs do not love Italy, but money and firm rule have done their work, and Arab soldiers, pocketing her pay, fought well for her in Ethiopia. A more moot point is the reputation which her Libyan policy has won for her outside Libya. Arabs admire might, display, determination, and success, and the Ethiopian victory has certainly won their respect, though it has also wakened their fear. At the same time, they admire consistency. And they think the Italians inconsistent. No one has forgotten the horrors of the conquest of Cyrenaica; I heard it mentioned by *Ulema* in Algeria, by the *Destour* in Tunisia, by a taxi-driver in Syria, and with quivering hatred by one or two Egyptians. All are on their guard against a sucking-dove policy which accords so little with past history, and with certain stories from Ethiopia which have found their way into the Egyptian press. 'Protector of Islam, indeed,' said one Cairo editor, 'we have heard that before. Napoleon said it here, and so did the Kaiser at Damascus. It's a bad precedent.'

He lives in a fool's paradise who thinks that these feelings are not secretly shared in Libya, for sentiment travels through Islam like the mysterious jungle message which reaches its destination while the white man is still writing out his telegram.

Libya—the Dodecanese—Pantelleria—Albania; the four scenes just described are intended to convey two impressions. The first is that Italy is for the moment secure in her strongholds. The second is that she is thus secure because she is dealing with problems of small magnitude—problems which pale to insignificance beside those of the French in Algeria, or of the British in Palestine. She is dealing with populations too meagre to lift up their voice, and she is doing so competently, though at times brutally.

Her success in Rhodes and Libya is no proof that she would be equally competent with a more resolute or a more unwieldy foreign population. Albania, where she most nearly meets her match, is the least successful of her Mediterranean experiments, and if she wishes to extend her dominance round the Mediterranean basin, she will have to deal with other Albanias, not other Libyas. For there is scarcely a soul left on the Mediterranean shore who would forego home rule, however bad, for the bread and circuses which are all that she can offer in exchange.

3. *Diplomacy and the Outlets*

'*L'appétit vient en mangeant.*' However greatly Italy increases her strength within the Mediterranean basin, she cannot recapture the self-sufficiency of ancient Rome, because science and speed have between them made men dependent on a world beyond. To achieve real mastery, she would need to control not only *mare nostrum*, but the bottle-necks at either end and at the Dardanelles. Such control is difficult, for each of the narrows runs between the shores of a foreign power—Spain, Egypt, Turkey. She hopes that she has not entered the arena too late to acquire, somewhere, the degree of control which Great Britain enjoys at Suez. Meanwhile, she has to depend on diplomacy to secure safe passage.

She receives 75 per cent. of her supplies from beyond the Mediterranean—through the Straits of Gibraltar, the Suez Canal, and the Dardanelles, in proportions, roughly, of 70 to 17 to 13. These percentages were calculated before Ethiopia had begun to yield produce; the Suez proportion is therefore expected to increase. Nevertheless, the greatest volume of goods must for years, and probably for ever, pass by Gibraltar, because, unless Italy acquires some region suitable for large-scale white settlement, her biggest overseas colonies will continue to be in New York and Buenos Aires. Her negotiations over the Gibraltar gateway are therefore dealt with first.

By the time Italy was ready to compete in the race for status at the western end of the Mediterranean, the draw for positions had taken place, and all were allotted except one—the city of Tangier. Great Britain, ensconced at Gibraltar since 1704, had been powerful enough to get her way on the opposite coast, and had kept it out of the hands of rivals. In the secret clauses of the Anglo-French 'Accord' of 1904, she had manœuvred France and Spain into dividing Morocco as she wished—that is, into awarding the coast opposite Gibraltar to the weaker and more manageable power, Spain. The status of Tangier was the only point left undefined.

Tangier had had a curious history. Its strategic position—commanding the Straits, but outside them—might well have singled it out as ideal booty during the European scramble for North Africa, but, by a miracle, its fate hung in suspense until after the World War. No European power had owned it since the seventeenth century. In 1661 it had passed from Portugal to England as part of the dowry of Catherine of Braganza, and had been greeted by Charles II as 'a jewell of immense value in the royall diadem', but in 1684 England had taken a decision rare in colonial history; she had cut her losses. After overspending men and money on the town, she had blown up her mole and sailed away, leaving the debris to the pashas of the Riff, who ruled it in the name of the Sultan of Morocco. He remained sovereign there, and is so to-day, simply because no one power could afford to see Tangier pass to any other.

But, during the years between the English departure and the present day, the town had assumed a special character. It was the home of the diplomatic representatives at the Sultan's court, and, as the port for most of Morocco's foreign trade, its harbour and business houses represented a large foreign investment. The British stake, which was the largest, was said to amount to £2½ millions in 1923. In order to protect these lives and treasures against the vagaries of the Moroccan government, the diplomatic corps took to making its own arrangements about municipal government, sanitation, and other matters affecting its creature comforts, and—as a result of some expensive wrecks—to buoying and lighting the coast. International management therefore grew up, but was never recognized in law. In 1911, negotiations over a permanent arrangement opened between Great Britain, France, and Spain, but the bargaining was slow, and was still in process when the outbreak of the World War put an end to such a minor affair.

Here Italy comes upon the stage. As a Mediterranean power, and as one of the victors in the War, she was ready to spread her interests. She asked to be invited to the three-power negotiations over Tangier when they re-opened in 1923. There were six hundred Italians living in Tangier, and the conferring powers had everything to gain by her co-operation. With regrettable lack of judgement, the British and French Foreign Offices refused her request. They nipped a chance of internationalism in the bud. She retaliated by refusing to recognize the international régime which they established under the 1923 Statute for the management of the Tangier Zone. Her refusal hampered—indeed, almost prevented—its effective working.

The Tangier snub, coupled with a simultaneous set-back over Corfu, caused the new Fascist Government in Italy to look round for a Mediterranean friend. The obvious ally was Spain. Both countries were monarchies; both kings had thrown in their lot with a dictator, and General Primo de Rivera, who was sensitive about Gibraltar, welcomed the Italian advances. Royal visits were exchanged in 1923 and 1924, and an Italo-Spanish treaty of friendship followed in 1926. One bond of union was Tangier. The international arrangement was, in practice, working out to the advantage of the French; the Spaniards were growing as anxious as the Italians to see it changed, and the new allies therefore set about undermining the French position. In 1927, Italy, taking a leaf out of the Kaiser's book, paid an ostentatious naval visit to the port. Her parade was less spectacular than the German manœuvre of 1905, for the Prince of Udine, the king's cousin, did not cut the dash of Wilhelm II. Nevertheless, he was more successful in achieving his country's object, for by 1928 the Statute was revised, and Italy was participating in the administration of the Zone. And there matters stand, presumably until the present Statute expires in 1948.

Italy gained her point, but the triumph was symbolic rather than useful. Equality of rights in the Tangier

Legislative Assembly and in the local courts-of-law could not be said to improve her strategic position in regard to the Straits. Were opportunity to offer, she would like to add some richer 'jewell to her diadem'. But suitable jewels are rare, and diplomacy alone is unlikely to secure them. The search for them is probably one of the reasons why, in 1936–8, she intervened in Spain.

The Italian policy of intervention in Spain has been ascribed to various motives, some political, others strategic. Undoubtedly some Italians started out inspired by genuine idealism. Evidence to this effect was collected by an Englishman who looked through the papers found on Italian prisoners, discovering among them some very human documents. 'Noiselessly the pirates of an ideal depart', records one Blackshirt's diary for January 7, 1936, 'on the most wonderful and most sacred adventure.'[1] This sentiment expresses the view of large numbers of young Italians, and was at the time constantly heard in private conversation in Italy.

The Italian leaders, no doubt, acted on more material grounds. They feared the Socialist tendencies of the Spanish left, and they were anxious as to developments in France. At the time when they first sent help to General Franco—in July 1936—Monsieur Blum's government was dependent on seventy Communist votes, and factories all over France were being occupied by the workers. Probably their chief reason for intervening was their fear that a barrier of Communism might bar their country's vital route to the west. Strategically, therefore, they needed a friendly Spain. Doubtless they also reckoned that if, in addition, they could secure an indebted and subservient Spain, they stood to strengthen their position not only as a Mediterranean but as an Atlantic power, that they would weaken Great Britain's hold over the Straits of Gibraltar, and that they would command France's communications

[1] Mr. Henry Blythe, *Spain over Britain*, Routledge, 1937.

not only from north to south, but from east to west along North Africa, where her road and railway run so near the Spanish Moroccan frontier.

But Italy's past motives for intervening are unimportant in comparison with the question of the future: will she see a return for her intervention? Among a host of conjectures, two facts are clear: the first, that she did not expect so long or so expensive a campaign; the second, that she did not lend men and material without hope of reward.

The Spanish campaign dragged its length along at a pace which could only have been foretold by a student of the Napoleonic or the Carlist wars. Spain was poor in war material. Most of her army equipment dated from before the War, and the nations who helped either side began by exporting out-of-date armaments which, while useless to themselves, represented trump-cards to the Spanish forces. But, from the moment in November 1936 when the Russians began to supply first-line aircraft, the situation changed. Italy and Germany were obliged in their turn to put their best foot forward. Italy could ill afford to do so. Her war material was already spread over Abyssinia and Libya, and she was short of the raw materials necessary for quick replenishment. The risk of war in Europe demanded that she should keep control over the equipment supplied to General Franco; she was therefore obliged to supply him with men as well. Hence her dispatch of whole units of the Italian army.

When this assistance did not bring the quick victory for which she hoped, she was caught in a vicious circle. The more she helped General Franco, the more she increased his chances of success, but the more she ran the risk of general war with her own armaments in a depleted state. On the other hand, to furnish insufficient help was to spin out a campaign the expense of which she could ill afford. By the end of 1937, voices at home were beginning to murmur against taxation for Spanish purposes. By 1938, when Germany had marched into Austria, they were suggesting that the Italians in Spain would be better employed in the Alps. But, despite their murmurings, Signor Mussolini found difficulty in withdrawing his troops, short of victory. He could not do so, because a dictator must go from strength to strength; like a man on a bicycle, he must keep moving or he will fall.

During the months in which the Duce was doubling and redoubling his Spanish stake, onlookers began to wonder whether the mere triumph of Spanish Fascism over Spanish Communism would enable him to give the required impression of perpetual motion. They feared that he might need some more substantial trophy—a Balearic Isle, for instance, or a foothold in Spanish Morocco, or, as a minimum, the promise of facilities at Spanish sea and air ports in time of war. Everything pointed to the Balearic Isles as his likely goal. Throughout the war, Italian ships and airmen were making themselves at home there, and, from the strategic point of view, Balearic concessions promised enormously to increase his Mediterranean strength. For the Balearics are not a group nestling under the coast of Spain. They occupy a fine commanding position in the midst of the sea; they bestride the shortest route from Marseilles to Algiers or Oran, and they are within flying distance of Gibraltar.

But, in the Agreement with Great Britain which he signed at Rome in April 1938, the Duce said that he renounced all such benefits. Provided that he could leave his troops in Spain until the end of the war—a proviso that was necessary, as we have seen, for his domestic purposes—he promised that his Government would seek no territorial, political, or economic privileges in Spanish territory.

This surprising end to the rumours and alarums of two years needs some explanation. The principal key to the riddle is his treatment at the hands of Herr Hitler.

When Germany displayed so scant a regard for his interests as to perpetrate the Anschluss without warning, he was forced to the bitter conclusion that he had put too much faith in his ally, and that he must draw in his Mediterranean horns in order to look to his northern defences. There is no honour among expansionists.

In any case, Spaniards will tell you that Italian hopes of securing a permanent footing in their country will always be vain, because the two nationalities are like oil and water. To a Spaniard, an Italian is a joke, from his language up. To an Italian, a Spaniard is not only irresponsible and a clown, but a brute who used to rule in Naples and Milan.

The martial tactics essayed in Spain have not so far been applied at the other outlets; Italy has maintained the gentler tones of diplomacy on the subject both of Suez and of the Dardanelles. But the reinforcement of Libya during the Italo-Abyssinian dispute, and again—'through necessities of an international character'—in October 1937, were warnings that sterner methods might one day be used at Suez. Egypt, for one, is nervous lest this should happen. Each strengthening of the Libyan garrison reminds her of her weakness, her riches, and her desirability. Her newspapers send anxious correspondents to interview the Duce, and her ministers demand and receive assurances of his peaceful intentions.

On paper, Italy is in a strong position at Suez. The Canal was internationalized by a Convention of 1888, and, as a signatory of that Convention, she is one of the guarantors of free passage to the ships of all nations, 'in time of war as in time of peace'. She can use it freely at all times, for it is never closed, even in war. In 1898, Spanish ships passed through during their war with the United States; in 1904, Russian ships used it during their war with Japan. Even during the World War, it was in theory open, except during the few days when it was threatened by Turkish troops, while, more recently, Italy herself used it without hindrance during her attack on Ethiopia.

But the talk of closure which then prevailed has caused Italians to take a new view of the situation. Their position, they say, may be strong in theory, but in practice it is weak so long as the two other Mediterranean powers—Great Britain with her troops and France with her money and officials—can in fact do as they please with the waterway. Italians point out that Great Britain's only claim to priority over other powers is her contention that the Canal is an essential imperial route, and that, since the conquest of Ethiopia, the same applies to Italy.

This feeling, which smouldered from the moment when the word closure was first breathed in 1935, became vehement when the text of the Anglo-Egyptian treaty was published in August 1936. The Italians read it with mounting resentment, for in their view it violated the old Canal Convention. The article to which they objected, which describes the Canal as 'an integral part of Egypt' and 'an essential means of communication between the different parts of the British Empire', goes on to provide for its defence by the establishment of 10,000 British soldiers and 400 British pilots on the banks. This arrangement, said Rome, might in the old days have passed muster as the 'legitimate self-defence' to which Egypt was entitled, but, once the idea of closure had been mooted, the modern meaning was clear. Great Britain had disregarded the clause in the old Convention whereby the signatories undertook to seek no territorial privileges affecting the Canal. She had placed herself in a position to close it, thereby proving that she was 'ready to waive any treaty in order to further her present or potential interests'.[1] To any British suggestion that Italy has torn up treaties, the Italian reply is '*Tu quoque*'.

[1] Ambrosini, *I Problemi del Mediterraneo*, Rome, 1937, p. 113.

The feeling among informed Italians is, therefore, that the old Convention is now valueless, and that a new arrangement ought to be devised to take its place. They advocate a genuine international régime, with mixed management, on the model of that at Tangier. 'Nothing short of such a settlement can quell anxiety and eliminate the potential danger of war.'[1] So writes the leading Fascist expert. He sets out a convincing case, but one which omits to mention that the defence of the Canal depends exclusively on the Egyptian Government, which is alone competent to determine how that defence shall be carried out, and to choose what allies it will for the purpose.

If internationalization of the Canal's defence were Italy's sole aim, she could doubtless get her way, for the arrangement could be made without loss of face to England or Egypt, and would add to the security of all three states. But so long as she is in her inflated, expansionist mood, the gesture presents difficulties. Who is going to make it in order to see it vaunted in the Italian press as an Anglo-Egyptian defeat and a glorious national victory?

In the Anglo-Italian Agreement of April 1938, Italy accepted reaffirmation of the 1888 Convention as sufficient guarantee for the future. Nevertheless, those who are acquainted with Italian political writings must feel that Suez is a potential source of trouble. The idea that the Anglo-Egyptian arrangement is hostile and provoking is no longer propagated in public, but it is still discussed in private—in offices, and over dinner tables. It is ready for wider use, and, if occasion arose, could be born fully equipped, like Pallas Athene from the brain of Zeus.

At both Suez and Gibraltar, therefore, Fascist diplomacy has never yet lost ground. At the Black Sea Straits,

[1] Ambrosini, *op. cit.*, p. 115.

on the other hand, Italy has been strangely clumsy in her handling of the presiding power. She needs a friendly Turkey, because a hostile Turkey can hamper her oil supply, yet she has so managed matters that her overtures are less welcome on the Bosphorus than either at Suez or in Spain. Some one has blundered.

Friendship with Turkey, or, failing Turkey, friendship with Greece, is essential to the power who wishes to influence the traffic through the Black Sea Straits. But, for years, Italy enjoyed neither of these privileges. Though Greece and Turkey were themselves bitter foes, and though the enemy of one was almost automatically the friend of the other until they made up their differences in 1930, Italian diplomacy contrived to antagonize them both. The Turks were frightened of Italian land-hunger; the Greeks were embittered by thoughts of the Dodecanese and by memories of a famous incident at Corfu. Italy traded in an atmosphere of hate, not only in the Straits but in the Aegean, until Signor Mussolini decided to improve his position in so important a waterway, and signed treaties with both states in 1928.

Looking back, it seems that these antagonisms could have been avoided. With Greece, in particular, Italy seemed to go out of her way to create bad blood, for, quite apart from the Dodecanesian question, her tactics at Corfu were as unnecessary as they were unwise. In 1923, the Italian member of a commission which was delimiting the Albanian frontier was murdered on Greek soil. Italy, who had a good case, demanded an indemnity, but she put herself in the wrong by her method of pressing the demand. The Fascists, newly in power and anxious to display that they were a force to be reckoned with in Europe, ordered some ships to the Ionian Islands and, on a flimsy pretext, bombarded the town of Corfu. They secured their indemnity, but the game was not worth the candle. The sum involved was no compensation for the liabilities incurred—a snub from their ex-Allies, and a lasting loss of Greek goodwill. The bombardment roused feelings which still emerge in conversation with Greeks, and which all the treaties and fair words of later years have never wholly effaced.

With the Turks, fraternization would have been more difficult, for Turkish hostility was more deep-rooted, being founded upon uncertainty and fear. Nevertheless, the history of Italo-Turkish relations reveals some missed opportunities—some chances of securing an important friend which Fascist diplomatists for some reason disdained or ignored.

The Turkish dislike of Italy dates back to the war of 1911–12, and to the capture of the Dodecanese and Libya. It simmered during the World War, and grew vehement after the Armistice, when Italy's war aims were discovered to include a province in Asia Minor. Her allies had promised her part of Anatolia in the Secret Treaty of St.-Jean-de-Maurienne, and Turkey's worst fears were realized when the Italian Government, chafing at the delays in Paris, took the law into its own hands and landed a force at Adalia in 1919.

But this threat was to come to nothing. The Italians did not, like the Greeks, fight a war for their promised land. They did not surge blindly forward alongside M. Venizelos. Had they done so, they might have changed the course of their colonial history. They grew hesitant when they saw that Turkey, instead of playing the submissive role of the vanquished, had turned into a two-headed Janus—an old head at Constantinople with whom they could deal as a victor, and a new head in Asia who regarded them as an Anatolian intruder. The rise of Mustapha Kemal with a fighting force behind him confronted them with a perplexing choice: Should they rely on their agreement with the British and French, promising them a 'zone' in the south of Asia Minor, or should they treat with the new Turkey and secure what they could from its leader before he was strong enough to be haughty? Dissension among the Allies at Constantinople decided them on the latter course. Reasoning that an Anglo-Franco-Italian agreement would in effect mean the dominance of Great Britain, because she had the biggest navy, they decided to make their own arrangements. In March 1921 they slipped off to Angora and signed a treaty with Mustapha Kemal. 'The Royal Government of Italy . . . undertakes to support efficaciously all the demands of the Turkish delegation relating to the Treaty of Peace, especially the restitution to Turkey of Thrace and Smyrna.' More than this, they smoothed his path to conquest. He too had promised them a 'zone' in Anatolia, but they waived this promise as he grew in power. When he swept the Greeks into the sea, and marched against the British police force at the Straits, they prudently withdrew to their islands. They retained nothing but the Dodecanese when he finally signed peace at Lausanne.

By comparison with the British and the Greeks, therefore, they had been positively accommodating, but they failed to reap the reward of their self-sacrifice. Instead of writing off Anatolia for lost, and exploiting a potential friendship, Fascism mourned aloud for the lost province, and included it in its list of grievances about the broken promises of the Allies. Naturally enough, such weeping and gnashing of teeth revived all Turkey's old anxieties. She forgot Italy's self-denial and remembered only her initial greed.

This period of Turkish animosity ended with the Italo-Turkish treaty of 1928. Both dictators were ready to come to terms, Mustapha Kemal because he felt that he had been leaning rather too exclusively on the arm of Russia, Signor Mussolini because he wished to improve his position in regard to the Straits. Six halcyon years followed. Italian shipping plied between Turkish ports;

Italian oil supplies flowed through the Dardanelles, and statesmen of both countries signed agreements, paid official visits, made flattering speeches, and indulged in all the paraphernalia of good relations.

But an event of 1934 proved that Turkey's old susceptibilities were still alive. In the spring of that year, Signor Mussolini made a speech in which he described the Near East as one of Italy's 'historic objectives'. The Turks reacted at once. Though the Duce was careful to explain that he meant economic and not political aims, and that he had no thought of territorial conquest, they did not accept his statements. They thought they recognized the old Anatolian spectre in the new guise of a dove, and they launched an anti-Italian campaign which kept their newspapers busy for a year. The Fascists were genuinely astonished at this reaction. They deplored Turkey's assumption that they were hostile to her interests; they reproached her for 'failing to take into account the repeated declarations of the Duce that his aim is to develop a policy of friendly comprehension', and they assured her that the Dodecanese islands were less a base than an outpost intended to 'promote the link existing between Italy and the peoples of the Near East'. But the Turks were not to be soothed. As the Ethiopian campaign approached, they felt that their fears had been justified, and they joined willingly both in sanctions, and in the agreements with Great Britain and France for mutual support in the event of attack in the Mediterranean. They drew away from Italy and closer to the League of Nations.

Once the Ethiopian war was over, Turkey and Italy resumed their former contacts, since mutual trade and shipping relations brought benefits to both parties, but on the Turkish side the approach was even warier than before. The Italians, on the other hand, were ready to resume the affable tones of 1928, but, try as they might, they could not revive the old atmosphere. They arranged diplomatic conversations in the spring of 1937, but the former warmth was lacking because, between times, they had made another psychological mistake. They had offended Turkey by their handling of her request to re-fortify the Straits.

The idea of refortification was not new. Turkey had been hinting that it was in her mind ever since the failure of the Disarmament Conference, but she took no active steps to implement it until two events of the winter of 1935–6 increased her chances of success. The first was the Ethiopian campaign, which proved that unarmed states could not rely on the League of Nations to defend their interests; the second was the German reoccupation of the Rhineland—in other words, the refortification of a similarly demilitarized zone. Her case strengthened by these two happenings, Turkey played her cards extremely well. Instead of further weakening the League and identifying herself with the treaty-breakers, she turned their lawlessness to account in order to gain her end by lawful means. In April 1936 she formally requested the signatories of the Peace Treaty to revise the demilitarization clauses. No one liked the Turkish request. No one enjoyed the idea of exchanging the amiable post-War arrangement for the exclusive Turkish control which had been the cause of so much trouble in the past, but Turkey met with general approval because no one was in a position to refuse her. All were obliged to accept the inevitable, and to derive such advantage as they could from the change. All—that is—except one. Italy alone refused to take part in the Straits Conference which met at Montreux.

Her decision is a piece of history which should interest any student of Fascist psychology. The date was June 1936. Sanctions, though they had failed, were still nominally in force, as were the mutual assistance arrangements between the other Mediterranean powers, and Italy, if she accepted the Turkish invitation, would have been obliged to sit at a table with her oppressors. On the other hand, she realized that her presence at the Conference would help to check the Balkan designs of Germany and the Black Sea designs of Russia. She had to make up her mind whether pleasing Turkey, and thwarting Russia, were considerations sufficiently important to warrant attendance, when attendance was bound to involve siding with Great Britain—the enemy who had been trying to ruin her by means of sanctions. She toyed with the idea of going to Montreux, for she booked provisional accommodation at an hotel, but two considerations finally decided her against doing so. The first was her conviction that no Mediterranean conference could reach a result unless she attended, and that, when pressed to come to the meetings, she could make her presence conditional on some concession to her own advantage—for instance, the expunging of the name of Ethiopia from the list of members of the League. But in this assumption she was wrong; the Turks were in a hurry and the Conference went on without her. The second reason for her refusal was less material. Fascism favours the cloak-and-sword school of manners which holds that a slight cannot be forgotten until its perpetrator has made his apology. Even when sanctions were called off during the Conference, Italy made it clear that she expected other amends before she could consent to treat with sanctionists. But the manners of d'Artagnan and Sir Percy Blakeney are out of place in the rough-and-tumble of modern diplomacy. The powers who are most successful nowadays are the realists who can waive formalities when more concrete interests are at stake; Japan, for instance, when it suits her, forgets that certain states have not recognized Manchukuo. Italy's inability to do likewise is a weakness, and that weakness was displayed when she allowed her sense of injury to run away with her and refused to go to Montreux.

Her decision did her nothing but harm. In the first place, it offended the Turks, and prejudiced her chance of influence at the Straits. Secondly, it enabled the Russians to mould the new Straits Convention to their liking, and to make arrangements for the passage of their fleet which were distasteful to any Mediterranean power. Of course, Italy cannot admit a mistake, but, when she accepts the Montreux decisions, as she will ultimately be obliged to do, she is bound to do so in the knowledge that they might have been more palatable had she assisted in their making.

At the end of 1936, therefore, Italy found herself in a slightly uneasy position at all three exits to the Mediterranean. She had antagonized the Turks; she had provoked an Anglo-Egyptian treaty over which Great Britain and Egypt had made friends, and, despite her help, General Franco was not achieving a quick victory in Spain. She was uncomfortably aware that powers at all three vantage-points would be hostile to her were the Spanish struggle to degenerate into war.

The Duce therefore decided to ease the position. With his Empire safely behind him, he could do so without loss of dignity. He decided to clear the course through the Canal and the Straits of Gibraltar by improving his relations with Great Britain. In a speech made at Milan on November 1, 1936, he held out a sprig of olive which, though proffered on the end of a bayonet, was nevertheless thrust forward with an eager gesture. The British Government responded at once. An agreeable atmosphere in the Mediterranean was a patent advantage to both states, and, after a few amiable preliminaries, London pleased Italian opinion in removing the British legation from Addis Ababa. From that moment relations began to progress favourably. British left-wing opinion was hostile, but the Italian press swung from bitter invective against England to coy acknowledgement of friendly speeches, and by the end of the year the outlook was—except for the Spanish danger—almost bright.

These were the preliminaries to the so-called 'Gentlemen's Agreement' of January 2, 1937:

> 'His Majesty's Government in the United Kingdom and the Italian Government recognize that freedom of entry into, exit from and transit through the Mediterranean is a vital interest both to the different parts of the British Empire and to Italy, and that these interests are in no way inconsistent with each other.'

The truth of the words is self-evident, yet the agreement did not last. Though it remained nominally in force, all the gentlemanliness had gone out of it before six months had passed, for Italy had decided that it was not enough.

Her first reaction to it was jubilant and self-assured. 'The two great powers have treated on an equal footing.' 'Here is an end to the position of inferiority which Italy has suffered through long years of British hegemony.' But on second thoughts opinion changed. The inferiority complex which is discernible in the phrases quoted above gained the upper hand as British rearmament proceeded and was unaccompanied by further recognition of Italy's new greatness. The idea that the British hegemony was not over began to creep into Fascist minds, and, since Great Britain took no steps to assuage it, Italy changed her Mediterranean tactics. She resumed her martial tones in the hope of gaining advantage by looking dangerous. She became brazen about her help to General Franco; she published lists of her Spanish casualties; she drew closer to Germany, and congratulated Japan on gangster successes in China. Further, she returned to her policy of defaming Great Britain. Her press and wireless trimmed the news to suit their purpose, loud- and soft-pedalling it as the policy of the moment demanded. The comment on England which is to be found in the file of any Italian newspaper for 1937 runs through the whole gamut of emotions from amiability to virulence.

Some Fascists had never been easy about this policy, feeling that it might permanently close the door to rapprochement with Great Britain. Even its protagonists found their faith shaken by the tone of the famous Hitler-Schuschnigg conversations which took place at Berchtesgaden on February 12, 1938. A week later, the resignation of Mr. Anthony Eden provided the Duce with an excuse for a *volte face*. He opened the conversations which led to the Anglo-Italian Agreement of mid-April.

Whether gentlemanly or ungentlemanly relations with Great Britain will best serve Italy's purpose at the Mediterranean exits only the next few years can show, but one prophecy can safely be made, and that is, that to alternate from one to the other is to defeat her own ends. For Great Britain is not the only power concerned. Turkey and Egypt are enjoying growing control at their respective bottle-necks; the Spaniards may do likewise when they settle down. The confidence of all three must be wooed if the Italian Empire is to be secure, and, judging by sentiments expressed both in Cairo and Ankara, wayward changes of policy are not the way to win it, either among Egyptians or Turks.

4. *The Mediterranean and Italian Expansion*

When Fascists speak of the Mediterranean as Italy's rightful field for expansion, they have in mind the eastern basin. They know that the western basin is the preserve of other nations, that France is strongly entrenched along most of its shore, and that Italian energy expended there would benefit no one but the French. But looking east, they see a different scene—a world to which they feel drawn not only for practical reasons but by sentiment.

This attachment was described by the Duce in March 1934, in a speech which is, of his many speeches, one of the most memorable. Addressing the great Five-Yearly Assembly of the Fascist Party, he inspired his Italian audience with enthusiasm, but filled the Levant in general, and Turkey in particular, with uneasiness as to his intentions, when he gave three material reasons why Italy should look to the Eastern Mediterranean for her development. First, it was on the high road to the rich regions of Asia—a door through which the nation could obtain Asiatic raw materials unhampered by the foreign dominance at Suez and Gibraltar; secondly, the coastal countries themselves were rich in products which Italy lacked; and thirdly, their ports were the natural destination of the great merchant fleets of Venice, Bari, Brindisi, and Trieste. What European power was more suitably placed for forging the much-needed link between east and west?

> 'There must be no misunderstanding upon this centuries-old task which I assign to this and future generations of Italians. There is no question of territorial conquests; this must be understood by all both far and near. The matter is one of a natural expansion which will lead to a closer co-operation between Italy and the peoples of Africa, between Italy and the nations of the Near and Middle East.'

Looking at this project from a strictly material standpoint, the field of action is well chosen. The nations in question are not only conveniently near, but inhabit an area upon which Italy already largely relies for the earnings from shipping and other investment which help to balance her international payments.

In the first place, the eastern Mediterranean is one of the few parts of the world in which she has almost succeeded in balancing her trade. True, the turnover is not very large; it amounts to but 10 per cent. of her total,[1] for her big transactions are not with the Orient, but with her immediate neighbours and with the commercial giants of

[1] For the U.S.S.R. (Black Sea trade), Rumania, Turkey, Greece, Bulgaria, Albania, Syria, Palestine, and Egypt, see Pace, *Gli Interessi dell' Italia nel Mediterraneo Orientale*, Milan, 1936.

the west. Germany, Great Britain, the United States, and Switzerland alone account for between 40 and 50 per cent. of the whole. But despite its small size, her Near Eastern trade is important, because, while the imports include more than half her oil and about a fifth of her iron and cotton, the exports—of which textiles, sold principally to Egypt, are the chief item—are, in good years, remunerative enough to pay the lion's share of the bill.

She fosters this trade by the usual means—commercial attachés and chambers of commerce—but also by a Fascist invention of some distinction, the Levant Fair inaugurated in 1930, and held every September at Bari. Tradition dictated the choice of site. Bari has ancient ties with the Levant owing to its position on the heel of the peninsula; it was once the capital of a province of Byzantium and, later, the clearing-house for eastern goods used by the Norman kings of Sicily. Remembering its past, Signor Mussolini decided to revive its old connexions, and, a few days before the March on Rome, he announced that he had destined it as the starting-point for 'Italy's pacific expansion in the eastern Mediterranean and beyond'. He has been a man of his word. Bari is to-day a blend of ancient and modern. The Byzantine basilica which houses the bones of Saint Nicholas is still hidden in the twisting streets of a medieval town, but to either side of it spreads a new metropolis shining with glass and chromium plating—the home not only of the Fair, which grows in size with every year, but also of a Benito Mussolini university, a Royal Institute for Commercial Research, and a wireless station from which Italy broadcasts nightly, in Near Eastern languages, the news of the world as seen through Fascist eyes.

Near Eastern shipping and air services are a second source of Italian income, and one from which Fascism, by strict rationalization, extracts the maximum of revenue. It has eliminated national competition by means of three successive amalgamations of shipping companies, and, since January 1937, four groups only serve the regular routes of the world—the *Italia* line for America, the *Lloyd Triestino* for beyond Suez, the *Tirrenia* for the western, and the *Adriatica* for the eastern Mediterranean. A similar amalgamation of air lines has transferred all business to the *Ala Littoria* concern. Of the shipping companies, the *Adriatica* is not so important as either of the trans-oceanic lines; it is smaller both as regards its share capital and the volume of its tonnage. On the other hand, being much used by foreigners, it represents both an advertisement for Italy and a source of foreign exchange. Its ships serve the first purpose effectively for they often ply on routes served by no one else. They go everywhere, and think of everything; they offer a quick service from Trieste to Palestine for the Jews of Central Europe, and they afford almost the only means of getting to or away from Cyprus. In the second, they set store by appearances. The oldest cargo boat has been rejuvenated in order to attract first-class passengers, and, with her clean paint and the burnished lion of St. Mark shining on her funnel, looks like a lady as she sweeps into the small harbours whose normal occupants are serviceable but grubby tramps.

The sting is in the tail of the story. Italian shipping heads the list of foreign callers at most of the ports in the Levant. In Turkey, for instance, it accounted in 1935 for 30 per cent. of the vessels entered and cleared, as against 18 per cent. from Great Britain. But the number of ships which call is not the only criterion of prosperity; for one thing, it is no guide to their earnings. The statistics for the port of Smyrna show that, in the first half of 1937, 77 Italian vessels called for 11,000 tons of merchandise. On the other hand, 24 German ships called for 17,000 tons, 26 Dutch ships for 14,000 tons, and 46 British ships for 14,000 tons. The figures suggest that, though Italy cuts the biggest dash, others surpass her in the knack of showing profits.

A third source of income is the interest on Near Eastern investment. Italy is a notoriously small foreign investor, and her interests look almost puny beside those of France or Great Britain, but if comparisons are set aside, and her enterprises are considered on their merits, they represent a welcome contribution to her supplies of foreign exchange.

She has attempted little public lending. Apart from her loans to Albania, which are political and are made without great expectation of a cash dividend, she holds but negligible shares in the public debt of eastern Mediterranean countries. On the other hand, she has a lively and growing interest in private ventures of several kinds.

Her money is mainly in banking and insurance. The *Banco di Roma*, which is the banking-house chiefly concerned, first opened a branch in Alexandria in the year 1905, destined for the convenience of the local Italian colony; the investment was part of the rush of capital to Egypt which followed the burying of the hatchet in the Anglo-French 'Accord' of 1904. But, not long afterwards, the bank put out a political feeler; in 1907 and 1909 it opened branches in Tripoli and Cyrenaica, in both of which it was conveniently ensconced when the time came for conquest of Libya. It spread its activities to Turkey in 1911, and to Syria and Palestine after the War. It has met with varying success. In Turkey, it has expanded relatively little, for Italy was unpopular at the time of its opening, and since the War it has, together with all its foreign counterparts, been relegated to second place by Turkish nationalism. In Egypt, on the other hand, it has shown a vigorous and promising development. In 1922, it combined with the *Credito Italiano* to set up an autonomous body called the *Banco Italo-Egiziano*, and this concern, together with the *Banca Commerciale Italiana*, has secured sufficient business to place Italy second only to Great Britain among the nations interested in commercial banking in Egypt.

Italian insurance companies have built up their business over a longer period, for the two largest—the *Assicurazioni Generali* and the *Riunione Adriatica*—both made their début in the Levant before the middle of the last century. Beginning from the Balkans, they worked their way eastwards, and, though the volume of business which they do is inferior to that of British and French companies, they have spread their net as far afield as Iraq, Iran, and Afghanistan. They run to imposing buildings in the larger cities. The *Generali* office, for instance, mitigates the horror of your first entry into the new Jerusalem, for it is the one building of distinction in the shambles of architecture which adorns the Jaffa Road. Moreover, their presence comes to your notice in lesser ways. In some small Turkish port, their affable agent, who has time on his hands, will heave his Byzantine body up the ship's side in order to press his card upon you. The company is no worse off because his motive is less to advertise its policies than to proffer his own services, not to mention those of his relations and friends.

The amount of foreign currency which these insurance companies bring into Italy is almost impossible to compute. In 1935, the premiums collected by foreign branches amounted to as much as 735 million lire, but this sum cannot be counted as net gain of foreign exchange, since from it must be deducted not only the companies' disbursements in payment of claims, but also the money which they reinvest in the countries of origin and in re-insurance, usually in London. Nevertheless, the original figure is sufficiently large to suggest that those who balance the nation's payments can look to the great insurance firms for some perquisites in the way of foreign exchange derived from transactions done by branches overseas.

They can also look to one or two enterprises outside the immediate field of banking and insurance, but, unfortunately for Italy, the number is woefully small. The principal earner is a contracting firm called the *Società Imprese Italiane all'Estero*, which, by organizing and financing the offer of tenders for public works abroad, has secured contracts in Turkey, Iran, and Iraq; but, apart from this concern, which is mainly financed by the leading banks, the large-scale Italian investor is a rare figure in the Levant. He has put money into the Yugoslav lumber trade, and into one or two farming concerns in Albania; he has invested with some success in the building trade and the mining of phosphates in Egypt, and—in the form of a great firm like Pirelli, Montecatini, or Fiat—he has opened an occasional Near Eastern branch, but the remainder of his ventures can be counted on the fingers of one hand. His contribution to the Italian balance of payments, therefore, is scanty and soon assessed, for, though a list of Italian businesses in the Near East looks imposing, its length is greater than its earning power. It is almost entirely composed of small agents and shopkeepers living from hand to mouth, who are too poor to do more than support their large families, and who have not a piastre to spare for the hungry maw of the Italian treasury.

On balance, however, Italy's economic position in the eastern Mediterranean is favourable. Her income from shipping, together with that from investment in banking and insurance, must more than compensate for her excess of imports over exports. She would be prosperous if she could say as much for her Atlantic or her Suez trade. The Duce's wave of the arm towards the Levant when he talks of 'natural expansion' is therefore dictated by something more substantial than his fancy or his sense of the past. The conception is one of his more solid projects, for it rests on the firm basis of a balanced economy in the area, and, could Italy but preserve this balance as she expanded, she would go far towards solving the problem of her poverty.

Italy's expansionist aims in the Levant are not confined to this material plane. Fascism also preaches a more exalted mission—the endowment of the former Roman Empire with the benefits which the Fascist renaissance has brought to the new Rome. When the Duce thundered out his instructions in his great speech of March 1934, the passages which most deeply moved his countrymen were those which gave the sentimental reasons for Italy's affinities with the Orient.

The appeal is one of tradition and history. Fascists are never allowed to forget that the eastern Mediterranean was once a scene of Roman greatness, and that it abounds with the marks left by their ancestors—whether great buildings like the temples at Baalbek, or the humbler monuments—small forts and soldiers' tombstones—which are strewn in an arc running from the Sahara through Transjordan and Asia Minor to Rumania.

The story is written on the wall for all to read in the form of five marble maps in the Via dell' Impero in Rome, four of which show the growth of the old Empire, and the fifth the extent of the new. They teach the belief that Fascism is not a new development, but a renaissance of former greatness, and, lest their significance should escape the passer-by, the theme is repeated elsewhere. It has found its way into text-books and novels, advertisements and films. It has swelled in a great *crescendo* as the Ethiopian Empire develops, and it reaches its highest expression in a magnificent exhibition of *Romanità*, or Roman-ness, for the opening of which the bi-millennium of the birth of Augustus served as pretext in the autumn of 1937. This exhibition, which is no doubt destined to be permanent, enshrines the idea which underlies all modern Fascist teaching. Shown with the Italian flair for showmanship, it leads the visitor from stage to stage until it brings him to a central statue which is not, as might be expected, Augustus, but a figure representing his spirit or genius. What that figure signifies is then made clear. It stands for Augustus's reconstruction of order out of chaos, his conception of civil service as an extension of personal service to a leader, and his restoration of Roman prestige in the Old World. But its firm, square-jawed face serves less to tell the old story than to throw into relief the new. The exhibition, while losing nothing as an artistic triumph, is a skilful and persistent reminder of the similar functions which the Fascist state and leader can fulfil in the twentieth century.

Moreover, Italy's historic link with the Near East did not end with the Roman Empire. Fascists also like to think of the eastern Mediterranean as the province of Italian traders and navies in the days of their great maritime republics. The relic preserved in a church of Venice or Pisa—bone of a saint or fragment of the cross—has taken on an added significance. To the peasant, it is still the sacred token of his faith, but to the ardent Fascist it is something more. He sees in it yet another tribute to the glory of Italy, for it represents the medieval Italian whose influence spread so far afield that he was able to bring the treasure safely out of the hands of the infidel.

In short, Fascism wishes to be considered as one with its great forebears. It resents the way in which western cultures have adopted Rome and the Renaissance as a common ancestor, and look upon Mussolini's Italy as something new. It is determined to prove its ancient lineage. And, since it has failed to carry its point by mere preaching, it turns east in order to demonstrate its heredity, in the hope that a rebirth of Italian greatness in the area where Caesars and Doges once flourished will waken the obtuse western nations to a realization of the grandeur that is Rome.

When Fascist Italy first set out on this mission of establishing a Near Eastern reputation, she found that the way was in part prepared, for Providence had supplied a ready-made starting-point. As a result of pre-War migrations, some of which dated back to the medieval republics, more than two hundred thousand Italians were clustered at intervals round the shore of the Mediterranean, of whom nearly 50 per cent. were in Tunisia and about sixty thousand in Egypt. With this nucleus to work upon, the first stage of her task was straightforward. She began to harness this potential force—to create local centres of nationalism.

At first sight the material looked unprepossessing, for the Italian emigrant was hardly an inspiring type. He was not, like his Greek counterpart, a thrusting, go-ahead trader, pushing this way and that in search of business, and suffering long years of exile up-country in order to make profits. He had no taste for such lonely experiments, preferring arc-lights, and cafés, and company; and thus, while Greeks became millionaires and built mansions in Alexandria or Smyrna, he eked out a hand-to-mouth existence as a stone-mason, knife-grinder, or waiter, and lived in a slum almost indistinguishable from the native quarter. He forgot his Italian origin, and accepted wages lower than did other westerners. In fact, he sank to the depths of poverty in everything but the size of his family.

Such was the creature whom Fascism set out to waken to a sense of national pride, and it did so by the simple method of making him feel important. It taught him to fly an Italian flag, and to display pictures of his King and Duce. It turned his ragamuffin children into spick-and-span Ballilas, complete with black shirt, blue neckerchief, and toy gun. It improved his bastard Italian, and built him bigger schools and better hospitals; it provided clubs and night schools and aftercare; it offered free holidays in Italy to his schoolboy and student sons, and it ran excursions from Cairo to the Suez Canal in order that he might see Italian troopships go by. In countries where the legislation decreed that locally-born children took on local nationality, it provided his wife with her fare to a maternity home on Italian soil. In fact, in every town from Istanbul to Tunis, it did all that was humanly possible to smarten and liven the Italian community, and to enable it to look its fellow westerners between the eyes.

The State paid the bill for this transformation, for the communities themselves were too poor to bear more than a fraction of the cost. It placed the burden on the national budget, and ran the campaign from a department of the Foreign Office called the *Direzione degli Italiani all' Estero*. It received help from two outside organizations. The great Dante Alighieri Society—which has no exact parallel in England, but which is, like the *Alliance Française* in France, an organization for promoting national culture—undertook the intellectual development of adults, while the Roman Catholic Church did its share through its Italian schools and charities.

The result of their joint labours is remarkable. The central office in Rome reports the usual 100 per cent. success, but here its superlatives are warranted. It has achieved a great work for Italy. The communities still live in slums, for standards of living cannot be raised in a day, and the older generation, which is conservative, has not appreciably changed its habits; but elsewhere a miracle has been worked. Their sons and grandsons are a new breed, radiating not only national loyalty but self-respect. Once a slipshod mass of inferior humanity, they now march through the foreign streets as the equal of all men, with bands playing, colours flying, and courage high.

But the rehabilitation of her own communities is not Italy's only objective in the Levant. Her self-imposed task extends to the people of other nations, whom she is anxious to draw into her orbit as admirers of her greatness and culture. Here she has found progress rather more difficult.

Any Fascist will tell you that the communities are the spearhead of her advance, that they win their way to local favour, and that they are more popular than their fellow foreigners, since their lowly way of life enables them to fraternize where the others command. The difference in relation, he explains, is that between *tu* and *vous*.

In this assumption, however, he is wrong. Far from creating sympathy and understanding, the Italian communities are not popular, because they compete with local labour. Egyptian, Syrian, and Turk are unanimous in disliking all foreigners, but on the whole they prefer the British or French capitalist, who offers them employment, to the indigent Italian, who takes the bread out of their mouths. Moreover, though this is a point that no Fascist can see from within his ivory tower in Italy, the very rehabilitation of the Italian communities has spoilt their chances of preaching Italy's cause. An Italian who is busy raising himself in his own esteem has no message for other nationalisms. On the contrary, he annoys them. The Tunisian or Egyptian, himself an ardent nationalist, does not want to listen to Fascist transports, and, if he must consort with any foreigner, prefers the company of an easy-going Greek or Englishman to that of an Italian brimming over with his new importance.

Those who doubt this assertion have only to visit a series of European schools. For instance, in the French *lycée* and English college at Alexandria, some 30 per cent. of the pupils are Egyptian; in the chief Italian school there are only 30 Egyptians among 1,000 pupils. The reason is not far to seek. In order to give his son a good education, the Egyptian will waive his dislike of foreign influence, but he would rather send the child into the cosmopolitan atmosphere of the British or French establishment than see him disappear into the stronghold of an alien nationalism, the chief purpose of whose curriculum is to build better Italians. Italy cannot have her cake and eat it.

Happily for her, the communities are not her only missionaries. She has other strings to her bow. She uses a whole network of propaganda devices in her attempt to win renown, some of them subtle and rather effective, others more blatant, and not everywhere successful.

At the head of the subtle class come her press and cinema propaganda, both of them far-reaching because they are moderate, and because their origins are well concealed. Apart from direct cash subsidies to foreign newspapers, her principal weapon is a news bureau in Cairo called the *Agence Égypte Orient*, which is run as a private concern, and which offers services at nominal rates to the Near and Middle Eastern press. The offer is widely accepted, especially by penniless local papers, and as a result the Arab reader gets most of his foreign news with a twist which enhances the greatness of Italy. The agency must be comfortably off, for it does not confine its services to newspapers. Its roneoed bulletins, posted at a piastre, seem to be circulated to any Arab of note, for you see their anonymous wrapper and guileless Egyptian postmark in the waiting-room of a Tunisian doctor and on the table of a Syrian cabinet minister.

The film organization is similar. Italian agencies offer free, or nearly free, newsreels to all cinemas who care to use them, and here again the news of the world is presented as Italy sees it. The camera cannot lie, but man can conjure with its results, and Italy does so without scruple and with malice aforethought. She shows herself at her most martial—helmeted Duce, massed tanks, roaring bombers—whereas she catches her rivals off their guard. During her anti-British campaign in 1937, one of her favourite scenes from British national life showed a ladies' archery competition in the garden of a Cambridge college.

To intellectuals she makes a different appeal. By means of books, articles, and even circulars, she points out that, just as the marriage between Ancient Rome and the Orient gave birth to what is now western civilization, so a similar marriage in the younger generation is capable of producing another and as great a culture. Suiting her action to her word, she flings open the doors of her universities to Near Eastern students. She offers them extremely easy terms and vaunts their presence. They enjoy the honour of a welcome from the Duce. 'Twenty centuries ago', he tells them, 'Rome achieved on the Mediterranean shore a union between East and West. . . . Once more to-day, thanks to the Fascist renaissance—a spiritual rebirth—Rome and the Mediterranean will resume this task of unification, and that is why the new Italy has summoned you to study here.' Flattered by this degree of attention, some 2,500 students are to be found obeying the summons in each recent university year, and though they are relatively few in number, they belong to an educated and influential class which, provided it is not overdosed with propaganda, might one day be a useful ally.

Italy reaches her widest public by means of her celebrated Bari broadcasts—the news bulletins issued nightly in three eastern European languages and in Arabic, which, not content with extolling Italian prowess, throw it into relief by belittling other nations. These bulletins are heard by an immense audience which has up till now had few other means of getting news. The spread of their influence is brought home to you when your police escort in the Syrian desert asks if it is true that the British Navy is not as mighty as it was, or when your Albanian chauffeur assures you that Mr. Eden is a Mason. (He does not know what a Mason is, but explains that he heard about it on the wireless, and that he believes it has something to do with witchcraft.)

All the same, Italy's wireless practices are not wholly to

her advantage, for she cannot pick and choose her audience. Unfortunately for her, the loud-speaker emits the same sounds whether it stands in a desert café or a Cairo government office, in a Cypriot village or in a club at Athens, and the same language is not suited to each. The exaggerations which she has taken to transmitting in order to bring her points home to the peasant listener are out of place in well-informed capitals. They impress the ignorant or unperceptive, because they are couched in lurid terms, but, at the other end of the intellectual scale, they defeat her object, for they provoke distaste and even derision.

Last, but not least, of her propaganda methods comes the more direct form of approach which she achieves by cutting a dash. The resplendent new buildings in which she houses her Near Eastern consulates, schools, and hospitals have created a general impression that she is well-to-do, and she has enhanced this belief by scattering largesse not only in money but in kind—a dispensary here, a newspaper subsidy there, a box of ammunition somewhere else. The Arab is delighted with something for nothing and, clasping his medicine, his cartridges, or his bag of gold, he is ready to cry 'Viva Mussolini', but this lip-service is thanks for a gift which he will use to further his own ends, not Italy's. Here east and west are still poles apart—as far apart as their differing conceptions of God, time, Mussolini, and the benefits of civilization can place them.

Does it pay Italy to advertise?

The yes-men of the Italian press claim that she is achieving a 100 per cent. success, that she is 'penetrating' everywhere in the Levant, and that she is fast becoming 'mistress of the antechamber of our African empire', but these statements, though widely believed in Italy, represent what psychoanalysts call wish-fulfilment. In fact, the result of her efforts forms a kaleidoscopic pattern, sometimes good, sometimes bad; sometimes furthered, at others diminished by outside events. For instance, she enjoys a more sympathetic hearing if Great Britain is using force in Palestine; on the other hand, she lowered her reputation in Egypt when, in her enthusiasm for autarchy, she decreed an independent Coptic church for Ethiopia. Not only Egyptian Copts, but Egyptian Moslems, were incensed at this brusque severance of an old connexion between Egypt and Ethiopia.

Her propaganda is most successful in the areas which are still controlled by a western ruler, and where she can win applause by upbraiding an unpopular government. It is least successful in the more developed, independent states, in which it arouses misgivings as to her intentions. But on balance it is worth her while, for it achieves publicity. She thrusts her way into the forefront of every conversation. 'What is Great Britain doing?' says your Byzantine host, drawing you with a cautious forefinger into the farthest corner of the café. 'Come and tell me why she is not stopping the mouth of Italy. Of course I know the Italians are not really great. I have known them all my life, for I was born in Smyrna. But, upon my soul (*de tout cœur*, *mademoiselle*) nowadays I am almost driven to believe the contrary.' During 1937 I listened to this view not once but again and again.

Yet much of Italy's propaganda would fall on deaf ears were it not for the extraneous factor which has won her a hearing—namely, her success in a war of conquest. The Near and Middle East is impressed less by her broadcasts, her bribes, or her newsreels than by the fact that she flouted Great Britain, and pursued her Ethiopian plans, despite the massing of the British fleet at Alexandria. Arabs draw the conclusion that she is a force to be reckoned with, and that they might be wise to listen to what she has to say.

Such was her reputation in 1936. Her problem is: how to maintain it, and this task is no light matter for an expansionist power who is surrounded by rising tides of nationalism. At every stage of her campaign, Italy is dogged by the difficulty which has already reared its head in this chapter—that of reconciling the language which she uses to hearten her own people with that which she needs in order to woo the rest of the world. She is setting out on her 'historic mission' just at the moment when the Near East is turning anti-missionary, when it is beginning to build a brave new world, but wants to do so unaided. She is pushing at a door which is gradually closing, not only against herself, but against the hated patronage of all western nations.

5. *Summary: Third Player Plays High*

Whichever way she turns, and however peacefully she seeks to expand, modern Italy cannot escape the fact that her geographical position is no longer the advantage it was in the days of Augustus or Trajan. In terms of twentieth-century trade and strategy, it is weak because it is dependent on the goodwill of states which have sprung into being in the years between—not only of great powers like Great Britain and France, but of smaller ones like Turkey, Egypt, and Spain.

Italy's strength in the Mediterranean of to-day is that of a blackmailer and potential destroyer. She occupies a magnificent strategic position astride the centre of the sea, and from a choice of bases on her mainland and her islands, in Albania and in Libya, she can cut all communications both with the Adriatic and along the main route from east to west. She has the strength of a Samson who can pull down the pillars of Gaza, but she is ill-placed for securing benefits out of the wreck.

For her position is otherwise weak. Even if she could lay in the stores to stand a siege, she has a very vulnerable coast-line, and she is separated from her new empire by two stretches of sea over which she has not full control, and which modern attacking power has turned into one long canal.

She therefore needs Mediterranean allies, and here her problems begin. If she would play for safety, the obvious choice is the Anglo-French combine, for, until she has rendered her East African Empire self-supporting, her interests coincide with theirs along the sea-route beyond Suez. But the new Italy, like all who are touchy about their status, resents the complacency of the established landowners. Moreover, the staid, conservative game they play is too slow for her. She scored below the line when she won Ethiopia, and, if possible, she would like to finish the rubber. Third player plays the highest he can.

Hence the nature of her policy. So far as the great powers are concerned, her problem is one of choosing the right moment and the right ally for improving her position. In 1934 she thought this was Germany; in 1935 she realized her mistake, sized up Monsieur Laval, and switched to Paris; by the end of 1936 she was negotiating with England; in 1937 Germany's turn had come round again; in the spring of 1938, the Germans had disappointed her, and she was back in her pre-War position, hovering between the central and the western European powers. The only constant factor in her calculations is her determination to keep open the road to every capital.

Among the small powers, she needs allies, and especially Mediterranean allies, in order to strengthen her bargaining power. In the west, she helps General Franco; in the east, she courts the Levant. But here her difficulties begin to accumulate. The quality for which small powers look in a great ally is consistency. Bewildered by Italy's vagaries in the great capitals, her small neighbours are shy of accepting her advances; they are polite, but reserved. Moreover, they see cause for alarm in the talk of historic missions and expansion with which she excites the emotions of her own people; it is distasteful to their ears, and a bad prelude to alliance. Her problem is to reconcile these conflicting aspects of her home and foreign policy. The task which she has set for herself in the Mediterranean does not depend upon Fascist driving power alone; it demands tact and skill in handling nations whose feelings are easily ruffled. Indeed, it seems to call for the subtlety of medieval Florence rather than for the grand manner which Fascism has borrowed from Ancient Rome.

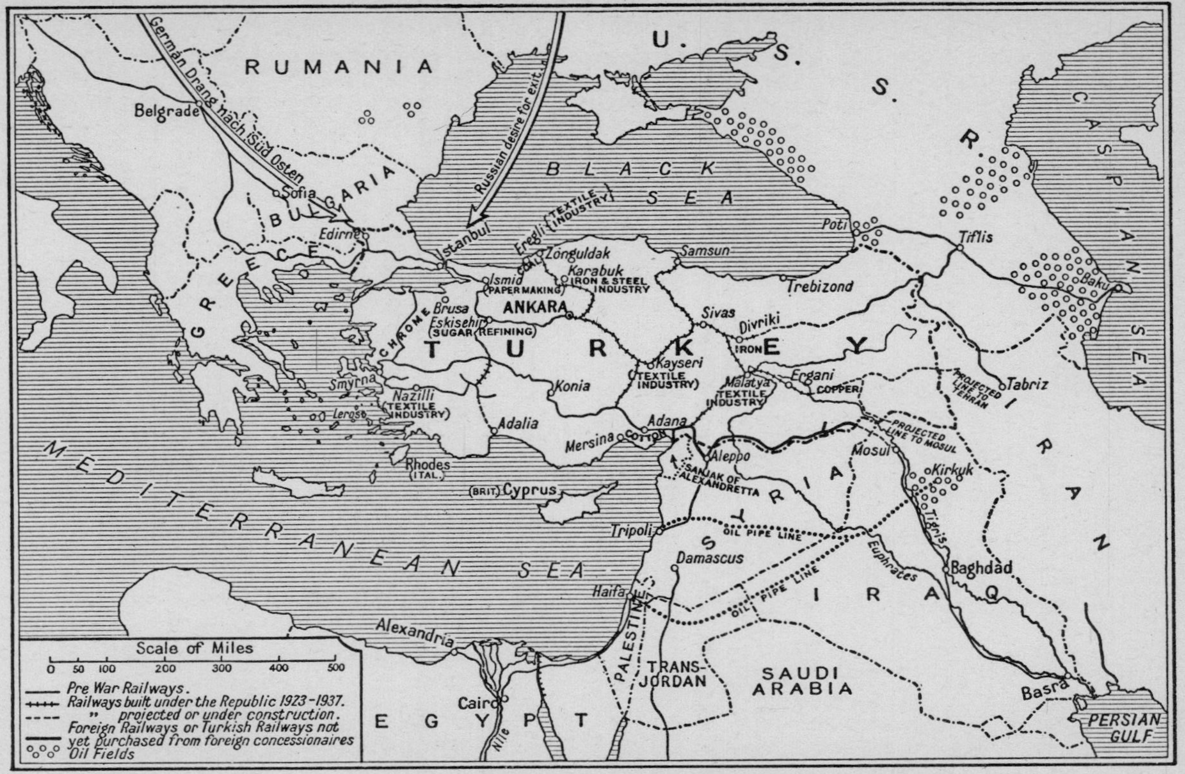

IV. TURKISH INTERESTS

CHAPTER V

NEXT OF KIN: TURKEY

At the moment, Great Britain, France, and Italy are the only three states who try to influence the Mediterranean peoples by means of strength, wealth, or culture. They used to encounter three competitors—Austria-Hungary, Germany, Russia—but of these, one has disappeared, one was crippled by the Peace Treaty and is only now returning to the fray, and the third, while she still dominates the Black Sea and is deeply interested in the arrangements made at its exit, has for years been too busy in her own vast territories to pay much attention to diplomacy in the sea beyond the Straits. On the other hand, three smaller powers can influence Mediterranean policy because they are geographically well placed. Egypt, Turkey, and Spain have all been great in their day; any one of the three may become so again. For some years to come, however, the most nearly great seems likely to be Turkey, who is more powerful than either of the others because her people are at one and her home politics stable, and because her state is directed by a man of wisdom, vision, and courage who is possibly the ablest statesman alive to-day.

Her renaissance deserves some description.

The old Turkey, as the seat of the Caliphate, belonged more to the Middle East than to Europe. The gulf which divides the new Turkey from the Middle Eastern countries has to be seen to be realized. She differs from the most advanced of them—Egypt—in every way except that both peoples are nationalist. Her distinctive features are not all the result of her president's will or originality, for some of them are inherent in the Turkish character; but, whatever their origin, they are very marked after fifteen years only of her new régime.

The difference is ascribable to various causes. A

modernizing movement had been longer afoot in Turkey than elsewhere in the Near East; the Young Turks of the Committee of Union and Progress had been making persistent efforts towards westernization for fifty years before the War. Again, in spite of the Caliphate, the Moslem faith was less part and parcel of national life than it is in the states which speak the language of the Koran. A ruler of Egypt, for instance, could not 'deliver politics from religion', and disestablish Islam, without shocking—indeed, outraging—opinion, whereas in Turkey the change happened nearly as easily as did the similar change in France. Again, the Anatolian peasant who now composes the bulk of Turkey's population offers good material upon which to work. For centuries he has excelled at nothing except soldiering, but in that profession he has learnt to bear burdens and to obey. Therefore, when he is told that he must drop his gun and become a bank clerk, an insurance agent, or a worker in a steel foundry, and to build a modern state, he downs the one tool and assumes the other to some purpose.

But ingredients alone do not make a dish; the crowning explanation of the difference is the hand of the master. Mustapha Kemal Atatürk enjoys the esteem of the Turkish nation to a degree which surpasses the feelings of Italy for Mussolini, or Germany for Hitler. Like them, he started to build upon ruins, but he is invested with especial prestige because he is a genuine *Ghazi*—that is, a victor who has proved his generalship in the field. He is the man who drove out the Greeks, stood up to the Allies, and secured the only non-dictated Peace Treaty. But above all, his position is superior to that of the Führer or Duce in that his people *trust* him, with never a twinge of uneasy fear that he might gamble too high. The Ghazi is sure of his aims; his strength lies in the fact that his people are sure of them too. They rely upon him, and on a band of good lieutenants who work with him—among them his present and ex-Prime ministers, Çelal Bayar and Ismet Inonü, and his Foreign Minister, Tewfik Rüshdü Aras. The plans which he has laid for fifty years ahead contain no element of risk; they stand upon a four-square national foundation, and do not depend for their execution upon one man's life or popularity.

Some of the changes made by the Ghazi were spectacular and are well known, especially those which altered the look or manners of the nation—the abolition of the veil and fez, the adoption of the European calendar, of Latin characters, and of new surnames. A bevy of changes, less obvious but just as fundamental, accompanied his renunciation of Islam. The Caliphate was abolished in 1924 as an institution for which there was 'no room in a national state'; in 1926 religious and family law were replaced by a western civil code; in 1928 Islam ceased to be the established religion; in 1929 the teaching of Arabic and Persian —the classical tongues equivalent to Latin and Greek in an English school—was replaced by that of European languages, and in 1932 the Koran and prayers were first read in Turkish in the mosques of Istanbul, and were broadcast from there to the nation. The sight of 'BUY TURKISH' written in neon lighting in a mosque suitably crowns this list of innovations.

Decree after decree has remoulded the private life of the individual, but each forming part of an ambitious long-term plan—the production of an independent, self-supporting Turkey. 'I am happy to declare to you that we shall tolerate no obstacle that could impede the march of our nation towards the level of civilization and happiness which it deserves.'[1]

The words ring familiar; we have heard them from Fascists and Bolsheviks. The striking feature about the Turkish dictatorship is that it has contrived to steer clear of both these extremes; that it is moderate; that it does not

[1] The Ghazi to the National Assembly, November 1, 1937.

dramatize its actions; that some of its reforms are so unobtrusive that the nation only wakes to them when they are achieved. By comparison with the Fascist or Nazi, the new Turk is tolerant. Just as Islam, though disestablished, is not frustrated, and is better off than the church in Germany, so self-sufficiency, though preached, is not a fetish. The Ghazi is not working for severance from the rest of the world, but for the creation of a state which could stand upon its own legs if required—for instance, in time of war.

Fortune favours him in that Turkey is endowed with adequate supplies of almost all the essential raw materials. She can feed herself; her soil produces fuel, the chief metals, and all the important fibres; moreover, she has a choice of accessible oil resources—Mosul, Rumania, south Russia. Few nations are so well off. Where she was not independent was in her business life; her industry was non-existent, and her public utilities, banking, and commerce were in the hands of foreigners. The pre-War Turk was either a pasha, a civil servant, or a peasant, and all other walks of life were occupied by Armenians, Greeks, or westerners.

Here the Ghazi's campaign became ruthless, for he was determined that Turks should fill all roles. He drove out the Greeks by means of a victorious war, by the sack of Smyrna, and by the famous exchange of populations with Greece, which drew life-blood from Istanbul, and filled Athens with people ranging from wealthy trader to humble boot-black who, when you ask them what part of Greece they come from, still answer: 'Je suis Grec de Constantinople.' The Armenians he either killed, dispersed, or drove towards the Caucasian republics. The only minority remaining in Turkey to-day consists of 1,200,000 Kurds, and even these are being forcibly Turkified.

To rid the country of these foreign elements was no light responsibility; the step caused the disappearance of much wealth and business experience, but the Ghazi and his lieutenants were full of confidence when they began to build their new republic out of the wreck. Wreck is the right word to use, for the country was devastated not only by the World War, but by defeat in wars waged almost continuously from 1911 onwards, and uncrowned by a single victory until 1923. It was like a man of property stripped naked and told to start life again.

'In order to achieve this feat within the shortest possible time,' says the Ghazi, 'we must cause thought and action to march hand in hand.' Action might have lagged behind had the Turk been left to himself, so the state began to supervise both industry and commerce in order to hasten the metamorphosis. In theory, private enterprise is encouraged in Turkey and private businesses still prosper; in practice, the state now manages so much of the nation's economic life that it strangles businesses which do not conform to its rationalization plans. Through a growing number of commercial banks founded with state capital—an Industrial Bank, a Mining Bank, a Maritime Bank, and so on—it is coming to control the whole mechanism.

The symbol of these drastic changes is the city of Ankara. Istanbul, for all its history and culture, stood for the Turkey of the Sublime Porte—a museum piece which reeked of foreign dominance and easy living, a lovely but seductive place where men had been accustomed to grow lazy and fat. The Ghazi made up his mind to remove the new generation from the clutches of this Circe. He transplanted the capital on to a windswept plateau in the middle of Asia Minor, whose invigorating air braces his people to greater energy and harder work. At the foot of an old brigand keep, a new city has sprung up, devoid of minarets, but full of stern, purposeful banks and ministries.

No one could fail to be impressed by the achievement which Ankara represents; that the miracle has been so quickly wrought is due not only to will but to wisdom. The Turkish state has not hesitated to spend its money on good advice, and has employed the best foreign experts available. For instance, it has consulted the American firm of Wallace Clark on business management, and it has profited by the banishment of many brilliant Jews from Germany to secure Hindemith for its Conservatoire, Nissen for its College of Surgeons, and Carl Ebert—who is well known to Englishmen for his productions at Glyndebourne—for its School of Dramatic Art. Moreover, it propagates the knowledge of these experts by an original method; it educates all students free of charge, but, for every year studied, each pupil is required to give two years of paid teaching or administrative service to the state.

Critics will tell you that Ankara is only a façade, since the rest of the country is still as poor and backward as in the days of the Sultans. It is true that other parts of Anatolia are far behind, that peasants live as their fathers lived, that more than half of them are illiterate, and that the nation as a whole is still pitifully poor. For proof, you have only to look at its budget, which, though the country is as large as France, is smaller than that of Paris, or at the low note circulation in proportion to the size of the population, or at the dilapidated farm-houses and towns which you pass even when travelling on a main line. Nothing can erase these impressions, though they are mitigated by the sight of a huge iron and steel works under erection in a wild tract of country, or by that of a wayside station littered with trucks and crates out of which bulge pieces of hyper-modern machinery. Study the whole picture and you will gain the impression that Ankara is not a façade but a kernel; it is the seed of a movement which will grow, but which, despite the determination of its apostles, must take decades to reach the more remote among a poor and ignorant people. However, there are signs of its progress. Among a choice of instances, one is a steady rise in the number of small savings-bank deposits; another, a curious sight which assails you as your train draws into a wayside

Anatolian station—boys running alongside the carriages begging, not for the baksheesh to which Near Eastern travel has accustomed you, but for '*Gazete*, *Gazete*, newspapers, newspapers', because they have no books and want something—anything—to read. Undoubtedly, Ankara's influence is spreading. All Turkey needs is fifty years of peace in which to let it spread, and possibly, the development of a little more self-criticism in her disciples. No mistake has yet been made at the centre, and the mental state of the younger Turk is that of an individual who has lived his life in a harmonious family directed by a capable father; it remains to be seen whether he is fitted to meet a set-back or a buffet from the wicked world.

Thus much of an account of Turkey's internal affairs is essential to an understanding of her position in the Mediterranean. She is united and sturdy, self-reliant, and potentially self-supporting; she has a first-class and well-equipped army, and her finances are sound. Her budget, though small, is balanced; despite her purchases for equipment, her trade balance has been favourable in every year since 1930 and, though taxation is desperately heavy, her revenues are increasing. So satisfactory a record at home inevitably increases her influence abroad.

During the first years of her reconstruction campaign, she was obliged to lean on a foreign ally. Great Britain was out of the question because she had encouraged Greek aspirations in Anatolia. The choice lay between France, Italy, and Russia, all of whom had helped Mustapha Kemal. Despite old enmities, he chose Russia, drawn to her by the common menace of Allied intervention. A close alliance between the two countries dates from 1921, when they alarmed Europe by signing treaties not only with one another but with Persia and Afghanistan, which seemed to point either to a Communist bloc in eastern Asia or else to the birth of another bogy, pan-Turanianism—that is, the uniting of the Turks of the Caucasus, south-eastern Russia, and Central Asia under the leadership of the Ottoman Turks. But these forebodings came to nothing, because Mustapha Kemal concentrated on home affairs, and because he contrived to embrace Russia without also embracing Bolshevism.

As Turkey grew stronger she became unwilling to depend exclusively upon one ally. She settled her chief quarrel with Great Britain when she accepted the Mosul Boundary decision in 1926; she signed a treaty with Italy in 1928; she patched her many bitter quarrels with Greece in 1930; in 1932 she joined the League of Nations, and in 1933 the Balkan Pact. She became a leader among her small neighbours and more independent of great power support.

The only subsequent threat to this position came from Germany. Reference has been made to the device by which Dr. Schacht captured the hesitating buyers of the Balkans and Levant. Turkey was at one time among its chief victims, so much so that Germany in 1936 enjoyed no less than 45 per cent. of her import and 51 per cent. of her export trade, and threatened her with a degree of dominance which approached a stranglehold. The device worked as follows. Profiting by the existence of exchange restrictions, German buyers offered for local products at prices above the normal world level. They found willing sellers and ran up large bills. Such goods as Germany did not need they re-exported at a loss to other countries; for instance, they resold Balkan tobacco in exchange for Swedish copper. But they recouped their losses in the Balkans. They told Turkey and others that, owing to the German exchange position, payment could only be made in blocked marks—that is, in German goods, and they offered these goods at inordinately high prices. Turkey had either to buy or else to whistle for her money. Simultaneously, some of the many Germans in Ankara, profiting by the position, began to behave rather dictatorially. The

Turks, their hey-day of selling over, began to feel that they had been tricked. In order to steer clear of further deceptions, and to reduce German influence, their subsequent policy has been to develop relations in other directions, notably with Great Britain.

The Turco-British *rapprochement*, which is now in full swing, is due to several factors, of which the chief is a shared desire for a long term of peace, and a consequent liking for the Mediterranean *status quo*. Its warmth is perhaps due to certain likenesses between the Turkish and English characters. At a time when political thought is distressingly lacking in half-tones, each likes and respects the moderation shown by the other; both are slow-thinking, phlegmatic, dogged peoples. In 1935 they were thrown together by disapproval of Italy's foreign policy and her methods in Ethiopia. In 1936 the Turks marked their appreciation by appointing the British firm of Sir Alexander Gibb as their consulting engineers for public works. In the autumn of the year, the visit of Edward VIII to their country caused excitement and pleasure. The number of times you hear this mentioned is flattering; so is the number of Turks who tell you that they are learning English since he came. The friendship prospers on all sides under the influence of a popular and successful British ambassador, Sir Percy Loraine. But it has disturbed none of Turkey's other relations; she is still allied to Russia and friendly with Germany. She is on good terms with all the great powers, but is independent of them—a feat which she has achieved by her straight dealing and her moderation.

Though Turkey is fully occupied at home, and is in no mood for risky foreign gambles, she has three times in the last few years used her new strength in order to improve her international position. On each occasion she has been successful, because the Ghazi chose his moment well, and played his cards with assurance—first over the Middle

Eastern Pact, then over the Straits Convention, and lastly over the Sanjak of Alexandretta.

The Middle Eastern Pact negotiations took place at Geneva in the autumn of 1935. Till then, Turkey had not been on good terms with some of her eastern neighbours. Iraq had been a British mandate, and frontier disputes with Iran had been a source of friction for generations. But Italy's expansionist policy quickened a desire for alliance in every Near Eastern state; hence a hasty settlement of differences between the three countries, and their signature, with Afghanistan, of a Four Power Pact on July 8, 1937. Iran was the initiator of the project, but Turkey, as the most developed of the four nations, is its leader and spokesman. The other three look up to her as a model of modernity, and a pattern which they hope to copy. She is busy building roads and railways which run directly from her territory into theirs, and when these are completed she becomes the western mouthpiece and outlet for the ideas and the trade of a compact and important group of states.

The Straits negotiations have already been described—how Turkey seized the moment in 1936 when the League had proved ineffective for the defence of small powers, and when the remilitarization of the Rhineland had provided her with a precedent; how she took advantage of these favourable circumstances in order to get her way by lawful means instead of by the *fait accompli* policy used by Italy and Germany, and how she earned moral prestige as the good boy of Europe.

The new Straits Convention is in many ways less desirable than the old. It is a step back to the pre-War *status quo*, and Lord Curzon would turn in his grave were he to see the rebirth of all the dangers which he laboured so hard to remove in 1923. On the other hand, Turkey benefits enormously by the change. It enabled her to do a good turn to her ally Russia, who was anxious to obtain (as she did) a one-way-traffic arrangement for her battleships—an arrangement which enables them to pounce out of their lair in the Black Sea, but which limits the number of ships that can pursue them into it. In other words, so long as Turkey and Russia are allies, the 1936 Straits Convention enormously strengthens Russia's Mediterranean position. But, above all, Turkey has gained in strategic strength. She has become the arbiter of the Black Sea traffic both in men-of-war and in petroleum. More than this, the article of the Convention which enables her to close the Straits to warships, not only in war-time, but upon 'general or special threat of war', in effect enables her to tip the scales in favour of one set of would-be belligerents, thus making her friendship highly desirable to Mediterranean powers and virtually essential to the Black Sea states. In fact, she is in a master position.

The tale of the Sanjak of Alexandretta is less straightforward. It goes back to an Anglo-French quarrel of 1921 as to the treatment to be meted out to Greek and Turk regarding Anatolia and the Straits, as a result of which M. Franklin-Bouillon bustled off to Ankara and offered favours and munitions to Mustapha Kemal. Among the favours was the settlement of a Turco-Syrian frontier which restored Cilicia to Turkey, but which left the semi-Turkish Sanjak of Alexandretta in Syria, in return for which the French guaranteed special language and cultural rights to the Turks in the area. France kept her promise, and those special rights were afterwards several times confirmed.

The story skips to 1936. The Blum government which came into power in the May of that year showed great sympathy for the Moslems under its rule, and promised a treaty on the Iraqi model to Syria, but, when that treaty was published in September, it was found to include no specific provision for the rights of the Sanjak Turks. Turkey saw her moment and seized it. To her, Alexandretta represented a valuable strategic and commercial prize. On the one hand, it is the best natural harbour in the Levant; on the other, it is a better outlet than is Mersina for the produce of eastern Cilicia, but such Turkish merchants as used it had for years been obliged to pay exorbitant freight rates on the twenty-five miles of French railway which led to it through Syrian territory. In October 1936, the Turks protested at the Franco-Syrian treaty and demanded a special status for the Sanjak. The quarrel hung on a matter of interpretation; France declared that her treaty with Syria covered the protection of all minorities, and that she would see that the Syrian Government observed the Sanjak guarantees. This declaration did not satisfy the Turks. They maintained that France had no right to transfer her engagements to a raw young government without asking so much as a by your leave of Turkey, while, in reply to France's assertion that she would supervise the guarantees, they pointed a warning finger to the fate of the Assyrians in Iraq, and pertinently asked her how she proposed to intervene if matters went wrong.

Many people would like to know whether France omitted to mention the Sanjak accidentally or on purpose. On the face of things, she seemed to be improvident, for she added to the complications of an already tangled international situation, and the best explanation of an apparent lack of foresight is that an impetuous Under-Secretary for Foreign Affairs, Monsieur Viénot, was in a hurry to secure Moslem approval for the *Front Populaire* government, and worked fast and thoughtlessly.

The dispute was laid before the League of Nations, under whose auspices France and Turkey reached an agreement in May 1937 on terms which benefited every one, and which were unpopular only in Syria. Turkey secured a free zone at Alexandretta for an annual rent of one gold pound, and an autonomous régime for her protégés. She also obtained the demilitarization of a potential foreign base on her border. France retained her supervision over that base through a French commissioner who was to represent the League in the area. Syria was freed of the burden of administering a dissident part of her territory which was bound to hamper her in the first years of her independence, while she retained control over its customs, monetary affairs, and foreign relations; her objection to the settlement was the loss of 'face' which she thought it involved. But the 'settlement' proved easier to sign than to operate, for when the League attempted to run elections in the territory, the Turks objected to its methods and its bias. Turk and Frenchman remained as hostile as ever until the summer of 1938, when the tempo of events in Europe caused them to sink their differences, to jettison the League, and, with Great Britain's blessing, to sign a treaty which provided for parity in authority. On the morning in July when triumphant Turkish troops marched in to share in garrisoning the territory, Turkey obtained all for which she had asked in the beginning. Once again she had struck at the right moment and gained her end.

Success is an attribute greatly admired in the Middle East, and Turkey's achievements at home and abroad have certainly increased her prestige, though they have not yet raised her to the rank of an authoritative power all over the Arabic-speaking states. Her influence carries most weight in the countries of the Middle Eastern Pact, all of whom admire the speed at which she has modernized herself, and who hope to follow in her commercial and industrial footsteps. Egypt and Saudi Arabia view her otherwise; there, she is respected rather than admired. Both countries are still shocked at her renunciation of the true faith, and Egypt, for one, cannot forget that the Turks were her enemies in the War and marched on her Canal in 1915. Antipathy of this kind dies hard. Hence, it is risky to argue that because the Iraqis show signs of entering the Turkish orbit, the other Moslem states are bound to follow suit. Iraq is a case apart; before the War, she was a district which sent many young men—now her leaders—to the military academy or university of Istanbul. Consequently, she feels affinities with the Turk which outweigh her distaste for his atheism. The other states, by contrast, remember him rather as a foreign oppressor. Thus, though Egyptian and Turk may display friendship, they are at bottom hostile; they would be rivals if a question of leadership arose. Perhaps it will not do so; Turkey, according to her statesmen, has no desire to champion a Pan-Arab movement; she does not think it has any chance of permanent success. Moreover, one slighter and more temporary factor at present precludes Turkish influence in the more religious Arab countries. Devout Arabs admire abstemiousness and dignity, and they hear that the Ghazi displays neither of these qualities. They appreciate his business achievements, but they tell you with distaste of his informal ways; the very behaviour which wins him admiration in Moscow loses him respect in Mecca and Cairo.

To sum up, Turkey's present strength lies less in her influence in Asia than in her superb strategic position in the Mediterranean, less in her membership of Balkan agreements or in her alliance with Russia than in her independence and compactness. And compact she is determined to remain until her self-sufficiency programme is complete. Therefore, her chief need is a long period of Mediterranean peace. Her excursion into the Sanjak of Alexandretta seems likely to be her nearest approach to an outside adventure for some time to come, and even that can scarcely be described as outside. Unlike some other powers, she prefers to observe the precept of Frederick the Great that 'a village on the frontier is worth a principality two hundred miles away'.

CHAPTER VI

SICK MAN OF EUROPE: SPAIN

THE superb strategic position with which nature and the Peace Treaty between them endowed the new Turkey is only surpassed by that of Spain. At first sight Turkey seems better placed. Whereas the Bosphorus looks like a river, and gives an impression of proprietorship because it is Turkish on both banks, the Straits of Gibraltar are unmistakably the high seas; what is more, their southern shore is Moorish rather than Spanish, and the Rock after which they were christened is in foreign hands. But Spain enjoys greater advantages. She stands at the junction of several of the world's main trade routes. She can threaten not only the Suez traffic, but the reverse stream bound from Genoa and Trieste to the Americas, and she can dominate the ocean lines from northern Europe to the Cape and Argentine, both from her Galician ports and again when they pass through the Canary Islands and along the coast of Rio de Oro. Her Balearic Isles command the route from Marseilles to North Africa, and her Riff mountains the bottleneck, called the Taza Corridor, through which French Morocco communicates with Algeria. In other words, forces operating from Spanish bases can bestride the main communications of both the British and French Empires. No wonder that Great Britain and France have striven for generations to keep Spain weak, amiable, and neutral. No wonder that Italy and Germany—both dissatisfied and both expansionist—have sought to secure her as an ally.

The civil war into which she was plunged in 1936 roused passions which, spreading far beyond her frontiers, penetrated to distant capitals and cabinet meetings. Regardless of nationality, Socialists and Communists supported the Spanish Left, Fascists and Nazis the Spanish

Right. Nor was partisan feeling confined to the political extremes; Catholics out of religious conviction, country gentlemen out of social prejudice, and intellectuals out of antipathy to totalitarian rule, each gave fervent support to one or other of the Spanish combatants.

Of the foreign capitals, therefore, only Rome, Berlin, and Moscow held clear views as to the side they wanted to win, and the losses or gains they stood to incur from its defeat or victory. London and Paris presented a contrasting picture. There, the repercussions of the war upon national strategy or diplomacy were dimly seen through a haze of conflicting emotions—emotions so strong that national interests were sometimes entirely lost to view. The object of the present chapter is to pierce that enveloping haze, and to survey the effect of the war and of intervention on the material interests of the Mediterranean powers.

Great Britain and France, who hoped to preserve the *status quo*, tried to limit the struggle to small dimensions, and therefore championed non-intervention. Since their ideal was a weak Spain, the result that would have suited them best was a stalemate—a situation in which the two Spanish factions, sickened with inconclusive fighting, and with insufficient help from their respective patrons, had turned to British and French bankers for reconstruction loans. Had this happened, the two powers would not only have remained strategically secure, but could have worked to recover any losses caused by the war among their considerable Spanish investments.[1] From a purely self-interested standpoint, any other result was less satisfactory to them. A victory for the extreme Left would have caused misgivings in Great Britain if it had encouraged Communist

[1] France is the larger investor; French interests hold perhaps 60 per cent. of the total foreign investment in Spain. The British share, representing about 20 per cent. of the whole, lies chiefly in mining, and was in 1937 estimated at £40 millions.

tendencies in France. But, once the expansionist powers were openly helping General Franco, a victory for the extreme Right presented even graver drawbacks. Won at the cost of Spanish subservience to Italy or Germany, or both, it threatened both the British and French Empires with strategic, diplomatic, and perhaps even economic difficulties.

Some Englishmen brushed aside the strategic threat as negligible. They held that the Italians would never retain a footing in Spain, because Spaniard and Italian could never agree, and that General Franco could be relied upon to eject his Fascist helpers as soon as he had won the war. The German menace they also dismissed. Spanish waters, they said, were an area in which the British and French fleets could deploy with effect. Spain was easy to insulate, and any German forces operating from there could soon be immobilized.

But these arguments are over-optimistic. The first disregards the tendency of totalitarian states to act together despite human dislikes. Italy is immensely powerful in the Central Mediterranean, but weak at its either end, and, were she to gain any kind of foothold in Spain, would shatter the present delicate balance of Mediterranean forces. The second, though true as far as it goes, overlooks the main advantage that Herr Hitler can derive from dominance in Spain. His arms or influence there achieve their maximum potency, not as a war force, but as a pre-war nuisance. In the game of poker to which diplomacy is once more reduced, he heightens his chances of winning a hand if his troops can glower at France from the Pyrenees as well as the Rhine, if they can hang, spectre-like, over the French mobilization channel, and if they can look briskly efficient in the hills on either side of the Straits of Gibraltar.

Germany's bold seizure of Austria in March 1938 brought this point home to the democratic states, where many of General Franco's former supporters begán to see disadvantages in a Right Wing victory. True, the *Anschluss* lessened one menace to Great Britain and France, for it weakened the position of Italy. The Duce revealed his anxiety as to German intentions when he opened conversations with London and Paris, and, once his fidelity to Germany became doubtful, such promises as he might have secured from General Franco were automatically rendered less sinister from the point of view of Germany's adversaries. As in Austria, so in Spain, it seemed that Herr Hitler might rake in the Italian stake with the nonchalance of a croupier.

On the other hand, the flourish with which Germany accomplished the *Anschluss* thrust German expansion into the limelight. Success in Austria gave point to stories of German prowess in Spain. The British and French public began to learn that German intervention, though less obtrusive than the Italian, had been more skilful and more telling; that, whereas the Italians had provided quantity and lent front-line troops, the Germans had concentrated upon quality; that, while to the fighting forces they had lent only pilots, yet, by providing technical, civilian help, they had contrived to gain a hold on all Spain's activities, from her police and post-offices to her civil aerodromes, and some of her industries and mines. Even the most optimistic Englishman felt a twinge of anxiety when he reflected that such 'help' need not come to an end with the civil war, and that, if it were to turn the new Spain into a German vassal or an efficient German ally, it would upset all Anglo-French strategic planning. He realized that it would burden Great Britain with fresh defence liabilities in the Atlantic and at Gibraltar, and that France—the greater sufferer—would feel the strain not only at sea, but in the Pyrenees and in North Africa.

His misgivings once roused, he began to see a menace in Germany's every move. He had known for some time that she was receiving Spanish ores from General Franco in payment for services rendered; he now began to envisage a future in which the German armaments industry would secure the whole mineral output of Spain.

This, if it were feasible, would be no mean acquisition, for the list of Spanish minerals is agreeably long and varied. The chief deposits lie on the Atlantic side of the peninsula. First among them are the great reserves of iron ore in the north, near Bilbao, and, second in importance, the copper and pyrites deposits in the south-west, behind Huelva. The same region, where the British-owned Rio Tinto company is the leading concern, also yields manganese and sulphur. The biggest mercury mine in the world is at Almaden, in central Spain; there are rich potash deposits in northern Catalonia, and subsidiary supplies of iron ore are mined in Spanish Morocco.

The rumour that the Germany of the *Anschluss* was in full possession of this wealth was a flight of fancy, but the story that she was procuring increasing quantities of Spanish ores was true. The position was roughly as follows: the buyers and sellers in the international mineral market are not governments, but business houses, and, during the war, brisk sale of all Spain's minerals had continued, almost without intermission. Most firms traded with their usual customers, regardless of the political colour of the part of Spain in which they were situated. Owing partly to rearmament, but, still more, to the general business recovery which marked the year 1937, the whole world was buying more minerals, and Spanish sales were interrupted only when the mineral deposits were actually in the battle-zone. For instance, the export of iron ore from the Bilbao district fell off while General Franco was actually capturing the area, but was resumed again, its direction little changed, as soon as the mines reopened work.

Only here and there were there exceptions to this

normal procedure, the copper-mining companies being the chief sufferers. The insurgents, after capturing the Rio Tinto mines early in the war, virtually requisitioned substantial amounts of ore, paying the company in paper pesetas of unpredictable value, and handing over the copper to Germany. Thus, at the beginning of 1938, the export of iron ore was continuing much as usual, but German copper imports from Spain were increasing, and the small British import was decreasing, because the Spanish ores were going to General Franco and his friends.

Had the Englishman-in-the-street appreciated this situation, he would have seen that the cause for anxiety lay not in the present, but in the future. A glance at Germany's economic plight would have convinced even the most ardent pro-Nazi that the Germans were bound to try to increase their dominance in Spain. They were short of foreign exchange. Therefore, instead of straining to find francs and sterling in order to buy ores from Lorraine or Canada, they were seeking a hold on mining areas which would accept a medium in which they could pay—that is, which could be made to take German goods or German services. Their object was to improve their general economic position rather than to swell their total import of ores.

At this no foreigner can cavil, provided that, once the war is over and a single government rules in Spain, the rights of foreign mining firms are respected. The British firms (almost all of which are subsidiaries of British industrial concerns consuming their whole output) are in a strong position, for British goodwill is important to Spain so long as the British consumer continues to drink sherry, and to eat his present large rations of marmalade, Spanish tomatoes, and Canary potatoes. Spanish firms, of course, may be forced to sell to Germany whether they like it or no, but to suggest that the imperial powers should use their money or influence to stop these sales is to provide the Nazis with a fresh reason for wanting colonies.

From the British and French point of view, the prospect of greater German influence in Spain is less disquieting in the matter of minerals than in that of markets. If German experts were to secure all the key positions in the country, Germany would be well placed for operating the device which she has already used so skilfully in south-eastern Europe—that is, she could run up bills, offer payment in German goods or not at all, and confront the British, French, or Italian exporter with crippling competition.[1]

Economically as well as diplomatically, therefore, Germany stands a chance of worsting the democracies, and seeing a substantial reward for her intervention policy. Moreover, these are not the only disturbances which Spain holds in store for Europe; there are others, of which the worst is the future of Spanish Morocco.

General Franco's use of Moorish troops creates a rod in pickle for the three Mediterranean powers. He did not force the Moors to fight for him; they were on his side from the start, for, like their brothers in French Morocco, they approve of the leadership principle, and are attracted by Fascist phalanxes and display. They fought willingly because to do so won them money and loot. A Moor wearing several overcoats and loaded with a sewing machine or typewriter on top of his equipment was a common enough sight after a new advance, and one Englishman, queueing in a telegraph office, was asked to sign a money-order for a Moroccan soldier who could not write his name, but who was wiring 60,000 pesetas home to North Africa. The trouble lies in the western experience they have gained. Months of modern soldiering have taught them new standards and revealed new horizons. By the time they return home, their ideas for their future will no doubt

[1] For the respective positions at present, see table on p. 253.

have outstripped those of their European rulers; they will probably ask for local autonomy as the price of their service.

Such a request sounds a domestic matter, but, in fact, raises international complications. The Spanish Zone is not an integral part of Spain, but a protectorate exercised by the Spaniards on behalf of the Sultan of Morocco. In law, the Sultan's consent must be obtained for any change of the territory's status, and the Sultan's foreign minister is the Quai d'Orsay. Whatever his personal view, France will use her influence with him to prevent the establishment in Spanish Morocco of a régime for which the French Zone is not yet ready, for she knows only too well that Tetuan is in close touch with Fez, and that any changes in the former will disturb her subjects not only in French Morocco, but probably in Algeria also.

What is more, harassed Spanish statesmen who are busy patching and rebuilding on the mainland will have little energy to spare for dealing with the Moors, and might be glad surreptitiously to transfer their burden on to other shoulders. Apart from a few Falangists who like the idea of empire, the average Spaniard would not oppose the step. He would wish to keep the towns of Ceuta and Melilla, and the islands of Alcehumas and the Peñon, which have been national property ever since Philip II captured them from Portugal, but, apart from these four points, he feels no strong ties with the North African shore. To him, it is an unmanageable strip of mountain country which cost him several national disasters during the long and expensive Riff War. He has often pressed for the policy which he calls *semi-abandono*.

But, supposing he were to 'semi-abandon' it to one of his friends, he would involve himself in a web of international intrigue, for several powers would dispute the semi-succession. Germany would claim preferential treatment, but rather than see her receive it, other contestants would enter the fray. Italy would be a candidate for favours in a territory so near the Straits; France would try to prevent the Riff mountains from passing into the control of an unfriendly power; Great Britain would prefer that the coast opposite Gibraltar should remain in weak hands. The Moroccans, backed by countless Moslem sympathizers, would seize the moment to clamour for self-determination. Moreover, Great Britain, France, and Italy would all have a legal right to speak, because any such change would affect Tangier, where the Moors have followed the fortunes of the civil war almost as keenly as have their cousins across the Spanish border.

Tangier and Germany, France and the Sultan: a troupe of pre-War players is waiting in the wings, ready to strut back on to the stage if the new Spanish régime is unable to maintain the Moroccan *status quo*. If they reappear, the play will doubtless run its course, and the characters repeat their smooth words and tense string-pulling. The only difference will be that a new generation of actors will fill the roles once played by the Kaiser and Bülow, Mulay Hafid and Delcassé.

Even when the fighting is over, therefore, the Spanish situation promises toil and trouble on every side. Spain will be the poorer in men, and money, and treasures, and perhaps also in national liberty. Will any one be the richer for his pains? At the moment, Germany seems to enjoy the greatest promise of gain, but to argue that an interventionist derives nothing but profit from his intervention is to take a one-sided view. Already, most Italians will tell you that it is an expensive and a thankless pursuit. The Germans may find their task more difficult, and their hosts less hospitable, when the war is finished and when lay, pro-Nazi Falangists and religious, pro-Italian traditionalists cease to share an immediate common objective. If Herr Hitler succeeds in establishing a hold on Spain, he is likely to wield his maximum influence in the months immediately following the truce, before Spanish gratitude wanes and Spanish quarrels weaken his tenure. National characteristics change slowly, and Spanish history will only be repeating itself if the end of the fighting is the beginning of the testing-time for the foreign patron.

CHAPTER VII

FURTHER OUTLOOK: UNSETTLED

'IF I have said a single word in this book that conflicts with good conduct, with the common opinion of reasonable men and with the word of truth, let it henceforth and from this moment be unsaid.' This sentence, borrowed from Grotius, is set up as a milestone. Up till now my map of national interests in the Mediterranean has been drawn on a basis of fact, or what I believe to be fact, whereas from here onwards it encounters an extra dimension. It must abandon firm earth for thin air, fact for conjecture, if it is to conclude with a bird's-eye view of the Mediterranean as a whole. So far, except for an occasional outburst of opinion, such as that on Palestine, the statements that I have made can be checked, and, if necessary, corrected. This final chapter, on the other hand, is full of guesses and opinions on subjects about which no one can be certain.

At present, four major forces are at work in Mediterranean politics—Italian ambition, Anglo-French conservatism, the German *Drang*, and the Arab awakening. The possible fifth, which is a Russian thrust southwards, is in welcome abeyance. Russia gave her help to Spain without strategic or economic motive, and she has not reminded the Mediterranean of her latent strength since the Montreux Conference of 1936, when she caused uneasiness by securing special terms for the passage of her navy through the Black Sea Straits.

Of the other four, the Pan-Arab movement is the least well-knit, and, probably for some time to come, the least powerful. Its strength lies in the instinct, inborn in every Arab, that a fellow Arab is preferable to other men.

Starting from this assumption, the Arab who thinks at all, beyond his prayers and his livelihood, conceives of the Pan-Arab ideal as something for which he would strike a blow if occasion came his way. Only a small percentage have thought more deeply than this. The men who have received a higher education, either in a European school or at a Moslem university, usually feel that some form of organization is desirable, and worth working for, but though the end is clear in most of their minds, few have considered the means. You meet a congregation of the younger spirits, assembled from Syria, Iraq, Palestine, and Arabia proper, when you visit the American University at Beirut. They talk freely, and with vigour, and the wide range of countries from which they come renders their ideas more interesting than those of a similar group in, say, Tunis. Local groups are usually too parochially minded to be constructive on general topics.

But, whether in Tunis or on the campus at Beirut, you will encounter the same blind spot in every spokesman. When you ask him how he intends to surmount some practical obstacle, he replies airily: 'That will be all right, you'll find.' He is so self-confident that your question seems to glance off him, without entering his mind. A handful only have thought out the intricacies of a far-reaching organization, and of these, the most logical seem to have their head-quarters in Europe—at Geneva, for the Near East, and in Paris, for North Africa. After hearing the different types, and asking them questions, you are left with the impression that the Arab, though he may change in the next generation or so, is still as he has always been since his great invasion towards the north and west nearly thirteen centuries ago:

'The first great rush round the Mediterranean had shown the world the power of excited Arabs for a short spell of intense physical activity; but when the effort burnt out, the lack of endurance and routine in the Semitic mind became as evident. . . . Their civilisations had been of an abstract nature, moral and intellectual rather than applied; and their lack of public spirit made their excellent private qualities futile.'[1]

The last sentence explains in a dozen words the chief obstacle that confronts the would-be unifiers in Geneva, Paris, or Beirut. They have to contend with an age-old tendency that is natural in people who have lived a hand-to-mouth existence, subjected now to desert hardships, now to the numbing military rule of the Turks. That tendency is the instinct to grasp at an immediate objective, to seize the bird-in-hand, to display most energy where there is greatest likelihood of gain, and, therefore, to be more interested in local than in general politics. As you talk to politicians or students in the different territories, you see that each fondly imagines that the other Arab states are interested in *him*, but has little time or thought to spare for *them*. In principle, he is interested in their causes; in practice, he seldom champions them unless he can turn the topic to local account.

This contrast between thought and reality might be less marked if the Arabic-speaking world were more homogeneous—if it were all as closely related as are the Arabs of Palestine and Syria, or those of Arabia proper. But it is not. Egypt, for instance, is separate from the other states. It is the richest, and the best equipped with unifying apparatus—wireless, newspapers—and its central position indicates it as an ideal rallying-point. Its neighbours, therefore, look to it for a lead, but that lead the Egyptian is unlikely to give. For one thing, much non-Arab blood runs in his veins. He felt like a stranger when he was drafted to Mesopotamia during the War, and he actively dislikes the Syrians who have emigrated to Cairo in search of business. For another, so long as he has secured tolerable political arrangements for his own country, he is far too lethargic to start shouldering the burdens of others. The

[1] T. E. Lawrence, *Seven Pillars of Wisdom*, p. 44.

influence which he exercises upon his neighbours is therefore passive, and not the active force they suppose.

Even in the more closely related states, lack of public spirit hampers any unifying process. Despite the pacts which are now fashionable between the Arab rulers, personal considerations still take pride of place. For instance, the Emir Abdullah of Transjordan often extols Arab solidarity, but, when partition of Palestine was proposed, he acquiesced in it, disregarding the vehement opposition of all other Arabs. He welcomed it because it offered him the chance of a nobler position and a larger kingdom, and any of his fellow rulers, similarly placed, would have done the same. It follows that Arabs pay more attention to Pan-Arab matters when in opposition than when in power. Those in the latter happy state must concentrate their whole energy on retaining office; the first have nothing to lose, and welcome any argument which might discomfit their foreign 'protector' or their political adversary; an Egyptian politician is seldom so loud in his support of the Palestinian Arabs as when he wishes to unseat a premier who is negotiating with Great Britain. Thus, when Pan-Arab enthusiasts hold a congress, as they did in Syria in 1937, the participants are malcontents rather than men of authority. The Arab kings are not represented, and the cabinet ministers who accept invitations are seized at the last moment with illness or pressure of work, and stay away. In fact, wherever you go, you see evidence that the centrifugal force of self-interest is stronger than the centripetal force of racial unity.

Whether these relative strengths will one day be reversed is a question that baffles every observer. As in French North Africa, unity of thought is bound to grow as education improves, wireless sets grow cheaper, and air liners increase the radius over which they deliver daily bundles of Egyptian newspapers. Already, the rift is narrowest where communications are best—that is, between Syria and Palestine, where cheap and frequent buses cross the frontier. On the other hand, distance is easier to conquer than is ingrained habit. Despite these contacts, a Syrian of Damascus is still more interested in a minor cabinet shuffle at home than in a cataclysm in Jerusalem. What is more, the nationalist ideas he is imbibing from Europe, and which whet his desire for an emblem, a coloured shirt, and an army, increase his tendency to concentrate on local ambitions. In fact, so strong are these growing that, if the idealists of the American University would rouse him to thoughts of a wider movement, they must quickly produce a Messiah of startling and unquestioned greatness.

Even were they to do so, the Pan-Arab movement would still be at a disadvantage *vis-à-vis* the west because of its scantier financial resources. The Koran forbids the lending of money upon interest. In Egypt, the Moslem is just beginning to disregard this precept, but, elsewhere, his practice is to hoard his gold for himself and his family rather than entrust it to other hands in hope of gain. Thus, when a Moslem state wishes to take an expensive step, it must look to foreign capital, because local money is not forthcoming. For instance, Syria, mistrustfully but of necessity, is negotiating with the Iraq Petroleum Company over prospection for its supposed wealth of oil. The same limitation applies to armaments. A state thus handicapped cannot hope to float a local armaments loan; on the other hand, armies are nowadays too expensive to finance out of ordinary revenue or a king's privy purse.

Yet even educated Arabs are oblivious to this weakness. Syrian graduates of the American University, displaying a parade of their local shirt movement in Damascus, will explain, in their fluent English, that it is the nucleus of their army; 'for we are to have an army, and become a great state'. When you ask who will meet the cost of equipment, they answer that the Government will pay.

You point out that, in order that Britain shall be great, you pay income tax at 5*s*. 6*d*. in the pound, but their polite, incredulous smiles show you that their minds cannot absorb news so undreamt-of and so strange. Weak in funds, and weak in armaments, the Arab world will for years be powerless against Europe so long as Europe is at peace.

Its importance as a force in Mediterranean affairs, negligible when the western powers are united, swells to quite other dimensions if they divide and go to war. But, even were this to happen, the Arabs are not necessarily capable of turning the situation to Pan-Arab account. Here again, the fatal interest of the individual in local and personal matters is likely to defeat the wider aim. Regardless of the alignments in Europe, each Arab area would be influenced by two considerations. Each would tend to side *against* the western power whom it associated most closely with past oppression, or else *with* the western power who proved readiest with supplies of money and armaments. Islam would probably fight on both sides, as it did in the World War; for, where the Caliphate was too weak to hold it together in 1915, the more ephemeral Pan-Arab movement is unlikely to succeed in the nineteen-thirties or 'forties.

To this impulsive, inchoate Arab movement, the world offers no more effective contrast than the mighty German machine, ticking over with clockwork precision as it pours a stream of goods into south-eastern Europe, officials into Spain, or soldiers and swastikas into their appointed places in Austria. The policy of *Drang nach Süden*, discarded, in *Mein Kampf*, in favour of a thrust towards the east and the Ukraine, has been taken down from its shelf, dusted of its cobwebs, and restored to favour.

The initial trials, carried out along the line of the Danube, led towards the Bosphorus and Aegean. In that direction, German policy has been bearing economic fruit since 1935. The system adopted—that evolved by Dr. Schacht—has already been described as capturing the trade of Turkey; the same device was applied to all the states producing raw materials, and, at its zenith, procured for the Germans a firm hold on the economy of Hungary, Rumania, Yugoslavia, Bulgaria, and Greece. In every state of south-eastern Europe, except Albania, Germany forged ahead at the expense of Great Britain, Italy, and other industrial exporters.[1]

She enjoys her hey-day when times are worst. She met with a temporary reverse in 1937, when a rise in the world price of Balkan products enabled a few sellers to evade her grasp, and to market their goods elsewhere, but only Turkey seems resilient enough to struggle against her in moments of real depression. The other peoples—even when, like the majority of the Greeks, they are unwilling victims—see no way of freeing themselves until prices show a general recovery.

Undoubtedly, Germany's Balkan policy increases her political as well as her economic strength. If creditors cannot afford to cut their losses, nor sellers to lose their German markets, most of south-eastern Europe must either ally with her, or else remain discreetly neutral. She can therefore count upon increased power of resistance to blockade.[2] Pursuing her efforts further, she might secure a door to the Mediterranean which would enable her to compete more effectively in Middle Eastern markets; she might even open a way to ports and aerodromes from which to glower at the Mediterranean Powers each time she contemplated a further essay in expansion.

[1] See table on p. 253.

[2] Even were she to dispose of the entire resources of the Balkans and Turkey, Germany would not be completely self-sufficient. Thanks to improved production, she would be a little better off than she was in 1914–18, but she would still lack fats and dairy produce, coffee and cocoa, and—among industrial raw materials—nickel, manganese, and three-quarters of her iron.

Happily for Mediterranean tranquillity, these last suggestions are suppositions only. Germany has achieved an economic advance, but she cannot convert it into a political victory unless she handles her vassals with skill. If she treats any one else as she treated Austria, she will alarm all the states who possess German minorities. If she administers too severe a dose of Prussianism, she may alienate, rather than subdue, the easy-going peoples of the Danube. After all, the methodical humiliations which her Storm-Troopers inflicted upon the Jews of Vienna revolted all well-bred Viennese.

If her purpose is to secure a footing on the Mediterranean, Germany has nowhere quite achieved her goal. She has a long way to go before she is invited to make herself at home in Greek or Turkish waters; if cordial receptions are any criterion, she is closer to success in Spain. But there is a third means to her end—the most satisfactory because it is the nearest home, and, both strategically and economically, the most convenient; she can fabricate a dependable alliance on the Adriatic. Couching her invitation in the tones in which the spider of fable addressed the fly, she can make advances to Yugoslavia. The other and better alternative is to bribe or mesmerize Italy. Herr Hitler will take his shortest cut to Mediterranean greatness if he can capture the allegiance of the Duce.

No one can understand to the full the horrid dilemma in which the *Anschluss* placed the Italians without making an excursion into their psychology and history.

One of Italy's ambitions is *mare nostrum*, but this is as nothing compared with another which is ever present in her mind—her desire to be looked upon and treated as a power of the first magnitude. Those who would account for this foible must bear in mind the humiliation which, in Italian eyes, the nation suffered at Versailles.

Foreigners may scoff at this interpretation of the Peace Treaties, and argue that Italy did as well as any of her fellow victors, in that she secured over seven thousand square miles of precious European territory, bringing with it one of the best land frontiers in the world. But whatever foreigners think, the fact remains that Italians consider that they were slighted. A whole room in the Exhibition of the Fascist Revolution is devoted to their chagrin, and people who suffer from such a complex instinctively turn to those who, by treating them as important, help them to erase a bitter memory.

These facts throw light upon the history of the last two years. By the beginning of 1937, Italy, proud and imperial, was ready to parley with all the world. But when the democracies refused to recognize her new Empire, she interpreted their refusal as a return to their old slighting attitude. Astutely enough, Herr Hitler stepped into the breach. The Germans, who still nurse memories of Italy's defection in 1915, instinctively mistrust and despise Italians, but a totalitarian state can surmount this difficulty. Displaying considerable psychological insight, the Nazis dispatched delegation after delegation to Rome. Be-medalled generals, uniformed labour corps, and detachments of German ex-service men saluted Italy's flag, paid homage to her unknown warrior, and shouted '*Duce, Duce*', in the Piazza Venezia, until the Italians believed that Germany, alone among the western powers, appreciated their greatness. The result was the Rome-Berlin axis.

Germany's action over the *Anschluss* revealed the falsity of this belief. At the time, some observers suspected a bargain between the dictators, but any one who happened to spend those March days in Rome knows that this suspicion is unfounded. Signor Mussolini is far too skilled a statesman willingly to have subjected his people to the shock they suffered when they heard the news. Nor would a man of his ability have deprived the cities of the north, without a word of warning, of the trade position he had so painstakingly acquired for them in Austria. He and they were nonplussed. 'Did our dead die in vain?' strangers asked one another, in cafés, in trains and—on the first day—even at street corners. 'For why did we fight the War, except to rid ourselves of great-power pressure on our northern frontier?'

Because it destroyed her faith in Germany, the *Anschluss* forced Italy to readjust her policy. As an immediate measure she protected herself by negotiating with France and Great Britain. But, taking a longer view, she was confronted with a perplexing question: Where did her ultimate interests lie? Would she be better advised to check the German *Drang nach Süden* by allying with the Anglo-French combine, or should she endorse Germany's programme, join in perpetrating expansionist *coups*, and hope that Herr Hitler would show her less cavalier treatment in the future?

Seen in the light of recent German policy, both courses present disadvantages.

Herr Hitler, of course, wants her friendship, not for its own sake, but as a contribution to Germany's bargaining power. Thus, if Italy shows signs of drawing nearer to the democracies, he will no doubt try to check her. Even if he keeps the letter of his promise about the inviolability of the Brenner frontier, he has several means of putting pressure on the Duce. He can stir disaffection among the compact German minority in South Tirol; he can undermine the prosperity of Trieste by deflecting to some other port the valuable transit trade coming from Austria, Hungary, and Czechoslovakia, or he can tamper with Italy's supremacy in the Adriatic by courting Yugoslavia.

On the other hand, to ally with Germany places Italy in a position of peculiar inferiority, for, however hard she may strike bargains about spheres of influence and division of spoils, she has no means of forcing the Germans to observe the conditions set. Her forty millions are no match for the seventy millions on her northern frontier, nor can she compete, in foreign states, with the efficient trading methods of Dr. Schacht. She can be bullied into submission whenever Germany sees fit to double-cross her.

The prospect would be less intolerable if she and Germany cherished different aims, but, unfortunately for her, their objectives are the same. Both wanted Austria as a satellite; both want to mother Hungary; both want Balkan influence and Balkan markets. In view of the rising tide of German trade not only in Greece and Turkey, but in Iran and Egypt, Italy has no guarantee that both will not want supremacy in the Mediterranean also. Once Germany enters the field, *mare nostrum* may be farther away than ever. Beset, either way, with patent drawbacks, Italy is, in many eyes, a German prisoner already.

Moreover, the advantages which she can derive from either alliance do not offset these liabilities, for they are speculative and imprecise by comparison. They would be clearer if she were sure what she wanted—if she could settle upon a single aim, instead of darting hither and thither, like an advertiser in the Agony Column who is prepared to 'go anywhere, do anything'. At one moment, she feels that she would do best to adopt a sober course, and consolidate her gains; when she is in this mood, the Duce's speeches direct national energies towards the development of Ethiopia. At another, she is tempted by visions of immediate, gangster successes—bold strokes which would enable her to snatch an advantage, perhaps in the Suez Canal Zone, perhaps in Tunisia. Her problem is the ancient choice between a bird in the hand, and two in the bush.

She wavers, for her experts are divided. One group, led by the military caste of which Marshal Badoglio is typical, points to the lesson of the *Anschluss*. Italy, they say, was caught napping, with troops and equipment spread over East Africa, Libya, and Spain. Experience should teach her that she cannot simultaneously maintain her authority in the north and pursue adventures to south, east, and west. They would prefer to see her play for safety, knowing that the opposite course may entail a war with the democracies, and feeling that this risk is unwarrantable until Italian East Africa is secure and self-supporting. Ranged in the opposite camp are the young bloods of the Fascist party—here the prototype is Count Ciano—who have acquired a taste for living dangerously, whose position depends on their popularity, and who know that their supporters, unless constantly stimulated, may grow indifferent and bored.

Caught between a series of fires, the Duce was virtually forced to adopt a middle course. His only means of avoiding the worst and gleaning the best of both alliances was to steer between them—that is, to return to the role of flirtatious neutrality for which history seems to have cast modern Italy. Seeing no way out, he put a brave face on his new policy. His beginning was almost flamboyant. In April 1938 he was winning cheers for an Agreement with Great Britain, and was deep in conversations with France. At the beginning of May he was sparing no expense to make a Roman holiday for Herr Hitler.

Englishmen could not forget the Austrian affair thus quickly, nor understand Italy's skin-deep emotions. When they saw the fears with which she had greeted the *Anschluss* converted, within a few weeks, into rousing cheers for the visiting Führer, they asked themselves—naturally enough—whether an Agreement with so capricious a people was worth the paper on which it was written.

When its terms were revealed, they condemned with some justification a document which secured them little beyond reaffirmations of old promises, and which, in exchange, jettisoned at least one important principle. For the British Government, in undertaking to remove the obstacles to recognition of Italy's Ethiopian conquest, waived its resolution, made at Geneva, never to recognize territory acquired by force. For expediency's sake, it abandoned a stand which it had always maintained over Manchukuo. Moreover, the Government's sterner critics were able to denounce a second moral lapse. They held that, in accepting the Duce's assurance that Italy would withdraw her troops from Spain in proportion to evacuations on the government side, and *in toto* at the end of the war, it had tacitly admitted the right of one nation to interfere in the civil war of another. Both concessions gave grounds for arguing that 'this decent people' (as Henry James described the English when, as a gesture, he took their nationality during the War) had abandoned something of its decency.

But decency was not abandoned for nothing. The main benefit derived from the Agreement did not appear in its written pages.

Enough has been said of the susceptibilities of Italians to show that to ostracize them is to throw them into the willing arms of Germany. English critics of the Agreement seemed to forget that to take advantage of a difference between the dictators is to lessen the risk of war. They seemed to disregard the danger of an Italo-German combination. For Germany alone is a powerful unit, and, in her expansionist mood, a menace to all her neighbours; but when to her strength is added that of Italy, stretching into and across the Mediterranean, the joint force becomes truly formidable—capable of striking, not only at the punier states of central Europe, but at the British and French Empires. The two dictatorships form a solid wedge stretching from the Baltic to North Africa. They are supreme in the central Mediterranean, whence they can cut the trade route from east to west, and attack the French mobilization channel or Egypt, while their submarines, based in Italian East Africa, can patrol the Red Sea and harry the alternative sea route to the Canal Zone and Palestine.

To state these facts is not to argue that the Rome-Berlin axis is invincible; the Anglo-French combine enjoys similar advantages elsewhere, and, were hostilities to break out, could offer not only a stout resistance but an equal power of attack. The result of a struggle between the two groups is uncertain. The certainty is that the war would be long, destructive, and useless, and that it would whirl into its hateful machinery millions of unwilling but helpless human beings. On balance, the Anglo-Italian agreement was worth a sacrifice if it lessened the likelihood of such a disaster.

Admittedly this is a dangerous argument, opening the way to endless international casuistry. Nevertheless, it need not constitute a precedent; rather, it can serve as a warning. It can point the lesson that, in modern politics, principles cannot be defended except before or during their overthrow, and that, once this moment is past, to insist upon them is merely to throw desperadoes together, thus reinforcing their hand and prompting them to attempt fresh expansionist gestures. To adopt a moral tone on the subject of last year's *fait accompli* is a luxury which no one can afford unless he is so fortunate as to live outside the bombing radius—for example, in the Middle West of the United States.

Yet many Englishmen were loud in their denunciation of Mr. Chamberlain's policy. Why, they said, must he go half-way to meet the Duce, since, once Italy had been flouted by her German friends, she must inevitably secede from the famous axis. But to argue thus is to misunderstand a dictator's psychology. He must be able to represent his every action as a success. Hence the foreign diplomatist who would induce a Fascist to climb down must, unobtrusively, provide a ladder. He must make an advance here, a concession there, and serve the whole with palatable compliments which will look well in the Italian newspapers. Unless he is skilled enough to do so, he will progressively discover that he is speaking to deaf ears; that Italy has forgotten him in her pride at the size and splendour of some newly arrived German delegation; and, finally, that the Führer, having recaptured Italian attention, is planning a further extension of his frontiers. History has said it, and will say it again. On the other hand, if our diplomatist handles his task with skill, he can outdo his Nazi rival. For he may be sure that Italy will, silently but thankfully, seize every chance of withdrawing from the menace of German dominance.

Juxtapose these four factors—German strength, Italian uncertainty, Arab unrest, Anglo-French diplomacy—and it becomes clear that two keys to successful British foreign policy lie, for the moment, in the Mediterranean.

The first is that which solves the miserable problem of Palestine. Until the British Government defines its policy, and—more important—until it carries out the policy defined, it will continue to engender disrespect and distrust throughout the Middle East. Procrastination is growing increasingly harmful; it is beginning to hamper the other western powers who rule Moslem territories; it is also beginning to provide Great Britain's ill-wishers with an all-too-easy means of sapping her strength.

The second key is to be found in Anglo-Italian relations. On Great Britain's approach to Italy, and on the Italian response to that approach, hangs Europe's best chance of a term of peace. Success depends largely upon the ability of each country to understand a foreign psychology which is far removed from its own. Unless both can do so, a cabal between the dictators becomes almost inevitable. To this, a clash with the democracies is the probable sequel, and, since the sides are well matched in their power of destruction, that clash portends havoc and disaster, not only for the Mediterranean, but for half the universe.

The last word rests with Uncle Leopold, penning industriously in the troubled winter of 1854, at a letter destined to convey to 'My dearest Victoria' the worldly wisdom which she often found tiresome, but which, for all her sighs, is still not one whit out of date:

'The plot is thickening in every direction, and we may expect a great confusion. The dear old Duke used to say: "You cannot have a little war." The Duke told me also once: "At the place where you are, you will always have the power to force people to go to war." I have used that power to *avoid* complications, and I still think, blessed are the peacemakers.'

STATISTICAL TABLES

TABLE 1

THE upper of the two tables opposite shows the principal supplies reaching Great Britain *from beyond Suez*, but should not be taken as a guide to the goods travelling *via the Canal*. There are no published figures showing the routes used for each commodity in each year, but at a rough estimate, less than two-thirds of the volume of goods shown reaches British ports *via* the short sea passage. Nor do the figures given show all goods arriving from the East, for they do not include re-exports; for instance, Great Britain imports from the Netherlands a large annual consignment of tin which, if traced to its origin, has probably come through the Suez Canal from the Netherlands East Indies.

The table should be used subject to one other reservation. Conclusions cannot be drawn from the figures for one year only. Particularly in the case of cereals, Great Britain shifts her purchases annually according to the abundance of local harvests. For instance, the large import of barley from Iraq, shown in the upper table, is by no means a regular annual purchase.

Both Australia and New Zealand now send quantities of their exports to the mother country by the long sea route. New Zealand goods (chiefly meat and dairy produce) are in part dispatched by Suez, but they have been omitted from the table on the ground that their journey to the United Kingdom is actually shorter *via* Panama. For lack of data as to the routes used, Australian supplies are included in full, though it is known that Australia dispatches at least half her huge export of wheat *via* the Cape.

One curious feature of the table is the high value of some of the foodstuffs; for instance, the tea reaching British ports through the Canal is worth over three times as much as the petroleum. In volume, on the other hand, the latter far exceeds any other commodity; moreover, the 'source' column shows that, since it comes chiefly from Iran, it would be faced with a bigger voyage-increase than the other goods were war to bar the way through the Mediterranean.

TABLE 1. GREAT BRITAIN, 1937

A. *Chief supplies received from beyond Suez*

(Excluding New Zealand)

	Value £000	*Tons* 000	*% of total import*	*Chief Sources*
FOODSTUFFS				
Barley . .	2,080	296	31·9	Iraq (27·9%), Australia (3·5%)
Butter . .	7,522	75	15·9	Australia (15·9%)
Coffee . .	602	9	47·8	British East Africa (41·8%)
Meat . .	10,245	225	14·4	Australia (14·4%)
Rice . .	703	71	61·6	India (53·6%), French Indo-China (8·0%)
Sugar . .	9,065	876	32·0	Australia (14·2%), Mauritius (10·4%)
Tea . .	29,413	216	99·3	India (56·4%), Ceylon (28·9%)
Wheat . .	14,721	1,435	29·7	Australia (23·1%)
INDUSTRIAL RAW MATERIALS				
Copper* .	6,181	110	28·1	Northern Rhodesia (28·1%)
Cotton .	5,745	108	14·7	India (13·9%)
Hemp . .	2,321	75	73·3	Philippines (44·7%), British East Africa (28·6%)
Jute . .	3,727	193	100·0	India (100%)
Lead . .	5,279	230	61·8	Australia (48·4%), India (13·4%)
Manganese Ore	1,006	235	85·6	India (85·6%)
Oilseeds .	7,828	604	32·4	India (19·3%), British East Africa (6·2%), Kwantung (4·6%)
Petroleum .	9,366	2,342	19·5	Iran (18·5%)
Rubber . .	11,448	129	90·8	British Malaya (64·0%), Netherlands East Indies (15·5%)
Tin* . .	1,461	6	26·6	British Malaya (25·1%)
Wool . .	22,472	154	44·0	Australia (38·5%), India (5·5%)
Zinc* . .	317	13	7·6	Australia (7·6%)
Zinc ore .	255	84	65·3	Australia (65·3%)

* Excluding ore.

B. *Chief supplies received from Mediterranean and Black Sea Countries*

	Value £000	Tons 000	% of total import	Chief Sources
Citrus Fruits .	4,314	410	65·5	Palestine (35·5%), Spain (30%)
Cotton . .	12,446	157	21·2	Egypt (17·5%), Sudan (3·7%)
Phosphates* .	397	271	63·2	Tunis (50·6%), Algeria (11·7%)
Iron ore .	2,510	1,607	20·0	Algeria (13·1%), Tunisia (6·9%)
Oilseeds &c. .	3,099	413	22·1	Egypt (16·4%), Sudan (5·7%)
Petroleum .	4,645	1,346	11·2	Rumania (4·5%), Iraq (3·8%), Russia (2·8%)
Wood-pulp .	1,374	352	16·4	Algeria (10·3%), Tunisia (5·4%)

* 1936 figures.

Source: United Kingdom: Monthly Trade and Navigation Statistics, 1937.

TABLE 2

Italy receives about 85 per cent. of her imports by sea, of which perhaps 10 per cent. come from within the Mediterranean and Black Sea, the remainder from beyond Suez and Gibraltar. Before the Ethiopian war, the proportions of Italian imports received *via* the three Mediterranean bottle-necks were estimated to be: Gibraltar, 70 per cent.; Suez, 17 per cent.; Black Sea Straits, 13 per cent.

There is some excuse for offering, in the table opposite, figures so old as those for 1934. Italian trade in 1935 and 1936 was dislocated by war and sanctions, and the full figures for 1937 are not available as this book goes to press. But the monthly data already published suffice to show that, except in the case of coal, petroleum, iron ore, and manganese, Italy has not substantially shifted her sources of supply.

Owing to the bitterness caused by sanctions, Italy's *coal* purchases from Great Britain have dwindled to half their former size; she has transferred much of her custom to Germany, and to Poland, who has risen to the new British level. Italy has also shifted her *petroleum* purchases, partly for political reasons (she has stopped buying from Russia), but partly also because she now needs more crude oil, as she is setting up an immense national refining industry. Where she refined 413,000 tons in 1936, she was able to refine 1,016,000 tons in 1937. For the necessary crude oil, she has turned chiefly to the United States and Iraq. For the refined oil which she formerly purchased from Russia, she has given extra custom to the Netherlands West Indies and Iran. In 1937, therefore, the percentages arriving by each route were approximately as follows:

Via Suez	*Via Gibraltar*	*From Mediterranean*	*From Black Sea*
16·3 %	47·8 %	12·3 %	23·5 %

The materials in which Italy is self-sufficient are not shown in the table; they are lead, zinc, bauxite (aluminium), mercury, sulphur, silk, and hemp. Nickel, too, is not shown, since she possesses an adequate reserve in her coinage. Foodstuffs also are omitted, as Italy can—in good harvest years—feed herself in all the main foods consumed except meat, fish, and coffee. Meat she could procure overland, though she usually buys largely from the Argentine and Denmark. Fish and coffee she also buys in large quantities, mainly from beyond Gibraltar—the former from Spain and the North Atlantic ports, the latter from the Caribbean and Brazil.

TABLE 2. ITALY: IMPORTS OF INDUSTRIAL RAW MATERIALS, 1934

Main sources of supply, shown as a percentage of total import of each commodity

TOTAL OR VIRTUALLY TOTAL DEFICIENCES

	Via Suez	*Via Gibraltar*	*Overland or via Adriatic*	*From Mediterranean*	*Via Dardanelles*
Copper .	via Portuguese E. Africa 22·4	U.S.A. 31·7 Chile 30·5			
Cotton .	India 17·0	U.S.A. 61·6		Egypt 17·9	
Jute .	India 99·9				
Petroleum .	Iran 12·2 Neth. E. I. 3·0	U.S.A. 11·0 Caribbean 10·4	†	Iraq 1·0	Rumania 31·2 U.S.S.R. 29·9
Phosphates .	Egypt (Red Sea) 7·8	Morocco 29·3 U.S.A. 11·3		Tunisia 40·7 Algeria 2·3	
Potash .		Germany* 69·1 Belgo - Luxemburg Union* 15·4			
Rubber .	India & Ceylon 47·8 Neth. E. I. 45·4 Br. Malaya 6·0				
Tin .	Br. Malaya 74·0 Burmah 7·2	Gr. Britain 11·9			
Wool .	Australia 44·4	Argentine 20·9 S. Africa 15·0			

PARTIAL DEFICIENCES

	Via Suez	*Via Gibraltar*	*Overland or via Adriatic*	*From Mediterranean*	*Via Dardanelles*
Coal and Coke		Gr. Britain 31·1 Germany* 38·9 Poland* 9·1		Turkey 2·0 France 1·2	
Iron ore .		U.S.S.R. 30·0		Algeria 21·5 Spain 11·1 Cyprus 11·1 Greece 8·9	
Scrap iron .		U.S.A. 27·4 Belgium 10·2	Switzerland 9·4	France* 38·4 Mediterranean countries 10·0	
Manganese .	Sinai 26·1	U.S.S.R. 60·0			
Oil seeds .	India 56·0				

† Albania's production was still neglible in 1934.

* Available overland.

Source: *Regno d'Italia, Importazione ed Esportazione, 1934* (volume figures).

TABLE 3

THIS table is chiefly interesting for its display of the remarkable rise of *German* sales in the Mediterranean countries during the last few years—a rise which is not confined to the exchange-restriction countries where Dr. Schacht's famous device[1] was worked, but which also extends to Egypt and the mandated territories. In 1937 it encountered a slight check in the Balkan countries owing to a temporary improvement in the world prices of some of their staple products.[2]

The table also shows the fate of two of the industrial exporters at whose expense Germany advanced. *France* suffered owing to her long retention of the gold standard; *Italy*, at first for the same reason and, later, owing to sanctions, although much of the ground lost for this second reason was regained in 1937. Germany's increasing sales in *mare nostrum*, and her progress in former Italian markets which she captured during the sanctions period, are an illustration of the fundamental clash of interests between the dictators.[3]

Up till 1937 *Great Britain* almost contrived to hold her own against the German onslaught, chiefly owing to the better quality of her goods.

[1] Cf. p. 214. [2] Cf. p. 237. [3] Cf. p. 241.

TABLE 3. GREAT-POWER MARKETS

Purchases of the Mediterranean States shown as a percentage of their total imports

		From Great Britain	From France	From Germany	From Italy
Albania	1929	7·0	2·0	4·9	46·2
	1935	9·8	2·8	8·1	28·5
	1936	8·4	3·2	6·1	24·9
Algeria	1929	2·6	77·4	0·9	0·8
	1935	1·8	80·5	0·7	0·4
	1936	2·7	77·7	0·8	0·2
Bulgaria	1929	8·9	8·2	22·2	10·7
	1935	4·7	1·4	53·5	3·1
	1936	4·6	1·2	61·0	0·6
Egypt	1929	21·2	9·9	7·3	9·8
	1935	22·8	5·3	8·9	5·6
	1936	23·9	5·2	11·1	3·5
	1937	21·7	4·5	11·0	8·6
Greece	1929	12·7	6·8	9·4	5·7
	1935	15·5	1·7	18·7	3·7
	1936	16·0	1·9	22·6	0·5
Morocco	1929	10·2	55·7	2·5	5·0
	1935	4·3	39·9	3·4	4·3
	1936	3·3	34·8	2·5	2·2
Palestine	1929	14·1	6·5	10·4	4·0
	1935	17·9	2·0	12·2	2·5
	1936	19·4	1·5	14·6	0·5
Rumania	1929	7·3	5·5	24·1	6·9
	1935	9·8	7·2	24·4	7·7
	1936	6·8	4·5	39·0	1·4
Spain	1929	13·0	12·8	10·5	3·4
	1935	10·4	5·6	13·7	3·0
	1936	?	?	?	?
Syria	1929	10·9	13·9	4·4	8·4
	1935	11·0	11·7	5·6	3·8
	1936	10·8	12·4	6·4	1·8
Tunisia	1929	2·9	64·0	1·2	4·5
	1935	2·7	64·2	1·5	6·2
	1936	2·7	62·4	1·1	1·3
Turkey	1929	12·2	10·4	15·3	12·5
	1935	9·8	4·7	40·0	6·4
	1936	6·6	2·5	45·1	2·2
	1937	6·2	nil	42·0	5·3
Yugoslavia	1929	5·6	4·0	15·6	10·8
	1935	10·1	4·3	16·2	10·0
	1936	8·5	2·5	26·7	2·5
	1937	7·8	1·7	32·5	8·2

INDEX

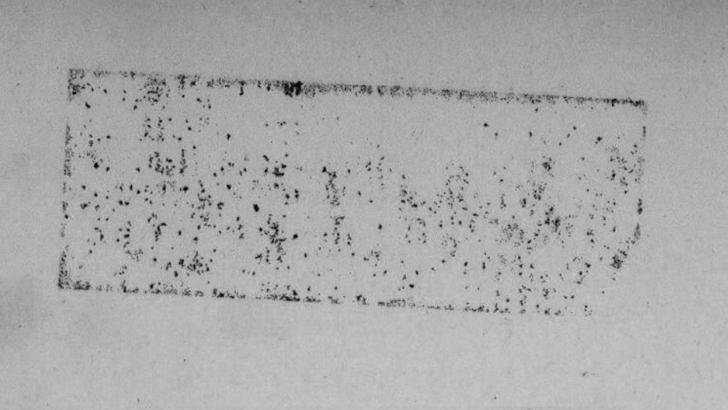